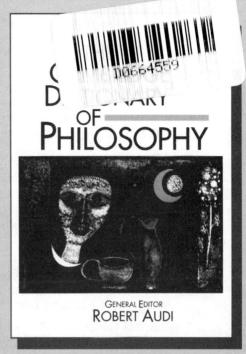

GRANTA 52, Winter 1995

EDITOR Ian Jack
DEPUTY EDITOR Ursula Doyle
MANAGING EDITOR Claire Wrathall
EDITORIAL ASSISTANT Karen Whitfield

CONTRIBUTING EDITORS Pete de Bolla, Frances Coady,
Will Hobson, Liz Jobey, Blake Morrison, Andrew O'Hagan

US FINANCIAL COMPTROLLER Margarette Devlin
SPECIAL PROJECTS DIRECTOR Rose Marie Morse
SPECIAL PROJECTS ASSISTANT Rachel Stoll
PROMOTIONS MANAGER Jenoa Brown
ADVERTISING MANAGERS Lara Frohlich, Catherine Tice
SUBSCRIPTION MANAGER Ken Nilsson
LIST MANAGER Diane Seltzer
PUBLISHING ASSISTANT Dario Stipisic

Granta, 2–3 Hanover Yard, Noel Road, London N1 8BE
Granta US, 250 West 57th Street, Suite 1316, New York, NY 10107

PUBLISHER Rea Hederman
US PUBLISHER Matt Freidson

SUBSCRIPTION DETAILS: a one-year subscription (four issues) costs $32 in the US; $42 in Canada (includes GST); $39 for Mexico and South America; $50 for the rest of the world. Telephone: (212) 246 1313. Fax: (212) 586 8003

Granta, USPS 000-508, ISSN 0017-3231, is published quarterly for $32 by Granta USA Ltd, a Delaware corporation. Second class postage paid at Charlottesville, VA. POSTMASTER: send address changes to Granta, 250 West 57th St., Suite 1316, NY, NY 10107.

Available on microfilm and microfiche through UMI, 300 North Zeeb Road, Ann Arbor, MI 48106-1346, USA. Printed in the United States of America. The paper used in this publication meets the minimum requirements of American National Standard for Information Sciences— Permanence of Paper for Printed Library Materials, ANSI Z39.48-1984. ∞

Granta is published by Granta Publications Ltd and distributed by Penguin Books Ltd, Harmondsworth, Middlesex, England; Viking Penguin, a division of Penguin Books USA Inc, 375 Hudson Street, New York, NY 10014, USA; Penguin Books Australia Ltd, Ringwood, Victoria, Australia; Penguin Books Canada Ltd, 10 Alcorn Avenue, Toronto, Ontario, Canada M4V 3B2; Penguin Books (NZ) Ltd, 182–190 Wairau Road, Auckland 10, New Zealand. This selection copyright © 1995 by Granta Publications Ltd.

Cover design by The Senate.
Photographs: Richard Kalvar/Magnum, Nigel Shafran
ISBN 0-14-014113-8

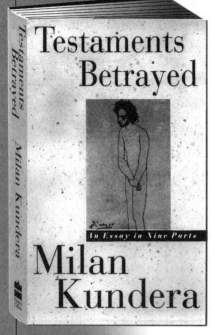

CONTENTS

OF THOUGHT

Free Exchange
Pierre Bourdieu and Hans Haacke

In this remarkable book by the leading social theorist Pierre Bourdieu and the artist Hans Haacke, the two men conduct a frank and open dialogue on contemporary art and culture. They range widely, from censorship and obscenity to the social conditions of artistic creativity, from the photographs of Robert Mapplethorpe to the debates over multiculturalism and ethnic diversity.
$14.95 paper $35.00 cloth

The Illusion of the End
Jean Baudrillard

"Vintage Baudrillard—compelling, diabolically clever, outrageous, wounded, ironic, refreshing, and certainly controversial. It is a most original meditation on the theme of history, on its shape or trajectory, and the human fate bound up with it."
—Mark Poster,
University of California, Irvine
$12.95 paper $32.50 cloth

Topographies
J. Hillis Miller

This book investigates the function of topographical names and descriptions in a variety of narratives, poems, and philosophical or theoretical texts, primarily from the 19th and 20th centuries, but including also Plato and the Bible. Topics include the initiating efficacy of speech acts, ethical responsibility, political or legislative power, the translation of theory from one topographical location to another, the way topographical delineations can function as parable or allegory, and the relation of personification to landscape.
$16.95 paper $49.50 cloth

Prosthesis
David Wills

"Most critical efforts look not only humble and constrained beside this magnificent book, but also simply dull—dull in the sense that they have not realized (realized in the sense of 'understood' but also in the sense of 'actualized') the implication of the epistemological revolution that is casually referred to as the coming of 'theory.'"
—Ross Chambers,
University of Michigan
$18.95 paper $49.50 cloth

GRANTA

GRAHAM SWIFT
THE BUTCHER OF BERMONDSEY

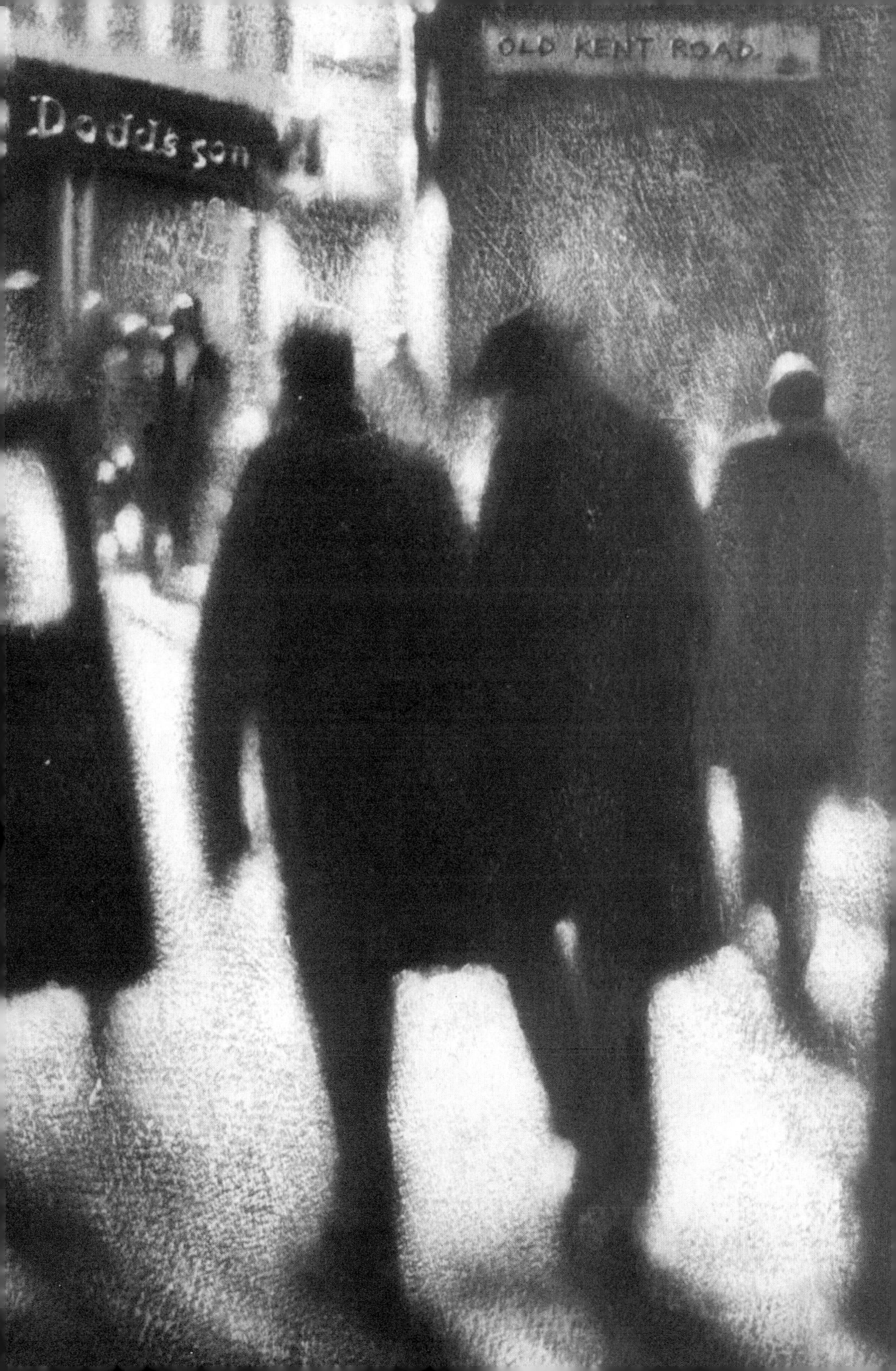

OLD KENT ROAD.
Dodds son

Ray Remembers

I said, 'I fancy seeing the Pyramids.'

He said, 'I fancy seeing the inside of the nearest knocking shop.'

It was Jack who first called me Lucky. It didn't have to do with the nags, that was later.

He said, 'Small fellers have the advantage, small fellers have the luck, hope you understand that. Less of a target for the enemy, less weight to carry in this fucking frying pan. Mind you, doesn't take away my advantage. I could knock your block off any time I like. Hope you understand that.'

Then he smiled, held out his hand, clenched it for a moment, grinning, then opened it again.

'Jack Dodds.'

I said, 'Ray Johnson.'

He said, 'Hello Ray. Hello Lucky. How'd you get so small anyway? Someone shrink you in the wash?'

It was out of consideration, that's what I think. It was out of wanting to make me feel easier, on account of I was new draft and he'd had six months already. But he didn't have to pick on me. I reckon he decided, for some reason I'll never know, to choose me. All that luck stuff was eyewash. But if you say something and think it and mean it enough then, sometimes, it becomes the case. Same when you pick out a horse. It's not luck, it's confidence. Which is something I'd say that, except in the rarefied business of backing a gee-gee, Ray Johnson's always had precious little of. But so far as Jack was concerned, I reckon I was like a horse. He picked me. That's how I became Lucky Johnson.

He said, 'Where you from, Ray?'

I said, 'Bermondsey.'

He said, 'You're never.'

I said, 'You know Valetta Street? You know the scrap merchant's, Frank Johnson's?'

He said, 'You know Dodds' butcher shop in Spring Road? I bet your Ma buys her meat there.'

I never said I didn't have no Ma. I reckon that would have

made him reassess my luckiness.

He said, 'Best bangers in Bermondsey. And, talking of bangers, I suppose you could say we're as safe out here as there.'

He said it was because I was lucky that he ought to stick with me, but it was the other way round. It was Jack who underwrote me. It wasn't that I was small so the bullets would miss me, it was that he was big, like a wall, like a boulder. And the bullets missed him anyway, they missed him so they missed me, except that once. It was because a small man needs speaking up for, like the old man saying I'd got brains and I ought to use 'em. I never knew I had them till he insisted on it, and till Jack went and made it a selling point. 'This is Ray, got it up here has Ray.' Except one way I knew I had it up here was in sticking with Jack.

I thought, Stick with this man and you'll be OK, stick with this man and you'll get through this war.

He passed me a ciggy.

He said, 'Tell you what, Ray, we could give the Pyramids a miss.' Then he took a crumpled card with an address scrawled on it from his wallet. 'Mate gave me this. Personal recommendation.'

I said, 'Maybe I could—'

He said, 'Pyramids are tombs, aren't they, Ray? Pyramids are for dead people. Whereas a tart's tackle. It's be-kind-to-your-pecker day.'

Then he led me out into the noise and the glare and the stink. As we dodged the touts and beggars, he said, 'Tell you what, Raysy, we'll go and see the Pyramids after.'

And so there's a photo of Jack and me, taken that afternoon, sitting on a camel, with the Pyramids behind us. There must be a thousand bloody photos of old desert campaigners sitting on camels with the Pyramids behind them, but this was Jack and me. And that camel was the nearest I ever got to being a jockey. He said, 'You sure about this?' I said, 'It's all right, I used to drive the old man's horse and cart.' He said, 'Yes, but this aint a horse and cart, it's a camel.' You wouldn't have thought it would've bothered him, of all things, a camel. I said, 'Trust me,' and he said, 'I trust you, I aint got no choice.'

So there we are, sitting on a camel, in the brass frame on Jack's sideboard, beside the fruit bowl. I'm laughing fit to bust.

Jack's trying to laugh. The camel aint even cracking its face.

It seems amazing now, like ancient history, that I was ever there, with Jack, in the desert. That I advanced with Jack from Egypt into Libya and retreated with him to Egypt and advanced again into Libya. A small man at big history. And somewhere in the same desert Lenny Tate was advancing and retreating, though we never knew him then. And Micky Dennis was killed at Belhamed and Bill Kennedy at Matrûh, and Jack said it was unfair that a pharaoh got a whole pyramid when there was a good half of Bill that wasn't even in that grave. Then on to Tripoli, and never a scratch, never a scratch. Save that once. And it wasn't me, it was Jack. Clipped him on the left shoulder, went crack over my own head. But he always said if I hadn't been there to pull him down smart off of those sandbags, he'd've copped it worse. He'd've been like Bill Kennedy. Smack in the wife's-best-friend.

I saw it when he was lying there after his op. The new scar on his stomach, the old scar on his shoulder.

See this nursey? Come a bit closer. Got it in North Africa. If it wasn't for my mate Lucky there I wouldn't be here.

Bermondsey

It aint like your regular sort of day.

Bernie pulls me a pint and puts it in front of me. He looks at me, puzzled, with his loose, doggy face, but he can tell I don't want no chit-chat. That's why I'm here, five minutes after opening, for a little silent pow-wow with a pint glass. He can see the black tie, though it's four days since the funeral. I hand him a fiver, and he takes it to the till and brings back my change. He puts the coins, extra gently, eyeing me, on the bar beside my pint.

'Won't be the same, will it?' he says, shaking his head and looking a little way along the bar, like at unoccupied space. 'Won't be the same.'

I say, 'You aint seen the last of him yet.'

He says, 'You what?'

I sip the froth off my beer. 'I said you aint seen the last of him yet.'

He frowns, scratching his cheek, looking at me. 'Course, Ray,' he says and moves off down the bar.

I never meant to make no joke of it.

I suck an inch off my pint and light up a snout. There's maybe three or four other early-birds apart from me, and the place don't look its best. Chilly, a whiff of disinfectant, too much empty space. There's a shaft of sunlight coming through the window, full of specks. Makes you think of a church.

I sit there, watching the old clock, up behind the bar. THOS. SLATTERY, CLOCKMAKER, SOUTHWARK. The bottles racked up like organ pipes.

Lenny's next to arrive. He's not wearing a black tie, he's not wearing a tie at all. He takes a quick shufti at what I'm wearing, and we both feel we gauged it wrong.

'Let me, Lenny,' I say. 'Pint?'

He says, 'This is a turn-up.'

Bernie comes over. He says, 'New timetable, is it?'

'Morning,' Lenny says.

'Pint for Lenny,' I say.

'Retired now, have we, Lenny?' Bernie says.

'Past the age for it, aint I, Bern? I aint like Raysy here, man of leisure. Fruit and veg trade needs me.'

'But not today, eh?' Bernie says.

Bernie draws the pint and moves off to the till.

'You haven't told him?' Lenny says, looking at Bernie.

'No,' I say, looking at my beer, then at Lenny.

Lenny lifts his eyebrows. His face looks raw and flushed. It always does, like it's going to come out in a bruise. He tugs at his collar where his tie isn't.

'It's a turn-up,' he says. 'And Amy aint coming? I mean, she aint changed her mind?'

'No,' I say. 'Down to us, I reckon. The inner circle.'

'Her own husband,' he says.

He takes hold of his pint but he's slow to start drinking, as if there's different rules today even for drinking a pint of beer.

'We going to Vic's?' he says.

'No, Vic's coming here,' I say.

He nods, lifts his glass, then checks it, sudden, halfway to his mouth. His eyebrows go even higher.

I say, 'Vic's coming here. With Jack. Drink up, Lenny.'

Vic arrives about five minutes later. He's wearing a black tie, but you'd expect that, seeing as he's an undertaker, seeing as he's just come from his premises. But he's not wearing his full rig. He's wearing a fawn raincoat, with a flat cap poking out of one of the pockets, as if he's aimed to pitch it right: he's just one of us, it aint official business, it's different.

'Morning,' he says.

I've been wondering what he'll have with him. So's Lenny, I dare say. Like I've had this picture of Vic opening the pub door and marching in, all solemn, with a little oak casket with brass fittings. But all he's carrying, under one arm, is a plain brown cardboard box, about a foot high and six inches square. He looks like a man who's been down the shops and bought a set of bathroom tiles.

He parks himself on the stool next to Lenny, putting the box on the bar, unbuttoning his raincoat.

'Fresh out,' he says.

'Is that it then?' Lenny says, looking. 'Is that him?'

'Yes,' Vic says. 'What are we drinking?'

'What's inside?' Lenny says.

'What do you think?' Vic says.

He twists the box round so we can see there's a white card sellotaped to one side. There's a date and a number and a name: JACK ARTHUR DODDS.

Lenny says, 'I mean, he aint just in a box, is he?'

By way of answering, Vic picks up the box and flips open the flaps at the top with his thumb. 'Mine's a whisky,' he says, 'I think it's a whisky day.'

He feels inside the box and slowly pulls out a plastic container. It looks like a large instant-coffee jar, it's got the same kind of screw-on cap. But it's not glass, it's a bronzy-coloured, faintly shiny plastic. There's another label on the cap.

'Here,' Vic says and hands the jar to Lenny.

Lenny takes it, uncertain, as if he's not ready to take it but he can't not take it, as if he ought to have washed his hands first. He don't seem prepared for the weight. He sits on his bar stool, holding it, not knowing what to say, but I reckon he's thinking the same things I'm thinking. Whether it's all Jack in there or Jack mixed up with bits of others, the ones who were done before and the ones who were done after. So Lenny could be holding some of Jack and some of some other feller's wife, for example. And if it *is* all Jack, whether it's really all of him or only what they could fit in the jar, him being a big bloke.

He says, 'Don't seem possible, does it?' Then he hands me the jar, all sort of getting-in-the-mood, like it's a party game. Guess the weight.

'Heavy,' I say.

'Packed solid,' Vic says.

I reckon I wouldn't fill it, being on the small side. I suppose it wouldn't do to unscrew the cap.

Vic says, 'Where's Bern got to?'

Vic's a square-set, ready-and-steady sort of a bloke, the sort of bloke who rubs his hands together at the start of something. His hands are always clean. He looks at me holding the jar like he's just given me a present. It's a comfort to know your own mate will lay you out and box you up and do the necessary. So Vic better last out.

It must have been a comfort to Jack that there was his shop, DODDS & SON, FAMILY BUTCHER, and there was Vic's just across the street, with the wax flowers and the marble slabs and the angel with its head bowed in the window: TUCKER & SONS, FUNERAL SERVICES. A comfort and an incentive, and a sort of fittingness too, seeing as there was dead animals in the one and stiffs in the other.

Maybe that's why Jack never wanted to budge.

Vic takes the jar and starts to ease it back in the box, but it's a tricky business, and the box slides from his lap on to the floor, so he puts the jar on the bar.

It's about the same size as a pint glass.

He says, 'Bern!'

Bernie's at the other end of the bar, usual drying-up towel over his shoulder. He turns and comes towards us. He's about to say something to Vic, then he sees the jar, by Lenny's pint. He checks himself and he says, 'What's that?' But as if he's already worked out the answer.

'It's Jack,' Vic says. 'It's Jack's ashes.'

Bernie looks at the jar, then he looks at Vic, then he gives a quick look round the whole of the bar. He looks like he looks when he's making up his mind to eject an unwanted customer, which he's good at. Like he's building up steam. Then his face goes quiet, it goes almost shy.

'That's Jack?' he says, leaning closer, as if the jar might answer back, it might say, 'Hello Bernie.'

'Jesus God,' Bernie says, 'what's he doing here?'

So Vic explains. It's best that Vic explains, being the professional. Coming from Lenny or me, it might sound like a load of hooey.

Then I say, 'So we thought he should have a last look-in at the Coach.'

'I see,' Bernie says, like he don't see.

'It's a turn-up,' Lenny says.

Vic says, 'Get me a large scotch, Bernie. Have one yourself.'

'I will, thank you, I will, Vic,' Bernie says, all considered and respectful, like a scotch is appropriate and it don't do to refuse a drink from an undertaker.

He takes two glasses from the rack and squeezes one up against the scotch bottle, two shots, then he takes just a single for himself. He turns and slides the double across to Vic. Vic pushes over a fiver, but Bernie holds up a hand. 'On the house, Vic, on the house,' he says. 'Aint every day, is it?' Then he raises his glass, eyes on the jar, as if he's going to say something speechy and grand but he says, 'Jesus God, he was only sitting there six weeks ago.'

We all look into our drinks.

Vic says, 'Well, here's to him.'

We lift our glasses, mumbling. JackJackJack.

'And here's to you, Vic,' I say. 'You did a good job Thursday.'

'Went a treat,' Lenny says.

'Don't mention it,' Vic says. 'How's Amy?'

'Managing,' I say.

'She hasn't changed her mind about coming then?'

'No, she'll be seeing June, as per usual.'

Everyone's silent.

Vic says, 'Her decision, isn't it?'

Lenny sticks his nose in his glass like he's not going to say anything.

Bernie's looking at the jar and looking anxiously round the bar. He looks at Vic like he don't want to make a fuss but.

Vic says, 'Point taken, Bernie,' and takes the jar from where it's sitting. He reaches down for the fallen box. 'Not much good for business, is it?'

'Aint helping yours much either, Vic,' Lenny says.

Vic slides the jar carefully back into the box. It's eleven-twenty by Slattery's clock, and it feels less churchy. There's more punters coming in. Someone's put on the music machine. *Going back some day, come what may, to Blue Bayou* . . . That's better, that's better.

First wet rings on the mahogany, first drifts of blue smoke.

Vic says, 'Well all we need now is our chauffeur.'

Lenny says, 'They're playing his tune. Wonder what he'll bring. Drives something different every week these days, far as I can see.'

Bernie says, 'Same again all round?'

As he speaks there's a hooting and tooting outside in the street. A pause, then another burst.

Lenny says, 'Sounds like him now. Sounds like Vincey.'

There's a fresh round of hooting.

Vic says, 'Isn't he coming in?'

Lenny says, 'I reckon he wants us out there.'

We don't go out but we get up and go over to the window. Vic keeps hold of the box, like someone might pinch it. We raise ourselves up on our toes, heads close together, so we can see above the frosted half of the window. I can't quite, but I don't say.

'Jesus Christ,' Lenny says.

'It's a Merc,' Vic says.

'Trust Big Boy,' Lenny says.

I push down on the sill to give myself a second's extra lift. It's a royal blue Merc, cream seats, gleaming in the April sunshine.

'Jesus,' I say. 'A Merc.'

Lenny says, it's like a joke he's been saving up for fifty years, 'Rommel *would* be pleased.'

Ray

Amy eyes me as I look up from reading the letter.

She says, 'I suppose he thought he'd get there in the end, one way or the other.'

I say, 'When did he write it?'

She says, 'A couple of days before he—'

I look at her and I say, 'He could have just told you. Why'd he have to write a letter?'

She says, 'I suppose he thought I'd think he was joking. I suppose he thought it would make it proper.'

It's not a long letter, but it could be shorter, because of the way it's wrapped up in language like you see in the small print on the back of forms. It's not Jack's language at all. But I suppose a man can get all wordy, all official, when he knows his number's up.

But the gist of it's plain. It says he wants his ashes to be chucked off the end of Margate Pier.

It don't even say, 'Dear Amy'. It says, 'To whom it may concern'.

Old Kent Road

We head down past Albany Road and Trafalgar Avenue and the Rotherhithe turn. Green Man, Thomas à Becket, Lord Nelson. The sky's almost as blue as the car.

Vince says, 'Goes along sweet, don't it?' And he takes his hands off the wheel so we can get the feel of how the car takes care of itself. It seems to veer a shade to the left.

He said he thought he should do Jack proud, he thought he should give him a real treat. Since it had been sitting there in the showroom for nearly a month anyway, with a 'client' who couldn't make up his mind, and a bit more on the clock wouldn't signify and it don't do to let a car sit. He thought he should give Jack the best.

But it's not so bad for us too, for Vic and Lenny and me, sitting up, alive and breathing. The world looks pretty good when you're perched on cream leather and looking out at it through tinted electric windows, even the Old Kent Road looks good.

It veers a shade to the left. Lenny says, 'Don't go and give it a dent, will you, Big Boy? Don't want you to lose a sale.'

Vince says he don't dent cars, ever, least of all when he's driving extra steady and careful, on account of the special occasion.

Lenny says, 'With your hands off the wheel.'

Then Vince asks Vic what they do in a hearse when they have to go on a motorway.

Vic says, 'We step on it.'

Vince isn't wearing a black tie. It's just me and Vic. He's wearing a red-and-white jazzy tie and a dark blue suit. It's his showroom clobber, and he's come from the showroom, but he could have chosen some other tie. He's taken off his jacket, which is lying folded on the back seat between me and Lenny. Good quality stuff. I reckon Vince is doing all right, he's not so badly placed after all. He says now they're feeling the pinch in the City they pop across in their lunch hours to do deals for cash.

Lenny says, 'Don't encourage him, Vic.'

Vic says, 'A hearse is different, everyone makes way for a hearse.'

Lenny says, 'You mean they don't make way for Vincey here?'

Vic sits in the front beside Vince, holding the box on his knees. I can see it's how it should be, Vic being the professional, but it don't seem right he should hold it all the time. Maybe we should take it in turns.

Vince looks across at Vic. He says, smiling, 'Busman's holiday, eh, Vic?'

Vince is wearing a white shirt with silver cuff links, and pongy aftershave. His hair is all slicked back. It's a brand new suit.

We head on past the gasworks, Ilderton Road, under the railway bridge. Prince of Windsor. The sun comes out from behind the tower blocks, bright in our faces, and Vince pulls out a pair of chunky sunglasses from under the dashboard. Lenny starts singing, slyly, through his teeth, '*Blue bayooo . . .*' And we all feel it, what with the sunshine and the beer inside us and the journey ahead: like it's something Jack has done for us, so as to make us feel special, so as to give us a treat. Like we're off on a jaunt, a spree, and the world looks good, it looks like it's there just for us.

Ray

Jack would say, 'Bunch of ghosts, that's what you are in that office, Raysy. Bunch of bleeding zombies.' He'd say, 'You want to come up to Smithfield some time and see how real men make a living.'

And sometimes I did. In the early mornings, specially when it was all falling apart with me and Carol, when we weren't even speaking. I'd slip out early and get the 63 as usual but get off two stops later and walk up from Farringdon Road, up Charterhouse Street, in the half-light. Breakfast at Smithfield. We'd go to that caff in Long Lane or to one of those pubs that serves beer and nosh at half past seven in the morning. There was Ted White from Peckham and Joe Malone from Rotherhithe and Jimmy Phelps from Camberwell. And of course, in the early days, there'd be Vince, being trained up. Before he joined up.

They'd say, What you need, Raysy, is a good feed-up, you're looking peaky. What you need is some meat on you. I'd say it was my natural build. Flyweight. Shovel it in, it don't make no difference.

Strange thing but you never see a thin butcher.

He used to give me all that old Smithfield guff, all that Smithfield blather. How Smithfield was the true centre, the true heart of London. Bleeding heart, of course, on account of the meat. How Smithfield wasn't just Smithfield, it was Life and Death. That's what it was: Life and Death. Because just across from the meat market there was St Bart's hospital, and just across from Bart's was your Old Bailey Central Criminal Court, on the site of old Newgate prison, where they used to string 'em up regular. So what you had in Smithfield was your three Ms: Meat, Medicine and Murders.

But it was Jimmy Phelps who told me that when he said all that, he was only saying what his old man used to say to him, Ronnie Dodds, word for word. And it was Jimmy Phelps who told me, when Jack was well out of earshot, when Jack and Vince were loaded up and on the way back to Bermondsey, that Jack had never wanted to be a butcher in the first place, never. It was only because the old man wouldn't have it otherwise. Dodds & Son, family butchers since 1903.

He says, 'Do you know what Jack wanted to be? Don't ever tell Jack I told you, will you?' And his face goes half smiling, half frightened, as if Jack's still there and might be creeping up behind him. 'When Jack was like Vince is now, being prenticed up, just like I was, he used to spend every spare minute eyeing up the nurses coming out of Bart's. I reckon it was the nurses that did it, he thought every doctor got a free couple of nurses to himself, but he says to me one day, and he aint joking, that he could chuck it all up and tell the old man to stew in his own stewing steak, because what he really wanted was to be a doctor.'

Jimmy creases up. He sits there in his smeared overalls, hands round a mug of tea, and he creases up. He says, 'He was serious. He said all it took was a change of white coats. Can you picture it? Doctor Dodds.'

But he sees I'm not laughing, so he sobers up.

'You won't tell Jack,' he says.

'No,' I say, sort of thoughtful, as if I might.

And I'm wondering if Jimmy Phelps always wanted to be a butcher. I'm remembering what Jack said, in the desert, that we're all the same underneath, officers and ranks, all the same material. Pips on a man's shoulders don't mean a tuppenny toss.

It wasn't out of wishing it that I became an insurance clerk.

But I never did tell Jack, and Jack never told me. Though you'd think when he was lying there in St Thomas's, with doctors and nurses all around him, it would have been a good time to let it slip. But all he said was, 'It should have been Bart's, eh Raysy? Bart's, by rights.'

And it seems to me that whether he ever wanted to be a

21

doctor or not, all those years of being a butcher, all those years of going up to Smithfield stored him up a pretty good last laugh against the medical profession. Because he tells me that when the surgeon came to see him for the old heart-to-heart, the old word in the ear, he didn't want no flannel. No mumbo-jumbo.

'Raysy,' he says, 'I told him to give me the odds straight. He says he aint a betting man, but I winkle it out of him. "Let's say two to one," he says. I say, "Sounds like I'm the bleeding favourite, don't it?" Then he starts up about how he can do this and he can do that, and I says, "Don't muck me about." I pulls open my pyjama top. I say, "Where'd you make the cut?" And he looks all sort of like his nose is out of joint and I aint playing according to the rules, so I say, "Professional interest, you understand. Professional interest." Then he looks at me puzzled, so I say, "Don't it say in that file of yours what I do for a living? Sorry, I mean 'did'." So he glances quickly down his notes—a bit sheepish now. Then he says, "Ah—I see that you were a butcher, Mr Dodds." And I says, "Master butcher."'

Blackheath

'So anyone tell me?' Vic says, 'Why?'

'It's where we used to go,' Vince says. 'Sunday outings. In the old meat van.'

Lenny says, 'I know that, don't I, Big Boy? But this aint a Sunday outing.'

I say, 'It's where they went for their honeymoon.'

Lenny says, 'I thought they didn't have no honeymoon. I thought they were saving up for a pram at the time.'

'They had a honeymoon later,' I say. 'After June was born. They thought at least they should have their honeymoon.'

Lenny gives me a glance. 'Must have been some honeymoon.'

'It's true, though,' Vince says. 'Summer of '39.'

'You were there, were you, Big Boy?' Lenny says.

Everyone goes quiet.

'From a meat van to a Merc, eh?' Lenny says. 'Come to think of it, Raysy, you weren't around either.'

Vince is watching us in the driving mirror. You can't see his eyes behind those shades.

I say, 'Amy told me.'

Lenny says, 'Amy told you. She told you why she aint come along an' all?'

Everyone goes quiet.

Vic says, 'Makes no difference, does it? Jack's none the wiser, is he? As a matter of fact, I told her if she wanted to forget the whole thing he'd be none the wiser either. If they scattered the ashes in the cemetery garden, he wouldn't know, would he?'

'And you an undertaker,' Lenny says.

I say, 'She's seeing June. Today's her day for seeing June.'

I look out the window. Blackheath isn't black and it isn't a heath. It's all green grass under blue sky. If it weren't for the roads criss-crossing it, it would make a good gallop. Highwaymen here once. Coaches to Dover. Your money or your life.

Vic's holding the box. I don't think he should hold the box all the time.

Lenny

Sunday outings in the meat van, as if I don't remember.

As if I don't remember them dropping our Sally off—half asleep she'd be sometimes—and my Joan saying, 'Won't you come in for a cuppa?' And Amy saying, 'Best not, we'd better get Vince home to bed.' As if I don't remember the sand between Sally's toes, and that toy bucket full of shells and bits of seaweed and dead crabs, and the smell of the seaside on her, in her hair, in her clothes, and the pints of calamine lotion Joan and I got through for her sunburn.

We'd have taken her ourselves, only we didn't have the train fare, and we didn't have no motor, of course. No motor, no shop, no house to speak of, scratching a bleeding living, that's what we was doing. I was better off in the Army if you ask me. And I remember that look Amy'd give—but maybe I imagined it, it don't do credit to a woman like Amy—when she said, no, they wouldn't come in. Like it was because we lived in a prefab and they lived in bricks and mortar. Like Amy was getting above herself. She and Jack had been to the sea for the day, and me and Joan had been to feed the ducks in Southwark Park.

Amy'd be standing there still holding on to Sally's hand and stroking her hair and stooping down to give her a kiss, so I'd feel like saying, 'That's one thing we've got that you aint got.' But I didn't. I just watched Amy kissing my daughter, and Joan would suck in her breath.

Well it wasn't our fault the bombs fell where they did. It wasn't my fault that all the old man left was three-and-six in the Post Office and a barrow in the Borough Market. And you had to remember that Jack and Amy had their hard luck too, and little Vince, of course, poor little pillock. There's luck and there's luck. So maybe I did imagine it, maybe it was me just thinking: Amy looks pretty good on a day out and some sea air, she looks pretty good. She still looks a cracker, Jack.

Jack would say, 'Come on then, Ame.' And Vincey would be sitting up there in the front of the van, ready for being carted off to bed, but he wouldn't look so sleepy because he'd be watching Amy and Sally too while they hung around on our doorstep, hoping like hell Sally was going to turn round and wave goodbye to him.

We could have done with a day out ourselves. I said the last beach I paddled on was at Salerno, I aint so keen on beaches, but we could have done with a day out. I could have done with seeing Amy in her bathing suit. But that's what parenthood is, I reckon, it's drawing the short straw deliberate. There wasn't no room for us too in the front of that van, it's a wonder the four of them managed to squeeze in. So it was all for Sally's sake. And for Jack and Amy's, of course, specially Amy. As if we didn't get the message.

Joan says, 'Them two kids are getting just like brother and sister, aren't they?'

But one day Sally comes in from school and says how they're starting to say things in the playground about Vince. How he aint all there in his head. Same as his *big sister*. How he ought to be in a Home too, a Barnardo's Home. Though when you think about it, it had to be one or the other, either the orphanage or the bin. She says Vince is getting into fight after fight and she don't know where she stands herself.

So we tell her. She must have been about ten years old. We tell her not to tell a living soul we've told her, but we tell her. It sounded half like a fairy tale, after all, half like what you'd make up to tell a kid.

How years ago when they first got married Uncle Jack and Auntie Amy, who weren't her real aunt and uncle, of course, but she knew that, had this little baby girl called June. But it wasn't a proper baby, it wasn't born right, it had to be looked after special. It happens sometimes, not so often, hardly ever, but it happens. And Auntie Amy knew she couldn't have another baby, at least not without running the same risk, so she wasn't a happy woman. Jack wasn't too chuffed either.

Then there was the war. Bombs dropping on Bermondsey and one of 'em drops on your ma and pa's old home, but that's a different story, because there's another bomb which drops on the house where the Pritchett family has just had a new arrival, called Vince. Vincent Ian Pritchett, if you want to know: V.I.P. Blame his parents. This was in Powell Road, where the flats are now, just round the corner from Wheeler Street where Auntie Amy lived then. It was June '44, a flying bomb. Another week and Mrs Pritchett and Vince would have been evacuated—taken somewhere safe. And it was five years to the month since June was born. That's how she got *her* name. Mr Pritchett was home on leave, which was bad luck, or perhaps not, depending how you look at it. And your dad and Uncle Jack were both away fighting Germans, though we hadn't even set eyes on each other then.

Well, there aint much left of the Pritchett family. Except Vince, who, being a little bouncy baby, bounces clear away without a scratch. And, if you haven't worked it out, it was Amy who took Vince in and looked after him and started to bring him up just like her own baby. Maybe you can work it out too, or you will one day, that she had more than one reason.

There's rules, there's laws about how you should bring up an orphaned baby, but this was wartime, remember, when rules get forgotten. So when the war's over a year or so later and Uncle Jack comes home, no one argues over the fact that he and Amy have got themselves an adopted child and Vince has found himself a new mum and dad. So you could say it all ended up neat and happy ever after. Except there's still June, who shouldn't be a baby any more but she is. You still following this? And Amy'd always wanted, she'd specially wanted, a girl.

'You aint to breathe a word of this,' we say.

But it was only a little while after that she tells us they'll be off again to Margate next Sunday but they don't want her to come with them. Joan says, 'What you gone and said?' getting all in a panic. And Sally says she aint said nothing, only it was getting to be a tight fit in that van, even with Vince travelling now in the back. I say, 'They put Vince in the back?' She says, 'Yes.' And a little while after that she comes home from school, tears in her eyes, and says that Vince knew now, anyway. They'd gone and told him themselves.

Well it had to happen sooner or later, and search me how you pick your time.

I should have known she was the type to get more trampled on the keener she got. Fact is, she was soft on Vincey, sweet as sugar, and I reckon she'd have made a good wife for him, it wasn't every woman would have taken him on, knowing the score. She could've done worse, too, than hitch up to Dodds and Son, all things being as they were. You could say it wasn't much to set your sights on, a butcher's shop, but when all your old man had was a fruit-and-veg stall, it was a notch up. Except Vince had his own ideas about Dodds and Son, like not having nothing to do with it.

I reckon every generation makes a fool of itself for the next one. Vince had his own ideas about Dodds and Son, but it was stretching it, even so, to do what he did, to sign up for five years just to keep out of Jack's reach, just at the time when every kid his age was thanking sweet Jesus there wasn't no call-up any more. I reckon a tour in the Middle East was a hard price to pay for not being a butcher's apprentice and for learning how to fix a jeep. Lad might even have had his arse shot off. I wouldn't have minded if he had.

I said, 'Well, Jack, you can't say he aint following in your footsteps. You were a soldier once, as well as a butcher.'

He looks at me like he's saying, I aint in no mood for jokes.
He says, 'I was a butcher by choice.'

But I knew a bit of conscripting had gone on there too. Like I'd been having a few private chats with Raysy.

He says, 'Soldier—bleeding defaulter I'd call him. Bleeding deserter. That's what I'd call him.'

I think, And you'd be right.

I say, 'It wasn't the only reason. What you think was his reason—it wasn't his only reason.'

But he doesn't listen. Hears me but he doesn't listen. Like there's only one reason in the word and that's Jack Dodds, family butcher.

I say, 'You don't own him, Jack. We don't own them, do we?'

He says, 'Talk sense.'

He looks at me and I think, You ought to be glad you don't own him, when you finally listen to what I'm saying, because you may be a big feller and it may be fifteen years since I stepped into a ring, but.

I say, 'We don't own 'em, do we? Even when we own 'em, we don't own 'em.'

He says, 'You're talking bollocks.'

So I say, 'The other reason was Sally. He left her a little leaving present. I'd say she's going to have to get rid of it.'

Vince

It wasn't like it is now, a quick race down the motorway and the taste of London still in your mouth halfway through Kent. It was like a voyage, only the other way round. So that instead of the waiting and hoping to sight land, you were moving over land in the first place, all impatient, all ready for that first glimpse. The seaside. The sea.

I watched Sally's legs. I watched the fields and the woods and the hills and the cows and sheep and farms and I watched the road, grey and hot, like elephant skin, coming towards us, always coming towards us, like something we were scooping up, eating up, but then I'd watch Sally's legs, resting on top of Amy's. Or not so much resting, because they were always moving, shifting, sliding, and when we got near the sea they'd start to jiggle up and down, her feet going under the dashboard, the way they did when she won at the spotting game, 'O' for orchard, 'P' for petrol station or, when Amy asked her if she needed to stop and have a pee, 'P' for pee. Then she and Amy would go off together, separate, behind a hedge, so I knew it wasn't just a case of pulling out your widdler, it was something different.

It wasn't so much the way they moved or even the way her cotton skirt would ride up sometimes so Amy would flip it down again if Sally didn't. It was their smoothness and bareness, their sticky-without-being-stickiness, and it was that they had a smell which you couldn't smell above the smells of going along the road but I knew it was there and I knew it was how Sally must smell all over, the bits you couldn't see. It was like the smell of the seaside, it was like the differentness of the seaside before you got there.

Sally on Amy's lap, me in the middle, Jack. We could've swapped round, I could've gone on Amy's lap, I wasn't so heavy. *Sally could've gone on my lap.* But that was how Amy wanted it. I saw that.

And one day he said anyway, 'You'll have to go in the back. You aint getting smaller, either of you. If you want Sally to come, you'll have to go in the back.'

So I went in the back where I couldn't watch Sally's legs, and all you could smell was the sweet, stale, stick-in-your-throat smell of meat.

It wouldn't be there at first. There was the picnic bag and the bag of beach things and the rug they put down for me and the soapy smell of whatever he used to scrub it all out with. But after a while the meat smell would come through, like something that had been hiding, and after a while more the sick feeling would start, and you'd have to fight it.

But I never said, I never said, and I don't suppose they even guessed, what with the windows down in front and the air rushing in, I never banged on the metal and said, 'Let me out, I wanna be sick.' Because I was doing it for Sally's sake, so she could be there. She was in the front where I couldn't see or smell her, I could only smell meat, but her being there where I couldn't see or smell her was better than her not being there at all, and when we got out at the other end she'd be there, really, and so would the seaside. The meat smell and the sick feeling would get blown away by the smell of the seaside, and though you knew it was still there in the van and there was the journey back, you didn't think about that till it happened. When something's one thing, it aint another. And when I got back in the van to go home, I'd think, It evens out, because in one direction there's what's ahead and in another there's the memory, and maybe there's nothing more or less to it than that, it's nothing more or less than what you should expect, a good thing between two bad things. Air and sunshine and, either side, being in a box.

I reckon she should've been impressed, that I did it for her sake. So I never said. But maybe she wasn't impressed, maybe she never guessed either, maybe she even thought it was something to laugh at, me being in the back like an animal in a cage, and maybe the real reason why they wanted me in the back was because they preferred Sally to me.

June aint my sister. I aint got no sister.

I'd get in, and he'd close the doors behind me, the one that said DODDS and the one that said & SON. Then he'd go round and start the engine, and I'd start to hate him. I'd hate him and hate the meat smell till they were one and the same. It was better than anything for fighting the sick feeling, better than thinking of good things, the seaside and Sally, because there wasn't no fight in those feelings. I'd lie there on the rug hating him and I'd think, I aint going to be a butcher never, it aint what I'm going to be. And as I lay there hating him I discovered something else, beyond and beneath the meat smell, something that made those journeys bearable. I'd put my ear to the rug. I'd feel the metal throbbing underneath, I'd hear the grind and grip of the transmission, the thrum of the shafts taking the power to the wheels, and I'd think, This is how a motor works, I'm lying on the workings of this van. I aint me, I'm part of this van.

But one day I sick up anyway. All over the rug and the beach bag and the picnic an' all. I never said, I just sicked up. So there aint the smell of meat, there's the smell of sick.

The next time, he says Sally aint coming so I can get in the front. So I think, I've done it now, Sally aint coming now ever again, and I say, 'I don't mind, I don't mind going in the back. I won't be sick again, honest.' But he says, 'She aint coming anyway, not this time. So hop in the front.'

Neither of them says much. It's like when I was in the back it was a sort of punishment but now I'm in the front again it's a punishment too. But then I think, It's not me who's sorry, I aint sorry, it's them who's sorry. They're sorry because they made me go in the back. They're sorry because they've been playing at being Sally's parents but now they've got me again. Then he takes a turn off the main road as if we aren't going to the seaside at all.

We stop near the top of a hill, with fields sloping away. It's all green. I think, I aint saying nothing, I aint saying, 'Why are we here?' There's an old windmill on the top of the hill, I remember that, and there's a view below: fields and woods and hedges and orchards, a farmhouse, a church tower, a village. It's spread out in different patches like someone's pieced it together.

We sit for a bit with the engine ticking and the breeze outside. Then they look at each other and he says, 'See down there. That's where your mum and me first met. Hop-picking.' But that don't mean much to me, because I know what it means to hop and I know what it means when he says 'hop in the van' but I don't have the foggiest what hop-picking is. So I say, 'What's hop-picking?', and he tries to explain, like he hadn't planned on that bit. And I aint much the wiser. And Amy says, 'They call Kent the Garden of England.' She's smiling at me funny. Then he says, like he hadn't planned on this bit either and he's only saying it so as not to say something else, 'It's like you've got to have the country to have the town. See them orchards. Uncle Lenny couldn't have no apples to sell, could he? See them sheep . . . ' Then he stops and goes quiet, looking at me. Then he looks at Amy and Amy nods, and he says, 'Come with me.'

We get out and walk into the fields and I'm scared. There are sheep bleating and staring. He stands and looks at the view. I think, It's because the sheep get killed. It's because the sheep get chopped up and eaten. The view's all far-off and little and it's as though we're far-off and little too and someone could be looking at us like we're looking at the view. He looks at me, and I know the reason I'm scared is because he is. And my dad Jack aint never scared. He doesn't look like my dad Jack, he looks as if he could be anyone. He takes a deep breath, then another one, quick, and I reckon he wanted to change his mind, but he was already teetering, toppling, on top of that hill, and he couldn't stop himself.

Amy

Well let 'em go, eh June? Let 'em do it, the whole bunch of 'em. Let 'em do without me. And you. Boys' outing. Do 'em good.

Jack should know that. All work and no play. Unless you count propping up the bar in the Coach.

That's what I told him all those years ago. We should give ourselves a break, a treat, we should give ourselves a holiday. His brave little Amy. When you fall off your horse you should get straight back on again. We should get ourselves out of ourselves. *New people.*

It might never have come to a choice between you and him. My poor brave Jack.

Vince

But a good motor aint just a good motor.

A good motor is a comfort and companion and an asset to a man, as well as getting him from A to B. A good motor deserves respect, treat it right and it treats you right. And if needs be, you can take it apart and see how it works. It aint no mystery.

People curse 'em. They say, curse of our time. But I say, aint it amazing? Aint it amazing there's this little thing that exists so everyone can jump in and travel where they please? Can't imagine a world without motors. There's nothing finer, if you ask me, there's nothing that shows better that you're alive and humming and living in this present day and age than when you squeeze the juice and burn up road and there are the signs and

31

the lights and the white lines all so it can happen and everything's moving, going. Or when you're cruising through town on a hot day with your shades on and your arm dangling out the window and a ciggy dangling from the end of your arm and some skirt to clock on the pavement. *Ridin' along in my automobeeel . . .*

And I always say it aint the motor by itself, it's the combination of man and motor, it's the intercombustion. A motor aint nothing without a man to tweak its buttons. And sometimes a man aint nothing without a motor, I see that. Motorvation, I call it. Fit the car to the customer, that's what I say. I aint just a car dealer, I'm a car *tailor*. I'm an ace mechanic too, as it happens. I know engines like you know your wife's fanny, but I've moved on from them days. A good motor's like a good suit.

Amy

But it wasn't the Pier, he even got that wrong. It was the Jetty. He ought to have remembered: the Pier and the Jetty, two different things, even if the Jetty looked more like a pier, and the Pier was only a harbour wall. Except there isn't no Jetty now, all swept away in a storm, years ago, and good riddance, I say, and amen. So maybe it wasn't his mistake, maybe it was his alternative arrangement. If he had to be chucked, if it was a case of chucking, if he had to be taken to the end of somewhere and chucked, but count me out, Jack, I won't be doing any chucking, then it had to be the Pier. Though it should have been the Jetty.

Vic

It's a good trade. It doesn't exist to buy cheap and sell dear, or to palm off on the nearest mug something he doesn't need. No one wants it, everyone requires it. There's shysters in any trade, and they're the worst kind of shysters who will take advantage of another person's misfortune. There's those I know will fleece a widow of less than a week for a solid oak coffin, satin lining, solid brass handles, the lot, when a plain veneer will do the job. I haven't heard a corpse complain yet. There's them that will flog coffins like Vincey here flogs cars. But the trade itself is a good trade, a steady trade. It won't ever run short of custom.

And it's a privilege to my mind, an education. You see humankind at its weakest and its strongest. You see it stripped bare of its everyday concerns when it can't help but take itself serious, when it needs a little wrapping up in solemnness and ceremony. But it doesn't do for an undertaker to get too solemn. That's why a joke's not out of place. That's why I say: Vic Tucker, at your disposal.

It's not a trade many will choose. You have to be raised to it, father to son. It runs in a family, like death itself runs in the human race, and there's comfort in that. The passing on. It's not what you'd call a favoured occupation. But there's satisfaction and pride to it. You can't run a funeral without pride. When you step out and slow-pace in front of the hearse, in your coat and hat and gloves, you can't do it like you're apologizing. You have to make happen at that moment what the bereaved and bereft want to happen. You have to make the whole world stop and take notice. There's times when an undertaker wields more clout than a copper. But you can't run a funeral without authority. When people don't know what to do they have to be told, and most people don't know left from right, they don't know back from front, it's a fact, in the face of death. It was the same at Jack's do as at a thousand others. When those curtains come across and the music plays, nobody knows when to turn round and go. There's no one to say, 'Show's over.' So there was Raysy, beside Amy, in the front pew, next to the aisle, looking straight ahead, and I go up to him and touch his arm and whisper in his ear, as I've whispered similar in I don't know how many ears, 'You can go now, Raysy. They'll all follow. Amy'll follow.' And just for that moment, Ray Johnson, known to those who know him as Lucky, was like putty in my hands, like a sleepy child I was sending off to bed.

I watched Jack clear off the meat trays, picking up the little sprigs of imitation greenery, then wash down the display counter, smoothly, without pausing, like he could do it all with his eyes closed, but carefully and deliberately, taking his time, it

33

being a hot day. And I thought, He's early, and it's a while since I've seen him do that himself, it's usually that lad, the one he said couldn't tell chuck from chine and couldn't keep a price in his head. Unless he's gone and paid him off too. And that red-and-white awning's looking tattier, it won't last the year out.

It's an old habit at the end of the day, to watch the other shops shutting up. A shop is meant to be looked at, that's why it's built round a window. You can eye the goods and watch the shopkeeper, like a fish in a tank, except that doesn't apply in the case of an undertaker's. A coffin shop's the one shop no one wants to peer into. They're laid out according, no pun intended. Curtain, screens. No one wants to see an FD going about his business.

So I stood where I've often stood of a quiet evening, behind the lace curtain which runs the width of the window, above the half-partition of dark panelling. It's a habit that comes with the trade too. Secrecy, seeing and not being seen.

Trev had the half day off, Dick was on a pick-up from Maidstone and the rest of the crew had slipped off, the hearses parked round the back, all waxed and polished for tomorrow. So I was alone on the premises. Excepting Mr Connolly, that is, who was waiting for his wife to come and view him.

I watched him step outside to wind up the awning, a few twists of the handle, then go back inside, then reappear to lock up and pull down the grilles. And all that must have cost a bit too, though I've never had the bother of it myself, because I haven't heard of an undertaker's being broken into lately. Not favoured in that respect either. Though I dare say there's more in my cash safe than there is in Jack's.

I thought, Now he'll turn right, pat his pockets, look at his watch, wave at Des there in the dry-cleaner's and head for the Coach, where I might well join him in an hour or so, if Vera Connolly isn't late. Thirsty weather. But I saw him walk instead to the kerb and look across, as if he could see me behind the lace curtain, as if I'd beckoned. Then he waited for the traffic and crossed over, so I stepped back inside quickly. Then I heard him rattle the door.

He said, 'Evening, Vic. You coming to the Coach?' And that

was strange, because either he'd see me at the Coach or he wouldn't, I could find my own way there. He knew if I turned up it was usually later, since I seldom finished the day like he did, five-thirty on the button.

I said, 'I was thinking of it.'

He said, 'Thirsty weather. Beautiful day.'

I said, 'Beautiful day. You come to tell me that?'

He said, 'First of June, Vic. Know what day it is?'

I look at him. He looks around.

He said, 'You all on your tod?'

I nodded. I said, 'Why don't you sit down?' He glances at me, uncertain, as if it isn't plain as pie he's come for a purpose, but he sits down, where my clients sit, where the bereaved sit and discuss their requirements. Then he says, 'Moment's come, Vic. First of June. I'm going to sell up the shop.'

He says it like he's confessing to a crime. Like he's come to arrange his own funeral.

I say, 'Well then I'll definitely come and have that drink, as there's something to celebrate. You buying?' And he looks at me, narrow-eyed for a moment, as if he wasn't asking to be made fun of, and maybe I'm not so different from all the rest of them. Scoffers.

He says, 'I'm telling you, Vic. I aint telling no one else. Not yet.'

I say, 'My privilege. Mum's the word.'

But I think, But what's the big secret, and what's the big shame? That he's going to quit when he's sixty-eight, which is not before time by most people's reckoning. That he said he'd go on till he dropped, but he hasn't dropped, though he's gone on. That he's going to do what even Vincey said he ought to do years ago: cut his losses before they cut him. Maybe that's the nub of it, that Vincey told him. And there's Amy who nigh on gave up on him.

I think, Pride's a queer thing. It puffs a small man up but that's nothing to a big man who's afraid of looking small.

He says, 'What's a butcher's shop, anyway?'

And I think, You tell me, Jack, since your whole face is saying it's everything, and it hurts to be admitting otherwise. You wouldn't think it was such a tragedy, taking your nose from the grindstone. I think, Cheer up, Jack. In my book butchers used to be jolly bastards, big fellers with big arms and big grins, like you once used to be. I'm supposed to be Mister Sad. It's retirement, not defeat. And it's only the nature of the trade that keeps me hanging on here, same age as you, lingering in the office, when I could be handing over to the boys. Because it's the age when most people start to have need of an undertaker, the age of widows in the making, and I know Mrs Connolly will appreciate it.

He says, 'There's more to life than bacon, aint there?' as if he's not sure what it might be. 'And it's only fair to Amy.'

I say, 'You told her?'

He lifts up his eyes, taken aback. He says, 'Hold on, Vic, I only made me mind up five minutes ago, swabbing down the trays.'

I thought, Well that's more like the Jack Dodds I know. So I was a witness, without knowing it, to the great Decision. There must be something that makes you look where you look when you look.

He says, 'So I thought I better tell someone fast, I better tell Vic fast, otherwise I'll go back on myself before I can tell Amy.'

That's more like the Jack I know.

I say, 'That puts me on the spot though, doesn't it? If you don't tell her.'

He says, 'I'll tell her,' indignant, but his face drops again, as though he hasn't worked out how he's going to cross that bridge, as if there's nothing harder in the world than telling good news.

There's an old clock in my office that ticks steady. It's a comfort.

He says, 'Boys OK, Vic?'

I think, Boys, they're both over forty. But it's what I call them: boys.

I say, 'I'm keeping them busy.'

He looks round at the deserted office and then at me, as though to say, 'Looks like they're keeping you busy, Vic.' But I know what that glint in his eye means, I've seen it before. It means, It's easy for you, Vic, isn't it, to give up, let go. With Dick and Trev. So it's still there anyway. It would be easy for me.

It means Vince.

Well you've scuppered your chances there, Jack. Not even help-me-outs there.

He says, 'You know what today is? First of June.'

I shake my head.

He says, 'June's birthday. June's fiftieth birthday. First of June 1939. You know where Amy is right now?'

I say, 'Seeing June.'

He nods, then looks at his hands. 'She didn't say nothing, but I knew what she was thinking. That I could make an exception. Fifty years is either special or it aint. A chance to do what I aint ever done before. She said, "I'm going to see June. It's not my normal day but today's special, isn't it?" She said, "I've bought her a present, a bracelet." She didn't have to say nothing else, just look. She don't give up. So I said, "I'll see, I'll see." Cost me a load, Vic, just to say that.'

I think, A load of what?

'I said, I could shut the shop early maybe and see you there. She said, "You're sure you know where it is?" I didn't say nothing definite, but it was like a promise. But when the time came—half an hour ago—I knew I couldn't do it, I couldn't change, not like that. Fifty years. June don't know how old she is, does she? June don't know what a bracelet's for. So then I thought, But I can change another way. She won't see me turning up at that hospital but I can have something to tell her. Something to compensate.'

I think, You might have done both.

He says, 'Amy don't give up.'

I think, Who's talking?

He says, 'June aint ever going to change, is she? Still a baby, aint she, a fifty-year-old baby? But maybe I can.'

I don't think anything.

He looks at me and at the thought I'm not thinking. He looks round the office again, cagily, as if he's half-forgotten where he is and that I'm Vic Tucker, undertaker, and not the parish priest.

He cocks his head towards the door at the back of the office. He says, 'Any lodgers?' Usual question.

I say, 'Just the one.'

And I can almost see him remembering it, that time when it was me who went running across to him. All on my own then too, short-staffed, and as luck would have it I had two in storage and one of them needed seeing to badly. It can be a two-man job. A hot day then too. So I thought of Jack across the road. I thought, Maybe a butcher. I said, 'Jack, can you do me a favour?' I had to steer him round to the back of the shop, out of earshot of a customer, to explain. He looked at me then he said, 'No problem, Vic,' as if I'd asked him if he could help me shift a piece of furniture. He said, 'Will I need this?' wiping his hands on his apron. We crossed back over, and I said before we went in, 'You sure about this?' and he says, looking at me sharply, 'I've seen bodies.' I thought, I saw them too, yours wasn't the only war. Heads bobbing in the oil. I said, 'Yes, but not women.' But he didn't turn a hair, didn't bat an eyelid, as if a seventy-four-year-old woman who'd died crossing the road wasn't any different from a joint of beef. I said, 'Thank you, Jack. It's not everyone.' He said, 'Any time, Vic. I aint everyone.'

And when the eldest son came to view I thought, You'll never know your mum was tidied up by the butcher across the road.

I suppose you'd expect a butcher not to be squeamish, you'd expect a man like Jack not to hold back. Jack Dodds was only ever squeamish about going to see his daughter. His own flesh and blood.

I say, 'Just the one. I've got someone coming to view.'

He says, 'Then I better hop it.' But he doesn't move. 'I suppose a man can change at the last minute.'

He looks at me and I look at him, as though I'm measuring him up. I think of Amy going to see June. Like Mrs Connolly.

I say, 'You sure you're going to tell Amy? I'm your witness now, Jack.'

'I'll tell her,' he says, like he's still got a trick up his sleeve. 'Or you can keep this.' And he dredges in his pocket and brings out a handful of crumpled notes. It can't have been much more than fifty quid.

'Day's takings,' he says. 'Double pledge. My word and my money. Now you can see how I can't afford to keep on the shop.'

He shoves the bunch of notes towards me. I don't refuse to take it.

Then he says, 'Do you know, Vic, what I once wanted to be?'

I look at him.

'A doctor.'

It's a good trade.

Dartford

Vic says, 'Well it's still a mystery. Why Margate?'

He's still holding the box. He shouldn't keep hogging it.

We're coming up to the M25 junction. The traffic's busy.

Lenny says, 'I reckon it was a try-on, just to see if we'd do it.'

Vince half-turns in his seat. 'You think he can see us?'

Lenny blinks and pauses a moment. He looks at me, then at Vic.

'Manner of speaking, Vincey, manner of speaking. Course he can't see us. He can't see nothing.'

Vic's hands move a little over the box.

The signs say SEVENOAKS, DARTFORD TUNNEL. The sky's clear and blue and clean.

I say, 'That box must be getting heavy, Vic, you want to pass it back here?'

Lenny chuckles. 'Mind you, Big Boy, if he can't see us, if he can't see nothing, why d'you go and borrow a Merc?'

Vince looks at the road ahead. He puts his foot down just a bit. We all feel the extra revs.

The sky's clear and blue. Jack can't see it.

Vic says, slow and gentle, 'It's the gesture, Vince. It's a fine gesture. It's a beautiful car.'

Vince says, 'It aint a meat van.'

GRANTA

J. M. Coetzee
Meat Country

Gandhi at a fruitarian luncheon at Grosvenor House, c1920

A kind of crankhood developed in the England of the 1890s, a creed of brisk cold showers, sandals in all weathers, free love, bicycle locomotion and the avoidance of alcohol and animal flesh. One associates it with Edward Carpenter and George Bernard Shaw, with the more peaceable anarchists, some of the theosophists, the early Fabians. In its political aspect the movement (if it had enough common purpose or direction to be called a movement) mixed ideals of communitarian socialism with extreme individualism and deep mistrust of the state. For inspiration it looked to Henry David Thoreau, Leo Tolstoy and, beyond them, to Jesus, son of Joseph the carpenter. The young Mohandas Gandhi, when he arrived in London to study law, fell into their company and carried some of their ideas into the wider world, so their historical influence was not nil. Nevertheless, in their high-minded naivety, their belief that the problems of the world were few and simple and easily solved, they now seem a comical lot. The internal combustion engine, and then the events of 1914, reduced them to a footnote in history.

Trying to live a life on Gandhian–Shavian lines in the United States today is both eccentric and dated, in an uninteresting way. Eccentric because one is a minnow swimming against the flow of the largest economy in the world, an economy based on the personal automobile and on getting people to consume more each year than the year before. Dated because it is a way of life without a future (in this respect it does not even qualify as 'alternative'). Uninteresting because the United States provides no more ideological resistance to it than to any other lifestyle, receiving it with the same momentary flicker of the mildest curiosity, followed by switch-off, as it receives any idea that isn't saleable.

Nevertheless, there are people deeply enough attached—or perhaps just habituated—to ways of living they have made their own to persist in them no matter how unsuitable the environment. On visits to the United States, visits which have sometimes stretched to months, I try obstinately to hold to a regimen which, although it does not include socialism or sandals or cold showers or even free love, does include a dislike for cars, a deep affection for the bicycle and a diet without flesh. I hold to these preferences as discreetly as I am able, aware of their comic potential. They seem perfectly sane to me, but I have no interest in making converts.

It is eccentric not to drive a car in the United States, doubly so in Texas. It is eccentric not to eat meat in the United States, doubly so in Texas. I write from Austin, capital of the state, where I am teaching at the University's Center for Writers. I do not write to make fun of Texas—a powerful state, almost a country in its own right, with a vigorous and varied culture that I see no reason to ridicule—and even less to assert a moral high ground over the locals. But if it is ever going to be possible to address the subject of dietary customs seriously—that is to say, not as part of the flippant cultural anthropology of tourism— then that attempt should be made from someplace like here. Austin is not Canton or Lyons, centres of the world's two great carnivore cuisines, or Chicago, historic hub of the meat trade. But it is in the heart of cattle country, and as close to the stockyards as I am likely to be for a while.

Summer in central Texas. Days dawn warm and steamy. Clouds build up and sit over the land like a lid on a pot. By ten o'clock the weight of the sun lies heavy on your limbs. It is a sun that burns white skins shades of wooden brown, from light oak to deep walnut, not unattractive but without any hint of the luminous honey-gold one sees under a temperate sun.

Nor is it like the sun of the African uplands, which whips the body dry as a bone. Here one moves in a pocket of humid warmth, sweat streaming from one's pores. Yet, surprisingly, the somatic imagination, the pre-verbal, reactive imagination of the desiring, craving body, turns not to the cold and moist—lettuce, berries, watermelon—but to the hot and dry.

I make the mistake of stranding myself on a bicycle on a country road near Bastrop, thirty miles east of Austin, with the late-morning sun already beginning to sear. It will take two hours and more to get home. I am carrying water, but the water is already at blood heat, warm enough to make one gag. My fantasies are anyhow not of water but of food: of a great dish of rice and peppers—*poblano, ancho, manzano, chimayo, serrano.* Peppers in all their hundredfold variety belong to the New

World. It was from Mexico, via the conquistadors, that they spread to the Orient. The wisdom of Mexico, which fights the fire of the sun with the flame tongues of the earth.

We are invited to dinner by a colleague at the University. Dorothy calls his wife to warn her of our eccentric dietary habits. 'Oh dear!' says our hostess. 'We're having ribs first and then chicken. You don't eat chicken? There won't be anything else.'

The Roman Emperor Vitellius gave a feast in honour of Minerva at which the *pièce de résistance* called for the brains of a thousand peacocks and the tongues of a thousand flamingos. A hecatomb of birds for one dish. In China a roast bear's paw is a delicacy. Four paws per bear: what of the rest of the beast?

In our time and place, tales like these evoke moral disapproval, even in deeply carnivorous circles. The death of the bear, the deaths of the flamingos, disturb us as the death of the beef ox does not. Why? Because there are so many more oxen than bears on earth, we say. Because we eat so much more of the carcass of the ox than of the carcass of the flamingo (do flamingos have carcasses or mere bodies?). The gourmet's nonchalant wastefulness, the disproportion between his pleasures and the slaughter that must take place to satisfy them, affront our sense of what is right. (What a relief we have a pet-food industry to grind up all the leftover flesh and put it in cans, so that no death occurs in vain!)

The sacrifice of the bear angers us because there are so few bears left. If we go on killing bears for their paws, we argue, bears will disappear as a species. Oxen, by contrast, are two a penny. They can be bred without end, their species is not threatened. The life of the species is of a higher order than the life of the individual.

This species argument is widely accepted today. Is it fair to remind ourselves of the Nazis, who divided humankind into two species, those whose deaths mattered more and those whose deaths mattered less? What does the ox think about being consigned— without consultation—to a lower species than the bear, or indeed than the spotted owl or the Galapagos sea turtle? It is one thing to say that man is of a higher order than the animals, another to say that among the animals there are higher and lower orders. Yet

45

once we concede that all animals have an equal right to life, we find ourselves in the company of the Jain sweeping the road before him so that he will not tread on an ant. An impossible position.

Life being nasty, brutish and short, Diogenes the Cynic believed that thinking men and thinking women should refuse to procreate. No one has ever taken Diogenes seriously, and rightly so. However sorry a business life may be, men and women cleave to each other, engender babies, bring them into the world. Having children is part of human nature; only a fool could imagine that mankind would change its nature for the sake of an idea.

Similarly, whether or not it is a good idea to kill fellow beings and eat them, that is the way of the world, the animal kingdom included. The few exceptions to the rule (cows, horses, deer) would probably follow suit if only they could find out how to digest flesh: it is certainly not for the sake of principle that they restrict themselves to grass. Our cousins the chimpanzees, whom we used to think herbivorous, turn out to prefer fruit with worms to fruit without.

The question of whether we should eat meat is not a serious question. The 'should' in the question is anomalous: bringing 'should' into contact with eating meat, as with bringing 'should' into contact with sex, is like asking, 'Should we be ourselves?' Interpreted to mean 'Should we be what we have made ourselves to be?' the question might perhaps be a real one. But we have not made ourselves to be creatures with sexual itches and a hunger for flesh. We are born like that: it is a given, it is the human condition. We would not be here, we would not be asking the question, if our forebears had eaten grass: we would be antelopes or horses.

Asking whether human beings should eat meat is on the same level of logic as posing the question, 'Should we have words?' We have words; the question is being posed in words; without words there would be no question. So if there is going to be any question at all, it will have to be a different question, one I have not even begun to frame.

Rationalist vegetarians like to point to the foolishness of feeding stock on grain. In energy terms, they say, it takes ten calories to provide one calorie when corn is converted into flesh.

But this is just a datum, without meaning in itself. There are two absolutely opposed ways of interpreting it, giving it meaning. One is that people are unenlightened and wasteful. The other is, in the words of Marvin Harris, who has written a history of mankind as a struggle for protein, that 'people honour and crave animal foods more than plant foods and are willing to lavish a disproportionate share of their energy and wealth on producing them.'

Nevertheless. It is only at the point of the 'nevertheless' that the whole sorry discussion begins to come to life. Despite the hypocrisy of wailing over dead bears and flamingos, despite the nonsensicality of the 'should' questions, there is something lurking here that will not go away. But how to approach it?

Let us begin at Central Market on North Lamar Avenue, Austin, Texas. Stores like Central Market, as large as two or even three football fields, are familiar to Americans, or at least to affluent, middle-class Americans. They are based on economies of scale and on a single, simple promise addressed to the customer: Everything you can conceivably want, in the way of things to eat and drink, is here, and more. You need go nowhere else.

The 'and more' is important. The cornucopia, the mythological horn of plenty, disgorges a *copia*, a torrent of goods, that is more than anyone can consume. Fundamental to Central Market and stores like it is the cornucopian promise that what is on offer is inexhaustible not only in sheer mass but in variety too: variety of flavour and colour and size, variety of origin, variety of method of cultivation. If the effect is dizzying, that is part of the plan.

Wandering around the first hall of Central Market, the atrium of fruit and vegetables, is indeed like being in the mythic Land of Plenty. Why, then, is the experience of the next chamber, the Hall of Meats (meat, fish and poultry), so different? Partly, perhaps, because the smell has changed. No longer does the air hold the scent of melons and peaches. Instead there is a smell of blood and death, and all the exertions of the smiling assistants behind the counters to scrub and sterilize will not chase it away.

The infernal atmosphere in which they have to operate is not their only handicap. However willing they are to advise, to chop and slice and weigh and pack, they cannot compete, as a show, with Fruits and Vegetables. The very current of modern marketing is against them. The modernist food hall consisting of nothing but rows and rows of gleaming refrigerated beds holding antiseptic packages, neatly labelled and priced, is becoming an anachronism. The new fashion is rough, homely, mock-rustic: fruit and vegetables cascading out of bushel baskets, with folksy handwritten signs planted in them telling where they come from, what they taste like, how to cook them. A spectacle, in other words, of origins.

In the old-fashioned supermarket of the 1950s, food was packaged and presented as pure commodity: germless, odourless, coming from nowhere. Central Market, on the other hand, is a vast mock-up of a rural street market. All that is missing is Farmer Brown, with no-nonsense country dirt under his fingernails, and his good wife by his side to help him sell the dew-pearled produce they harvested that very morning.

How is the Hall of Meats to move with the times? How can it rival this pageant of origins? Ineluctably the meat halls of Texas and the rest of the United States are being tugged towards the model of the Cantonese market, where you can pick out a goose and have its head chopped off before your eyes; or of the Riviera restaurant, where in their aerated tank lobsters await the distinction of being selected for the cauldron; or even of those Hong Kong establishments where a live vervet monkey is brought to your table and trepanned so that you can spoon out its warm brains (good for potency or longevity or sagacity, I forget which). Towards theatre, in other words.

Yet there is something in the Anglo-American way of life that baulks at such a prospect. For centuries its table culture has been moving in the opposite direction, towards greater discretion, greater delicacy regarding the unpleasant off-stage business of the slaughterhouse and kitchen. The climax of the feast in Petronius's *Satyricon*—the arrival of a giant goose built out of pork, with quail in its belly—would call forth no admiring applause today. On the contrary, the dish would be regarded as vulgar and even offensive. The pig—tail and trotters and eyeballs and all, with an apple in his mouth—has been removed from his showplace at the centre of the table, and replaced with euphemistically or metaphorically named *cuts* (butterfly chops, veal scallopini, tenderloin) whose relation to the bodies they come from is a mystery to most of the family. The art of carving, which used to be part of a gentleman's repertoire, proving that he was a huntsman and knew how to deal with a dead animal, has become a quaint and faintly comical accomplishment rolled out for Christmas or Thanksgiving; the diner's personal knife has evolved into the table knife, a dull, blunt-pointed tool for pushing food around. The United States in its present mood would simply not stomach the metamorphosis of the meat hall into a theatre of execution, disembowelment, flaying, quartering.

Respect for life, one might call it, but for the fact that the same customers who might shrink from the spectacle of locusts being de-winged or ants being fried alive—to say nothing of pigs being stuck—will unblinkingly call in the pest exterminator to their homes. It is not death that is offensive, but killing, and killing only of a certain kind, killing accompanied by 'unnecessary pain'. Somehow the imagination knows what the other's pain is like, even the ant's pain. What the imagination cannot encompass is death. Death, it says to itself, is the end of pain. Death is a relief.

The Book of Leviticus is filled, chapter after chapter, with proscriptions: no camel flesh, no pig flesh, no hyraxes or hares, no shellfish or crustacea, no vultures or storks, no bats, no tortoises, no lizards or chameleons. The bans spelled out with such maniacal exactitude are all on animal flesh. There are no proscriptions on plant foods. The branch of human knowledge that tells which plants may be eaten and which are to be avoided seems to be separate from the branch that tells which kinds of flesh may be eaten and which are unclean. The basis of plant lore is experience, passed down by word of mouth. To the extent that it is indistinguishable from herbal lore (knowledge of the medicinal properties of plants), plant lore belongs to folk science. Flesh lore, on the other hand, belongs squarely to tradition, to taboo, and therefore to religion (this despite efforts to persuade us that, for instance, the rabbinical ban on pork was a public health measure, an effort to control the spread of trichinosis).

Even in the case of so-called clean meat, like beef, the same people who eat the muscle flesh of cattle are revolted at the thought of eating their eyes, their brains, their testicles, their lungs. They would vomit if they had to drink blood. Why? The question is pointless: distaste for certain body parts, and particularly for body fluids in their fluid state, belongs to the penumbra of taboo, well outside the realm of rational explanation.

The letter of Levitican law is dead in American culture, the spirit by no means so. The same late-twentieth-century consumers who, leaving behind the cautious eating habits of their ancestors, eagerly experiment with baby white aubergines, oyster mushrooms, pumpkin flowers, will not touch frogs' legs, snails, rabbit flesh, horse meat. The standard for allowing unfamiliar vegetable matter into the body seems to be of a quite different order from the standard for unfamiliar flesh. In the first case, the criterion is taste alone: if it tastes good, I will eat it. In the second, a deep-seated resistance has to be overcome, a resistance which is intimately related to taboo and the horror to which food taboos give expression.

What is the nature of this horror? It has something to do with the essential distinction between plants and animals in our everyday understanding: that animals are alive and plants are not, that animals cannot or should not or dare not be eaten while they are alive, while plants can be eaten with impunity because they have never been, in the full sense of the word, alive.

But the matter is more complicated. In the visceral imagination there appears to be some mistrust of the alive/dead distinction itself, some reluctance to accept that what is dead is henceforth and for ever devoid of life. At its deepest level, this mistrust expresses itself as a fear that forbidden flesh—flesh that has not been properly killed and ritually pronounced dead—will continue to live some kind of malign life in one's belly—that it will be, as Leviticus calls it, an abomination inside one. Hence the intimate relations, in so many religions, between priests and butchers, and the requirement for a priestly presence in the slaughterhouse. Hence too, perhaps, the custom of praying before eating: an effort to placate the angry spirit of the sacrificed beast. (After he first ate meat, Gandhi could not sleep: he kept hearing the goat he had eaten bleating in his stomach to be let out.)

Of course it is just superstition that meat is a different kind of thing from plants. Plants are food, meat is food—a particularly good food, rich in protein, B-group vitamins and amino acids. Beef is good for one, chicken is good for one. Fish is particularly good for one. Pork is good for one too, good even for Jews and Muslims. Frogs are good for one, or at least frogs' haunches. Prawns are good for one, once their digestive tracts have been cut out. Even roaches are good for one, once their hard wings have been pulled off.

People who extend their superstitious horror of roaches to cover prawns (which look so much like them!) and then frogs and then fish and ultimately chicken and beef don't know where to draw the line. The question is: To whom should they go to learn where to draw the line?

Marvin Harris's thesis that the history of mankind is a struggle to capture and control protein resources is controversial: protein is not everything, say other scholars.

Protein may not be everything; but if asked for a truly down-to-earth, materialist explanation for the peace that reigns, by and large, in western democracies, the best answer available may be that these are societies that have made available enough animal protein to satisfy the cravings of the overwhelming majority of their citizens. (Enough and more: the amount of gross obesity in the United States seems to point to people stuffing themselves with protein—and fat—simply because it is cheap and plentiful.) Europeans emigrated to the Americas, to Australasia, to the more hospitable parts of Africa, because they wanted better lives. Better lives meant, most immediately, meat on the table seven days of the week. It was not the well fed who left behind their birthplace, but the hungry and, specifically, those hungry for meat.

One of the most bitter, unremitting and unremarked social struggles in European history, stretching from the Middle Ages to the early twentieth century, was over the right to hunt, over access to game. When warlords took possession of great tracts of land and became landlords, they took over the wildlife as well, and defined as criminals those commonfolk who continued to treat wildlife (which of course knew no boundaries) as a common resource. Robin Hood may have been a proto-insurrectionary

51

preying on the rich in the name of the poor, but at a more mundane level he was a poacher who challenged the claim of the Crown to ownership of the deer of the forests. European legend is full of stories of poacher heroes, just as the records of European law courts are full of draconian sentences for poaching. What these records memorialize is generation after generation of class warfare over access to meat.

Africa is the last continent where poaching goes on on a grand scale. No longer is it the king's game—'royal game'—that is being poached. Instead, tribespeople poach from the game parks, the refuges where those who have enough flesh for themselves hoard up the edible beasts of the savannah for motives that make no sense to the protein-hungry.

Europeans emigrated to the colonies for a host of reasons. Most vivid among these was the promise that there they could have meat whenever they wanted. It did not escape the notice of the colonial authorities that, from being peasants who lived on a diet of milk and grain to being hunters who lived on meat and not much else, these new colonists were tracing an evolutionary reversal: hunting, after all, belonged to an earlier stage in human progress than agriculture. This rather abstract concern of the authorities about cultural retrogression was matched by a more specific anxiety about control: free-ranging hunters were harder to keep track of, and therefore to tax, than static cultivators.

Dietary habits took hold in early colonial times that would not thereafter be easily shaken off. Egalitarianism came before democracy, and egalitarianism meant an end of the stratification of society into those who hogged the supply of meat and those who had to stuff their stomachs with grains. America typifies the triumph of the common people in their historical drive for animal protein, and Texas is, in this respect, the capital of America. The Texan family sitting down to a meal of chicken and fried steak with french fries on the side is making up, atavistically, for European forebears who had to make do with milk and bread, or polenta. Day after day, meal after meal, their diet celebrates the New World. Life is good here: no amount of argufying is going to change that. 'Ribs first and then chicken. There won't be anything else.'

GILES FODEN
IDI'S BANQUET

Idi Amin

I did almost nothing on my first day as Idi Amin's doctor. I had just come in from one of the western provinces, where I'd run a bush surgery. Kampala, the city, seemed like paradise after all that.

Back in my old neighbourhood, I'd seen to Idi once. On his bullying visits to the gumbooted old chiefs out there, he would drive a red Maserati manically down the dirt tracks. Walking in the evenings, under the telegraph poles where the kestrels perched, you could discern his passage—the green fringe of grass down the middle of the track would be singed brown by the burning sump of the low-slung car.

On this occasion, he'd hit a cow—some poor smallholder had probably been fattening it up for slaughter—spun the vehicle and been thrown clear, spraining his wrist in the process. The soldiers, following him in their slow, camouflaged Jeeps, had come to call for me, and I was required to go and splint it on the spot. Groaning in the grass, Idi was convinced the wrist was broken; he cursed me in Swahili as I bound it up.

But I must have done something right because a few months later I received a letter from the Minister of Health, Jonah Katabarwa, appointing me to the post of General Amin's personal physician—Medical Doctor to His Excellency—at Nakasero Lodge, his residence. That was Idi's way, you see. Punish or reward. You couldn't say no. Or I didn't think, back then, that you could. Or I didn't really think about it at all.

I explored the planes and corners of my gleaming office, which stood in the grounds of the Lodge and came with a next-door bungalow thrown in. I felt rather pleased with its black couch and swivel chair, its green filing cabinets, its bookshelves stacked with medical reports and back issues of the *Lancet*, its chrome fittings and spring-loaded anglepoise lamps. My immediate tools—stethoscope, a little canvas roll of surgical instruments, casebook and so on—were laid out tidily on the desk. The neatness and general spotlessness of the place were the work of Cecilia, my nurse. She was a remnant of the regime of my predecessor, Ironside. After suffering my attentions at the roadside, Amin had summarily dismissed him. I knew I ought to feel guilty about this, but I didn't, not really. Cecilia made it quite plain that she didn't like or approve of me (I reckon she must have been half in love with old Ironside), and that she would soon be going back herself, back to Ashford, Kent.

Let the old girl go, I thought, pushing aside a paper on disorders of the digestive tract—my private study, my little problem. I was just glad to be out of the bush and to be earning a bit more money. The sun was shining, and I was happy, happier than I'd been in a good many months. I stared out of the window on to a cultivated lawn which swept down Nakasero Hill towards the lake, glittering in the distance. A light breeze moved the leaves of the shrubbery: bougainvillea, flame tree, rhododendron. Through the slatted blinds, I could see a group of prisoners in white flannel uniforms cutting the grass with long, pliable sword-like implements, curved at the end. They were guarded by a sleepy soldier, leaning on his gun in the dusty haze. Swish, swish, the noise came quietly through to me. I watched the prisoner nearest to me, slightly hypnotized by the movement of his cutter and the articulation of his bony arm. I shouldn't think they were fed too well: a bit of steamed green banana or maize meal, some boiled-up neck of chicken if they were lucky.

Turning away from the window, I resolved (since there didn't seem any likelihood of a presidential consultation that afternoon) to walk into town. I just used to wear shorts and shirt in the bush, and needed to get a nice linen suit run up for tonight. The Indian tailors—their ancestors had been brought over to work on the Uganda Railway—these chaps, with their push-pedal, cast-iron Singers, their bad teeth and worse English, were just the fellows for the job. They could sort you out a suit in a couple of hours, while you looked round the market or went to one of the laughably understocked grocers. Not quite Savile Row, but good enough for here, good enough for Idi, anyway. Though he himself did wear Savile Row tailoring, with its luscious, thick lapels and heavy hem-drop. Zipped up in their polypropylene bags, the suits came in on the weekly flight from Stansted, hung on racks among crates of Scotch, golf clubs, radio cassettes, cartons of cigarettes, bicycles tubed in cardboard, slimline kettles, sleek toasted-sandwich makers with winking lights. And plain things, too, sugar and tea: products that might well have come from here in the first place, swapping their gunny sacks for cellophane packaging on the return trip.

I needed a suit quickly because this evening Idi was to host the Ambassadors' Dinner, the annual beanfeast at which he entertained Kampala's diplomatic corps, assembled local dignitaries, senior civil servants, the wealthier concessionaires (Lonrho, Cooper Motors, Siemens), senior figures from the banks (Standard, Commercial, Grindlays) and tribal chiefs from all over the country. Katabarwa, the Minister, had told me that His Excellency had given specific orders that I should attend. 'As you know,' he had said (I had read Amin's medical records, such as they were—chaos really, since His Excellency insisted on editing them himself), 'General Amin occasionally suffers from a slight gastric difficulty.'

As I shut the door of the office behind me, the draught from the corridor set the blinds tinkling, like little cymbals. The noise reminded me of something I once saw on holiday in Malta—a set of tiny, shiny knives hung up like wind chimes outside a knife-grinder's shop. I was with my friend Philip Fry. 'Aeolian sharps,' he remarked at the time. He's dead now, from you-know-what: 'slim', 'the illness', as they would call it here in years to come.

I took a shower in the concrete-lined cubicle in my bungalow. The big steel rose spurted out only a single stream of tepid water, under which I held up my hands, sending it spattering, planing down my back. Afterwards, as I went through the rough archway that separated the steamy bathroom from the sweltering bedroom, it was like going from one dimension to another. Fresh sweat mixed with the runnels of shower water.

I then found myself, to my irritation, needing to defecate, which I always hate doing just after a shower—it seems like a form of sacrilege. As usual, I inspected what I had produced: it's the easiest way of determining at an early stage the presence of a parasite, which can take hold in that fetid climate in a matter of days. This evening's offering, I was worried to notice, was paler than usual, suggesting that bacteria had been absorbed into the bowel. I made a mental note to run some tests on myself in the morning.

The effort of expulsion had caused me to perspire even more, when I put on my new suit I was already wearing what I called my African undertaker's outfit: the envelope of moisture which covered the body day and night. This tropical monster, ghostly presage of a thousand sallow malarial deaths, squatted on one's shoulders and then, trickling down, concentrated its peculiar force in the hollows of the knees and ankles.

It was in this morbid state that I strolled across the lawn to the Lodge—hair brushed and shining nonetheless, a blue, short-sleeved shirt and natty green tie under the new cream suit. On my way, I saw that the gardeners were being herded into the lorry that would take them back to the jail on the outskirts of town. One by one, they disappeared through the canvas flaps of the tailgate. The guard lifted up a short stick, acknowledging me as I passed. A marabou stork was poking about nearby in a pile of rubbish, and I gave it a wide berth. These birds, the height of a small child, stood on spindly legs, their large beaks and heavy pinkish wattles making them look as though they might topple over. They were urban scavengers, gathering wherever there was pollution or decay. I hated them, yet I found them intriguing; they were almost professorial in the way they sorted through the heaps of rotting produce scattered all over the city, the organic mass mixed in with mud and ordure, scraps of plastic, bits of metal.

Going through a gate in the wall that divided off the ceremonial parts of the Lodge, I walked to where the big black cars of the ambassadors, the Mercedes of the richer Indian merchants and various white Toyotas and Peugeots with a smattering of dirt about the wings were beginning to pull up outside a cavernous portico. An official in a red coat with brass buttons (it was too tight for him; the buttons strained to close the gap) ushered them into parking spaces, smiling and inclining his head.

Once inside, Katabarwa, the Minister, beckoned me impatiently from the top of a wide staircase. He and various other ministers and senior army officers were waiting there to greet the guests and progress them through the great ebony-panelled door into the main hall, where the banquet was to take place.

He was definitely one of the solemn ones, Katabarwa, his young face (he couldn't have been much older than me—about twenty-eight) frowning with the burden of office.

58

'Ah, Garrigan, you have arrived. I was hoping that you would be here in good time. You must be on hand if any of the guests are becoming unwell.'

'Of course,' I said obligingly.

He looked ridiculous, my boss—somehow he'd got hold of a dress suit, but the sleeves were too short, and his cuffs, fastened with twisted bits of fuse wire, stuck out like little birds.

Already a long queue had formed down the stairs as the dignitaries waited for a handshake from Idi—he was wearing a blue uniform today, Air Force I supposed, with gold trim and lacy epaulettes. He looked splendid.

Katabarwa propelled me into a little knot of three people in the straggly queue. One of them was Spurling, the boyish attaché at the British Embassy, who had logged me in his book on my arrival in the country, before I went into the bush. The other couple, I supposed, were the Ambassador and his wife. She was small but sinewy, in a dress printed with flowers. Coming closer I studied her covertly from over Katabarwa's shoulder; then her eyes, long-lashed in a composed but unsmiling face surrounded by a dark bob, were suddenly meeting mine, and I had to look away. Her mouth was pursed like a little fig. Her face momentarily registered some expression as she looked at me. Not a totally unpleasant one, I thought.

She must have been about thirty, at least ten years younger than her husband, who was standard Foreign Office issue: plastered-down hair, a large body shifting in its bristly suit, round glasses in a round face—a sponge of official easing-along, ready to soak up whatever discord the world threw at him.

Katabarwa introduced us.

'Ambassador Brown, you have met our new doctor at the Lodge, Nicholas Garrigan?'

'I haven't in fact, but Spurling here has told me all about his good work out west. So you've come to keep things in order back up here? We've been a bit lost since old Ironside went, I can tell you.'

He looked meaningfully at Katabarwa.

'This is my wife, Jenny. And Spurling you already know.'

Spurling lifted his nose up in the air at me.

'Hello, Mrs Brown.'

She held out a hand to me, leaning her head to one side, her teeth showing slightly between her lips.

'It's so nice to have a doctor nearby again. One gets so terribly worried.'

I wondered whether she was teasing me.

When it was the turn of our little group to take its salutations from Idi, he clapped me on the shoulder with one great hand and waved the other in front of my face.

'So you see, Doctor, I am fully recovered from my tumble. But although I am as strong as lion, I have some small wounds in my belly which you must fix for me.'

Greeting each of us in turn, relaxed and charming, he chuckled as we moved past, beneath the twinkling chandeliers. We searched out our seats at the long mahogany table, which was already filling up with grim-faced Army officers and assorted civilians. There were a couple of journalists dashing around with notebooks, and a photographer, his camera hanging round his neck on a broad canvas strap. Some guests were in dinner jackets and evening gowns; some were in linen suits, cotton dresses, safari suits, saris; some (though by no means all) of the chiefs were in traditional garb; and several matrons wore wraparound dresses of colourful printed cloth. One lissom Ugandan maiden—a princess, I was later informed—was wearing a trouser suit of what appeared to be pink cashmere. But she didn't, under those whirring hardwood fans, seem to be any hotter than the rest of us.

The company hovered, ill at ease, behind the tall chairs, waiting for the greetings to come to an end and the meal proper to begin. I discovered my place card. Name spelt wrong, in uneven type: DR GARGAN. Mrs Brown was next to me on one side, Katabarwa on the other. Brown and his American counterpart, Todd ('Nathan Theseus Todd', if you please) faced us. Beyond: the Italian, Cueva, the Spanish, Ricaba, the Portuguese, Dias. All were fat, or fattish, and full of savoir faire: they must make them in factories, these ambassadors.

I looked down the table, over the rows of silver and crystal, towards the kitchen, where processions of waiters were bustling in and out. A slight aroma of woodsmoke, a whiff of reality, drifted up the table, fanned by the kitchen doors. All this—the china, the doilies, the display of tropical flowers, the perfumed finger bowls, most of all her, Jenny Brown, next to me—all this was a bit much to take after those long months in the west; it all promised, it all suggested too much.

Wine was poured. Conversation bubbled quietly as we waited for Idi to finish greeting the guests. Eventually, he bowled in, smiling genially as he made his way up to the top of the table, to the carver chair. Behind him on the wall was a large disc of golden metal, emblazoned with the country's emblem, a Ugandan crested crane.

Idi was seated at the head of the table, a couple of places up from our party. Brown and Todd were the most significant emissaries, politically speaking, but as they had presented their credentials only relatively recently, ancient diplomatic practice decreed that they not be placed hard by the seat of local power. About which, I suspect, they were secretly ecstatic. It's a lesson worth noting that apparently burdensome convention can sometimes work to individual advantage.

So there he stood, Idi, solid as a bronze bull, almost as if he, too, was waiting for something to happen. What did happen was that a greying official in tails, some sort of major-domo who had been scuttling up and down ever since we entered the hall, sounded a gong and then, straightening up, read from a paper:

'His Excellency President for Life Field Marshal Al Hadj Dr Idi Amin Dada, VC, DSO, MC, Lord of All the Beasts of the Earth and Fishes of the Sea and Conqueror of the British Empire in Africa in General and Uganda in Particular welcomes the Court of Kampala and assembled worthies of the city to this his annual banquet.'

I looked down at Jenny Brown's hands resting in her lap.

'I wonder how long this bloody business is going to last,' I muttered.

'I know what you mean,' she said, turning towards me. But at that moment, the toastmaster's voice rose to a crescendo:

'Ladies and gentlemen, welcome. Field Marshal Amin has requested that you should begin eating only after he has made a few introductory remarks concerning domestic and international affairs.'

Amin drew himself up to his full, impressive height, the light of the chandeliers dancing on his shiny dome, his sharply planed cheeks. The girl in pink was seated next to him.

'My friends, I have to do this because if I do not speak now, you will become too drunk to hear my words. I have noticed there can be bad drunkenness in Uganda and indeed across the whole world, from beer and from spirits. This is true of the armed forces especially. For example, looking at the faces of the Entebbe Air Force Jazz Band, I know straightaway they are drunkards.'

The diners tittered, turning to look at the jazz band, seated on a podium in a shadowy corner. Having looked doleful at the outset, and then worried at Idi's remark, the musicians were now laughing energetically.

'Yes, some people look as though they are painted with cosmetics just because of too much drinking of alcohol. And cosmetics too can be bad themselves, and wigs: I do not want Ugandans to wear the hair of dead imperialists or of Africans killed by imperialists.'

He patted the pink princess on the head. For a moment, he paused, blinking as if confused, or unsure of what he was seeing—his eyesight, I knew from the files, was bad. Then he sniffed the air and continued.

'No member of my own family is to wear a wig, or she will cease to be my family member. Because we are all one happy family in Uganda, like it is we are gathered around this table in our single house. Myself, I started cleaning the house until I succeeded in placing indigenous Ugandans in all important posts. Can you remember that even cooks in hotels were whites? Except for me: I myself sold biscuits on the roadside as a young boy and was a cookpot stirrer in my first Army position, before I became General. Otherwise, insecurity prevailed before. Now, if you go into the countryside you will see we have enough food. We are growing crops for export and we are getting foreign exchange. Also I have received a report from the Parastatal Food and Beverages Ltd: it says we are selling Blue Band, Cowboy, Kimbo Sugar, salt, rice, Colgate, Omo and shoe polish. So you see, you do not hear anywhere Uganda has debts, only from the British press campaign to tell lies.'

Brown wiped his fork on his napkin, then lifted it up close to his face, examining the prongs. He looked slightly green, as if the wine had touched up his liver.

'Because the World Bank is very happy with Uganda. In fact, I have decided to help the World Bank. I have decided to offer food relief to countries with food problems: millet, maize and beans shall be sent in sacks to all thin countries. And cassava also.'

I thought of the terraced plots back in the west; I used to watch the women set out to work as I ate my breakfast on the wooden veranda. They carried strange, broad-bladed hoes on their shoulders and had children strapped to their backs and bundles balanced on their heads, their chatter floating up to me as they walked by.

'Ambassadors who are here, please ensure that the food delivered in your countries is equitably distributed. Even you who are from superpowers. Remember this: I do not want to be controlled by any superpower. I myself consider myself the most powerful figure in the world and that is why I do not let any superpower control me. Remember this also: superpower leaders can fall. I once went for dinner with the Prime Minister of Britain, Mr Edward Heath, at his official residence Number Ten Downing Street. He fed me very well. However, he is now very poor, having been relegated from Prime Minister to the obscure rank of bandmaster. I understand he is one of the best bandmasters in the United Kingdom. I saw the picture of Mrs Thatcher in one of the East African papers. From the photograph she appeared very charming, happy, fresh, intelligent and confident. I think she must eat well. I would like to marry her.'

'I don't think we need give too much credence to that,' muttered Brown. His wife fiddled with her spoons, putting the dessert spoon into the curve of the soup spoon. And then she changed the arrangement around.

'Indeed, I would like to marry all of you. As I have repeatedly emphasized, there is no room in Uganda for hatred and enmity. I have stated I will not victimize or favour anybody.

Our aim must be unity and love. And good manners. So guerrillas against the country will be met with countermeasures. You will forgive me for ending my speech here. I have said it before: I am not a politician but a professional soldier. I am therefore a man of few words and I have been very brief throughout my professional career. It only remains for me to draw your attention to one thing more: the good foods coming to the table before you. A human being is a human being, and like a car he needs refuelling and fresh air after working for a long time. So: eat!'

With this last declamation, he threw up his arms and stood there motionless for a second, like a celebrant at the Mass. Behind him, his raised arms were reflected dully in the great gold dish on the wall, altering the pattern of light as it fell on the tablecloth.

And then he sat down.

The diners hardly stirred, staring at him still. Idi savoured the sight of it, his own lips moving silently, as if he had carried on speaking.

The rattle of the trolleys, bringing in the starters, broke the spell, and everyone began to applaud.

The hors d'oeuvres were placed in front of us, a triple choice: fillets of tilapia, thick gumbo soup made from okra and crayfish, or, most disturbingly for the Europeans (it was the kind of thing Idi would do on purpose), a variety platter of *dudu*—bee larvae, large green bush crickets, cicadas and flying ants, fried with a little oil and salt. They were actually quite delicious—crisp and brown, they tasted like whitebait.

'I think I'll stick to the gumbo,' said Todd, horrified, as Katabarwa and I crunched up a few.

Katabarwa pushed the *dudu* platter towards him.

'But these are a local delicacy. You may not be knowing, Sir, that gumbo is an imported dish even in our own Uganda. It is from just over the fringe of our south-western province, into Zaire, where, as you may know also, many of the border peoples speak Swahili like our Ugandan soldiers here, and come to trade fish or to be treated medically by such fellows as Doctor Garrigan, who was in those parts before.'

'That's right,' I added, lamely. 'I was in the west before I came to Kampala.'

'I guess it must have been quite rough to live out there. I went down there on tour last year,' said Todd.

'But in Zaire it is too bad more,' interjected Katabarwa. 'They are real savages in that place. In that country, Sir, this gumbo, it is called *nkombo*, which means "runaway slave" in the Nkongo language—it is how he, this dish here, came to your country America. I am sure you were not knowing this.'

'No, I can't say I was aware of that, Minister Katabarwa. Of course, American cuisine is nourished by all manner of national traditions: Dutch, German, English, but also Korean and, as you say, there's the whole Afro-American thing. The melting pot, you know. It is fascinating, isn't it, this gourmandizing business? Every plate tells a story.'

'I thought you chaps just ate hamburgers.'

'Don't mock me, Spurling. I had a Paris posting when I was young. They'd call you Monsieur Rosbif over there, or John Bull.'

'But in Zaire, too, those people eat monkey meat,' Katabarwa said loudly, laying it on thick, piqued at no longer being the centre of attention.

Suddenly Amin himself, overhearing, called down from the top of the table.

'And what is your fault with monkey meat, Minister of Health? I, your President, has eaten monkey meat.'

Katabarwa, craven, toyed with his cutlery.

'And I have also eaten human meat.'

This His Excellency almost shouted. A silence fell over the table—acute, nearly tangible, throwing over the tureens and salvers a shroud of embarrassment. We looked at him, not sure how to react.

Idi stood up.

'It is very salty, even more salty than leopard meat.'

We shifted in our chairs.

'In warfare, if you do not have food, and your fellow soldier is wounded, you may as well kill him and eat him to survive. It can give you his strength inside. His flesh can make you better, it can make you full in the battlefield.'

And then he sat down again.

The candles fluttered light on to the silver, which threw off distorted images of the faces round the table.

I found myself thinking of ants, clay mounds, the distribution of formic acid.

No one said a word until the waiters wheeled in the centrepiece of the main course. It was a whole roast kudu hind. Her little stumped-off, cauterized legs stuck up in the air like cathedral spires, and she was stuffed, so the menu told us, with avocado and sausage meat. The latter spilt out, crusty and crenellated, at one end, the Limpopo-coloured fruit-vegetable at the other.

The display rolled up to Idi. We watched him rub knife against steel, rhythmically, the noise marking out still further the silence over the table. Then he slit the torso and, with a rough majesty, hacked off a ceremonial slice of meat for himself, flipping it on to the gold-rimmed plate. A little spatter of grease flew on to the princess's cashmere, causing her to jump back in her seat and then, when Amin looked down, smile at him obsequiously. Finally, he handed the knife to one of the waiters, who proceeded dexterously to layer slice after effortless slice—the meat falling away like waves on a beach—on the edge of the platter, while others shuffled them on to plates. Yet more waiters, moving swiftly behind the chairs in a complicated shuttle system, sliding along the parquet, brought them to each guest.

I prodded the kudu steak in front of me. A thin trickle of juice came out of it. I thought about how the beast must have been stalked and shot, dragged or perhaps carried home slung on a pole, flayed and jointed, the crouching hunters palming prize portions (heart, kidney, liver) into bloodied banana leaves to take home to their wives. And this cut in front of me, too, might well have been so wrapped for transport by lorry back to Kampala: as well as keeping off flies, the banana leaf is said to contain a tenderizing enzyme. Out in the bush, I'd often mused about analysing and isolating it, selling the formula to make my fortune back home.

Nathan Theseus Todd attacked his steak with gusto. He cut off such a large piece that the dark meat, darker than beef, covered his mouth as he forked it in, making it seem—ever so briefly—like a gag.

Nauseated, I turned to Jenny Brown.

'What's really nice about all this is that none of the meat is chilled at any point: refrigeration breaks down the cell structure you know. That's why it tastes different from English meat.'

She looked at me slightly quizzically.

'You're so lucky, being a man of science. I sometimes wish that I had a better idea of how things fit together.'

The accompanying dishes for the kudu began piling up: a little ramekin of chilli relish; mounds of vegetables—sweet potato rissoles, yam chips, fried groundnuts, pigeon peas; and a chopped mess of green I called jungle salad: spinach, *shu-shu* and cowpea leaves.

'Watch out for this foods,' called out Idi, tapping a dish. 'There is an old Swahili proverb: if you give pigeon peas to a donkey, he will fart. That is why I never eat this foods.'

I thought of the donkey I had as a child in Kirkcaldy. It died from bloat, having eaten grass cuttings I'd left in a bin outside the paddock. They'd fermented in its stomach, blowing it up like a balloon. The only way to cure it was to stick the point of a knife between the beast's ribs, cutting into the stomach wall where it pressed up against them. I remember how the green liquor came out, when the stable lad did it, but the animal was too far gone—we couldn't save it.

Nathan Theseus, excited by mouthfuls of meat, waved his fork in the air.

'We saw these wonderful cows when we went down to the Rwanda border. You know, the ones with the long horns and humped backs. Herds and herds of them. It was like New England, I tell you.'

'They are called zebu,' said Katabarwa. 'The hump is for storing fluid during drought.'

'Like a camel, I suppose,' said Brown. 'Don't cows have two stomachs, Doctor Garrigan?'

'That's right. Grass is very difficult to digest. Though I believe the digestive structure of zebu is even more complicated than that of the European cow—more like buffalo or wildebeest.'

'You have buffalo cheese in Italy, don't you, Cueva?' asked Todd, leaning forward.

'Yes, mozzarella. But it is mostly made from ordinary cow's milk these days.'

Amin cut him off, booming: 'Only in Africa are there real buffalo, strong like me.'

'Nice flowers,' Jenny Brown whispered to me, touching the display. It was the first time I had seen her smile. I lifted up my glass of wine and looked straight into her eyes over the rim.

The sweet, like the starter, was a choice of three: guava fool, pumpkin pie with cream and, as the menu put it, 'Delicious Pudding'—some kind of blancmange, each portion moulded into a quaint little castle shape.

This last Idi himself had, scooping it up swiftly, closing the distance between mouth and plate with every spoonful. By the end, he was almost bent double.

'All gone,' he said then, pushing his dish aside like a little child.

As I finished my own Delicious Pudding, the waiters began to bring in the coffee and liqueurs, and the jazz band struck up for the dancing. I watched transfixed as, in one fluid and totally seamless movement, Nathan Theseus brushed a bead of sweat off his brow, reached into his jacket, pulled out a cigar from one pocket, a clipper lighter from the other, cut and lit the cigar and put the silver contraption away again. All in a matter of seconds. It was a quite astonishing piece of prestidigitation. I almost felt like asking him to do it again, to prove that it had happened at all. But it was final, this perfect execution: the tip of the cigar glowed fiercely.

Much later that evening, I took a walk down to the lake. The first birds had begun calling from the rhododendrons, the flame trees, the bougainvillea. As I looked out over the water, I supposed the crocs were moving in the dark shallows that stretched out towards the fires and lamps of Tanzania on the other side. And I fancied, standing there, that I could see the circles of tilapia rising to the surface for crane-flies, rising as if coming up for air; denizens of the lake, our scaly forebears: white eyes, blind mouths.

GRANTA

JOAN SMITH
PEOPLE EATERS

'*A Cannibal King's Larder*', 1907

In 1777, a butcher's assistant from Cheshire, Samuel Thorley, was tried for murder at Chester Assizes. Thorley was accused of killing Ann Smith, a twenty-two-year-old ballad-singer, in circumstances that one report described as 'too shocking to relate'. In fact, as the writer and radical Joseph Ritson recorded twenty-five years after the event, Thorley had treated the unfortunate Smith like one of his master's animals: 'He decoy'd her, lay with her, murder'd her, cut her to pieces and ate part of her.' Thorley was convicted, executed and hung in chains as a warning to anyone who might be tempted to follow his example.

Thorley was a freak, the only instance of cannibalism in England, so far as Ritson knew, since the ancient Britons. Ritson's rather macabre interest in the subject arose, paradoxically, from his passionate belief in vegetarianism; existing on a diet of vegetables, biscuits, tea and lemonade, he was nevertheless fascinated by the habits of carnivores. A friend of the philosopher William Godwin, Ritson helped him research his novel *Caleb Williams* and, in 1794, a daring article in defence of a dozen political reformers accused of the capital offence of high treason. Yet Ritson's antiquarian studies did not instil a rigorously critical approach when it came to writing about cannibalism. His extensive catalogue of horrors recklessly mingled attested, anecdotal and mythic examples, from sources as diverse as Homer, Juvenal and Captain Cook's journals. He knew of relatively few homovores in Europe, finding only a band of fifteenth-century Scottish outlaws from Angus who were said to have eaten their victims. They were eventually captured and burnt to death; the only survivor, a one-year-old girl, was fostered and brought up in Dundee until, on reaching adulthood, she began to show the same gory tendencies as her parents and was punished in the same manner. (It is not clear from Ritson's text whether this account refers to the notorious Sawney Beane, who was executed with his numerous relatives in Leith in 1435 after bloodhounds led pursuers to a cavernous lair where, according to legend, joints of human meat hung neatly from the roof as if in a butcher's shop.)

Ritson did claim to know of a more recent outbreak in France, where some women had unaccountably embarked on a ravenous rampage through their immediate kin: 'A woman of the

city of Chalons in Champagne ate her own sister; another devour'd
her husband; and a third, having murder'd her children, salted
their bodies and ate of them every day as a delicious morsel.' But
most of his accounts came from further afield, such as this one
taken from the memoirs of a Spanish explorer in Peru:

> About twenty-five or thirty soldiers, going abroad
> marauding, or, to speak plain, to steal what they could
> find, lighted on some people that fled, for fear of being
> seen and taken by us. There they found a great pot, full
> of boil'd meat, and their hunger was so great, that they
> thought of nothing but eating; but when they were well
> satisfy'd, one of them pulled out a hand, with all its
> fingers and nails; besides which they afterwards discover'd
> pieces of feet, of two or three quarters of men that were in
> it. The Spaniards, beholding that spectacle, were sorry
> they had eaten of the meat, and their stomachs turn'd at
> the sight of the hands and fingers; but it pass'd over with
> them, and they return'd satisfied, having gone out hungry.

Another Peruvian tribe, according to Ritson, was so keen on
human flesh that when foraging for food, its hunters would
ignore flocks of sheep and devour the shepherds where they
stood. Similarly, the 'savage Indians of the Ladrone ilands are
say'd to eat white men, if they can take them, and drink their
blood, devouring all they catch raw.' Ritson believed the habit of
eating prisoners of war to be widespread and linked it explicitly
to revenge; one of his most vivid examples concerns the Caribs,
the West Indian people whose fearsome reputation for eating
their enemies turned their name into the source, in a corrupt
Spanish transliteration, of the word cannibalism:

> When the Caribbians brought home a prisoner of war
> from among the Arouagues, he belong'd of right to him
> who either seiz'd on him in the fight, or took him
> running away, so that being come into his iland, after he
> had kept him fasting four or five days, he produc'd him
> upon some day of solemn debauch, to serve for a
> publick victim to the immortal hatred of his countrymen

toward that nation. If there were any of their enemies dead upon the place, there they ate them ere they left it. They had heretofore tasted of all the nations that frequented them, and affirm'd that the French were the most delicate, and the Spaniards of hardest digestion.

A striking feature of Ritson's cannibals is that, far from showing remorse, they generally polished off their victims with exhibitionist relish. 'Aroe Tanete, King of Soping and the Bouginese' in the East Indies reputedly fattened his prisoners for a few days, then cut their hearts out and ate them raw 'with pepper and salt'. Few of the people Ritson listed had been driven to eating their fellow humans by necessity, a motive he viewed more leniently than sheer bloodlust; reporting incidents from Ireland in the 1650s, when plague and famine were said to have driven the desperate population to cannibalism, he observed drily: 'Such were the blessings of Ireland under the protection of English humanity!' But there is another, probably unconscious, reason for his relaxed attitude towards Irish anthropophagy, which emerges as soon as he turns his attention to Africa:

> The negros, from the inland parts, are, almost without exception, *anthropohagi*, have a terrible, tiger-like, scarcely human aspect, and pointed or jagged teeth, closing together like those of a fox. Most of these are so fierce and greedy after human flesh, that they bite large pieces out of the arms or legs of their neighbours and fellow slaves, which they swallow with great avidity.

Cannibalism is, in other words, an index of savagery. Ritson had never seen the inhuman and indeed unlikely creatures he described, and his credulity is surprising in someone with his political background. Yet the literature of cannibalism reveals that his belief in the widespread existence of cannibal tribes in the non-European, 'uncivilized' areas of the world is shared by a number of authors. Two centuries after Ritson, in his avowedly modern and scientific book *The Psychology of Eating*, Lewis Robert Wolberg included a section on 'The Modern Savage and His Menu' which asserted:

In places where human life is held in low esteem, a man may be regarded by his companions as a convenient source of food. Thus on the coast of West Africa, among the Fuegians, and in certain islands of Northern Melanesia, the eating of human flesh has been considered until fairly recent times a matter of necessity. The ferocious Fiji islanders relished human flesh with such gusto that murder became a daily transaction, and relatives and friends were converted habitually into table delicacies.

Another author, Garry Hogg, adopted an anthropological approach in his book *Cannibalism and Human Sacrifice* (1958), but allowed an unintentionally comic glimpse of his preconceptions when he assured readers that 'there is no limit to the tortuosities of the mental process of the so-called "simple savage".'

Hogg's intention was very different from Ritson's, whose list of cannibals was compiled in support of a broader argument: that slaughtering and eating animals was the first step on a road which led to full-blooded cannibalism. This notion, although transparently disprovable, has a surprisingly long pedigree; some sections of Ritson's *An Essay on Abstinence from Animal Food as a Moral Duty* resemble passages in Plutarch's *De Esu Carnium*, two short articles attacking meat-eating which appear at the end of the *Moralia*. Plutarch, an early advocate of vegetarianism, suggested that 'when our murderous instincts had tasted blood and grew practised on wild animals', they naturally progressed to the slaughter of other humans—and that the taboo on eating friends and guests might eventually be broken.

Cannibalism was a popular theme among ancient authors, but the assumption that it was a real rather than a mythic phenomenon was usually a precondition for its more important function of emphasizing the superiority of their culture over the savage 'other'. Plutarch's Roman contemporary Juvenal devoted the whole of one of his satires to the subject, describing 'an act of mob violence worse than anything in the tragedians' which was supposed to have taken place in Egypt. According to Juvenal, the citizens of two rival towns, Ombi and Tentyra, had fought running battles which ended in an unfortunate Ombite being captured:

. . . The victorious
Rabble tore him apart into bits and pieces, so many
That this single corpse provided a morsel for all.
They wolfed him
Bones and all, not bothering even to spit-roast
Or make a stew of his carcass.

Another Roman author, Julius Caesar, claimed personal knowledge of an incident in the Gallic War when his enemies, facing defeat and starvation during the siege of Alesia in 52BC, very nearly resorted to cannibalism. According to Caesar, the Gallic warlord Vercingetorix called a council of war at which one of the nobles, Critognatus, made a speech which 'deserves to be recorded for its unparalleled cruelty and wickedness':

When [our ancestors] were forced into their strongholds by the Cimbri and Teutoni, and overcome like us by famine, instead of surrendering they kept themselves alive by eating the flesh of those who were too old or too young to fight.

The Gauls decided to adopt Critognatus's proposal only as a last resort, but the passage is, in any case, hardly to be taken at face value. It is a classic example of history being written by the victors, a devious piece of self-justification on Caesar's part for extending the war in Gaul way beyond the authority given him by the Senate. Few allegations would horrify educated first-century Romans as much as the 'revelation' that the Gallic leaders were prepared to save themselves by eating their own young and elderly; thus a war of rampant colonialism, undertaken for reasons of personal ambition, is neatly transformed into a principled campaign to save Roman civilization from the barbarian hordes.

Julius Caesar's conquest of the supposedly anthropophagous tribes that occupied parts of what is now France, Belgium, the Netherlands, Germany and Switzerland is often known by an alternative title, the *pacification* of Gaul, which sets up a series of crude oppositions: war/peace, savagery/civilization, nature/culture. The latter was more vividly expressed by the French anthropologist Claude Lévi-Strauss in the title of his celebrated study of myth and ritual, *Le Cru et le cuit* (*The Raw and the Cooked*); the cooking metaphor is peculiarly apposite, given that Caesar chose to condemn his opponents through their alleged eating habits. It also illuminates a bizarre common feature of many cannibal narratives, which is the protagonists' alleged preference for eating meat raw or crudely cooked. In a telling detail, Juvenal condemns the Egyptians not just for eating their fallen enemy but for failing to turn him into a stew, perhaps unconsciously contrasting their rapacious appetites with the Romans' highly sophisticated culinary practices.

Cannibal narratives, according to this hypothesis, are one of the ways in which colonial cultures differentiate themselves from other races—particularly ones they regard as troublesome or unwilling to accept their subject status. (Joseph Ritson quotes the case of a tribe in New Guinea, the Dahomes, who defiantly chopped up their English governor, Mr Testesole, grilled the pieces over hot coals and ate them. 'That English beef was very good!' they are said to have boasted afterwards.) This is not to argue that cannibalism does not exist but to suggest that its unacknowledged function in supporting an otherwise dubious hierarchy of racial superiority has predisposed too many commentators to believe almost any anecdote, no matter how vague or unlikely the details. Homovores are a staple ingredient, so to speak, of narratives as diverse as the *Thousand and One Nights*, fictional product of an expansionist medieval Muslim culture, and the memoirs of Marco Polo, thirteenth-century apologist for the Mongol emperor of China. The latter's account of his travels, improved by his fanciful collaborator, Rustichello of Pisa, features several encounters with cannibal tribes among his employer's subjects:

> The people are idolaters subject to the Great Khan . . .
> They live by trade and industry and are amply provided
> with the means of life. There is abundance of game here,
> both beast and bird, besides lions of great size and
> ferocity . . . Furthermore, you must know that the
> natives eat all sorts of brute beast. They even relish
> human flesh. They do not touch the flesh of those who

have died a natural death; but they all eat the flesh of those who have died of a wound and consider it a delicacy . . . They carry lances and swords and are the most blood-thirsty lot in the world. For I assure you that they go about every day killing men and drink the blood and then devour the whole body.

In the *Thousand and One Nights*, Sinbad the Sailor is shipwrecked with his men and rescued by a king who offers them strange meats which turn Sinbad's stomach. His sailors eat the food, fall into a stupor, are transformed into beasts and led into the fields to graze:

> My horror at this spectacle knew no bounds, especially when I soon discovered that our captors were cannibals who fattened their victims this way before slaughtering them. The King feasted every day on a roasted stranger; his men preferred their diet raw.

The final detail makes an interesting distinction between the cannibal king who, being higher up the social scale, does at least cook his victims, and his more uncouth men. Explorers and adventurers who went in search of cannibals in the nineteenth and early twentieth centuries had less luck than Marco Polo or Sinbad. Robert Louis Stevenson was disappointed by his encounter with a homovore—'the last eater of long-pig in Nuka-Hiva'—in the South Seas, an episode he described thus:

> Not many years have elapsed since he was seen striding on the beach of Anaho, a dead man's arm across his shoulder. 'So does Kooamua to his enemies!' he roared to the passers-by, and took a bite from the raw flesh. And now behold this gentleman, very wisely replaced in office by the French, paying us a morning visit in European clothes.

A less celebrated traveller, Captain J. C. Voss, records a similarly deflating encounter in his memoir *The Venturesome Voyages of Captain Voss*, published in 1913. Voss and a companion were in a small boat, approaching the entrance to

Port Resolution in Melanesia, when a much larger vessel bore down upon them. Bearing in mind that 'the inhabitants of the New Hebrides in former days had a very bad reputation for cannibalism and treacherous manners in their intercourse with whites', the two men lifted their rifles, only to discover to their chagrin that the 'natives' had been sent by a local Christian missionary, Mr Watt, to tow them safely into the harbour. After a pleasant dinner with the missionary, his wife and an English trader called Mr Wilson, Voss demanded to know whether cannibalism was still practised in the area:

> This question was immediately answered by the trader who assured me that they ate a native man there only a few days previously. And Mr Watt added that it was very difficult to stop this horrible custom. Mr Wilson further explained that on the last occasion the younger missionary had gone to the place where the feast had occurred in order to reason with them. But instead of taking his advice they had picked up some of the bones and throwing them at the missionary gave him to understand that he had better mind his own business.

The Victorian explorer Mary Kingsley went in search of a cannibal tribe called the Fans in the equatorial forests of Africa in the 1880s but, according to her biographer Jean Gordon Hughes, did not find any evidence of their flesh-eating habits. An earlier visitor, the French explorer Paul Belloni du Chaillu, who had explored the area thirty years before, claimed to have encountered a woman carrying a piece of human thigh, 'just as we should go to market and carry thence a roast or steak'. He then discovered that the local people were dividing the body of a dead man—'The head,' he was told, 'was always saved for the king!'—and the following day, found a 'pile of human bones including the skulls'.

What emerges from these credulous and strikingly similar narratives is greater evidence of a prurient curiosity within *developed* cultures about cannibalism than of its widespread practice outside them. The smugness with which 'civilized' people regard cannibal natives is summed up by Ritson's casual remark about the extermination of the anthropophagous tribes of the Caribbean: 'They are now nearly extirpated by the Christians.' (Reay Tannahill, writing in *Flesh and Blood*, expands this point to show that the Caribs' undoubted cannibal practices were exaggerated by the invading Spanish—they were said to salt and dry their victims' flesh at a time when this practice was unknown to them—and used as an excuse for 'reducing their numbers to only a few hundred and their temperament to a state usually described as mild and melancholy.')

Lewis Robert Wolberg took a paternalistic line in *The Psychology of Eating*, observing that 'ecclesiastical pressure has forced the savage to restrain his appetite and to give up his tasty human dishes.' He does not seem to have stopped to consider the irony of so-called savages being persuaded out of their supposed cannibal habits by emissaries of a religion itself so firmly rooted in anthropophagous ritual. For, as Mark's Gospel recounts, Jesus laid down the form of the Church's central act of worship in terms that are overtly cannibalistic:

> As they were eating, he took bread and blessed and broke it and gave it to them, and said, 'Take; this is my body.' And he took a cup, and when he had given thanks he gave it to them, and they all drank of it. And he said to them, 'This is my blood of the covenant, which is poured out for many.'

The obvious distinction between, say, the Caribs and the Spanish Christians who converted or exterminated them is that for the latter, 'cannibalism is metaphorized', in Gian-Paolo Biasin's striking phrase. Yet the Roman Catholic Church is resistant to this interpretation; in 1215, the Fourth Lateran Council firmly rejected symbolic interpretations in favour of the doctrine of transubstantiation, declaring:

> There is one universal church of the faithful, outside which no one at all is saved. In this church, Jesus Christ himself is both priest and sacrifice, and his body and blood are really contained in the sacrament of the altar under the species of bread and wine, the bread being

79

transubstantiated into the body, and the wine into the blood by the power of God, so that to carry out the mystery of unity we ourselves receive from him the body he himself receives from us.

In future, anyone who suggested otherwise would be guilty of heresy, creating the curious situation in which a religion that would later use cannibalism as an excuse for declaring war on indigenous tribes nevertheless insisted that its adherents pretend they were regularly taking part in an anthropophagous act of worship. Perhaps unsurprisingly, the slippage between metaphor and reality was so great that in the late Middle Ages, churches all over southern Europe had to be locked against *religieuses* who obsessively consumed communion wafers, refusing other forms of sustenance in favour of what they genuinely believed to be the body of Christ. Even before the Fourth Lateran Council, Mary of Oignies turned her hunger for the host into the central passion of her life, as her hagiographer James of Vitry explained:

> The holy bread strengthened her heart; the holy wine inebriated her, rejoicing her mind; the holy body fattened her; the vitalizing blood purified her by washing. And she could not bear to abstain from such solace for long. For it was the same to her to live as to eat the body of Christ, and this it was to die, to be separated from the sacrament by having for a long time to abstain.

The fourteenth-century saint Catherine of Siena went even further. Caroline Walker Bynum, in her book *Holy Feast and Holy Fast: The Religious Significance of Food to Medieval Women*, describes Catherine's frequent bouts of anorexia and her need to substitute 'the filth of disease and the blood of Christ's agony' for ordinary food:

> Several of her biographers report that she twice forced herself to overcome nausea by thrusting her mouth into the putrifying breast of a dying woman or by drinking pus, and the reports stress these incidents as turning points in her developing inedia, her eucharistic craving,

and her growing compulsion to serve others by suffering. She told Raymond [of Capua, an early hagiographer]: 'Never in my life have I tasted any food and drink sweeter or more exquisite.'

The curious aftermath of these episodes was a vision of Christ in which he uncovered the wound in his side and drew Catherine towards it. '"Drink, daughter, from my side," she heard Him say, "and by that draught your soul shall become enraptured with such delight that your very body, which for my sake you have denied, shall be inundated with its overflowing goodness." Drawn close . . . to the outlet of the Fountain of Life, she fastened her lips upon that sacred wound, and still more eagerly the mouth of her soul, and there she slaked her thirst.' The swift transition from anthropophagous imagery to a scene that resembles fellatio is peculiarly shocking in this context, but it is also a salutary reminder of the extent to which our sexual practices, although we shrink from viewing them in this way, mimic the act of eating another human being. Lévi-Strauss made the same point, and indicated the existence of a similar set of taboos, when he described cannibalism as a form of 'alimentary incest'.

This raises the intriguing possibility that cannibal narratives fascinate developed cultures not only because they validate notions of cultural superiority but because they embody our darkest urges and fears about sex. Cannibalism involves the literal incorporation of the other, that fusing of two into one which is at the heart of so many sexual fantasies; at a crude level, it appears to defy the precipitous return to isolation that follows orgasm and is the origin of the sensation of *petite mort*. Few novelists have captured this cannibalistic element of the erotic impulse so graphically as Italo Svevo in his novel *The Confessions of Zeno* (1968):

> I had a curious dream: I was not only kissing Carla's neck, I was positively devouring it. But though I was inflicting terrible wounds on it in my mad lust, the wounds did not bleed, and the delicate curve of her neck was still unaltered under its soft white skin. Carla, prostrate in my arms, did not seem to suffer from the bites.

The final sentence is crucial, marking Svevo's recognition that his character's erotic and alimentary fantasy belongs safely in the symbolic order. An equally disturbing expression of the narrowness of the gap between hunger and lust appears in Italo Calvino's *Under the Jaguar Sun* (1986), about an Italian couple in Mexico; here, the narrator links the lovers' urge to consume each other with a fleeting—and in this context comic—realization of the fragility of the taboo which prevents human beings being turned into food:

> Our teeth began to move slowly, with equal rhythm, and our eyes stared into each other's with the intensity of serpents'—serpents concentrated in the ecstasy of swallowing each other in turn, as we were aware, in our turn, of being swallowed by the serpent that digests us all, assimilated ceaselessly in the process of ingestion and digestion, in the universal cannibalism that leaves its imprint on every amorous relationship and erases the lines between our bodies and *sopa di frijoles, buachinango a la veracruzana* and enchiladas . . .

The passage is funny precisely because it jolts the reader into recognizing, momentarily and therefore safely, the dark origins of love talk like 'I could eat you up'. For a few seconds, people who understand themselves to be 'cooked' in the metaphorical sense are able to flirt with the notion that they might literally become so and eaten. The return to the normal order of things is swift and comforting.

In the twentieth century most actual instances of cannibalism take place in desperate circumstances, the most famous being the Uruguayan rugby team who resorted to eating their dead friends when their plane crashed in the Andes in 1972. Occasionally, though, evidence comes to light of a case of voluntary anthropophagy in which the gory details appear to defy understanding. A notorious example is Jeffrey Dahmer, the serial killer known as the Milwaukee Cannibal, whose apartment, at the time of his arrest in 1991, contained three severed heads, two skulls and a skeleton. An obituary in the *Guardian*, after Dahmer was beaten to death by another inmate in a Wisconsin prison in November 1994, revealed his bizarre housekeeping habits, reporting that he had stored lungs, intestines, a kidney and a liver in his freezer. 'Prosecutors believed that Jeffrey Dahmer was serious about his cannibalism. Besides the contents of his freezer, they found no food in apartment 213—only condiments.'

There is an echo here of Joseph Ritson's account of Aroe Tanete, the cannibal king who liked to ingest his victims raw with a sprinkling of salt and pepper; the familiarity of the detail hints that Dahmer's practices have already begun to be mythologized. That this is happening is confirmed by the precise if repellent account of Dahmer's activities in Brian Masters' book *The Shrine of Jeffrey Dahmer*. The killer once 'ate a bicep which he had fried in a skillet, tenderized and sprinkled with sauce'; in all, he prepared six meals using body parts from his seventeen victims.

This is horrific enough but it does not add up to the exclusively anthropophagous diet implied in the *Guardian*. But Masters' book is revealing in another way; it reports testimony at Dahmer's trial that he was lonely, unstable and unable to form steady relationships with the men he picked up in bars or on the street. Masters suggests that killing became, for a man whose lovers always left him the following morning, a macabre way of keeping them with him. Eventually, when his loneliness failed to subside, Dahmer resorted to the desperate remedy of ingesting them. 'Many of these young men,' Masters concludes, 'died because Jeff Dahmer liked them.' The theory is plausible, as far as it goes, but it overlooks the sensational and most revealing aspect of Dahmer's crimes, which lies in the racial profile of his victims. Whether or not it is true, as Dahmer's stepmother claimed, that something happened to him in prison in 1989 which made him hate black men, it is undeniably the case that the vast majority of his victims were black or Southeast Asian—very different physical specimens, in other words, from the weedy, fair-haired Dahmer.

Ever since they were brought to the American South from Africa as slaves, black men have been invested with mythic attributes of physical strength and sexual potency. A more complex explanation of Dahmer's actions is that, in killing and eating his victims, he was ritually acting out fantasies of subjugating and incorporating the all-powerful other—even, perhaps, hoping to confer some of their potency on himself. Whether Dahmer would have recognized these impulses is, since his own murder, impossible to know. That he regarded himself as a freak is clear from his plaintive enquiry to doctors after his arrest, when he asked whether there was anyone in the world like him, or was he the only one? The final phrase is ambiguous, implying 'special' as well as 'isolated' and turning Dahmer into a quasi-heroic figure, treading a solitary path that would have been familiar to our common tribal ancestors. Yet the reality behind the image of the lonely cannibal, cursed inheritor of a savage tradition that can no longer be understood by his deracinated peers, is far more gruesome. What motivates people like Dahmer is a catastrophic failure of the imagination, an inability to think metaphorically which compels them to act out the symbolic order regardless of the cost, to themselves and others, in horror and degradation. Unlike the rest of us, they don't know or don't care that, except in dire emergencies, eating people is wrong.

GEORGES PEREC
ATTEMPT AT AN INVENTORY
OF THE LIQUID AND THE SOLID
FOODSTUFFS INGURGITATED BY ME
IN THE COURSE OF THE YEAR
NINETEEN HUNDRED
AND SEVENTY-FOUR

Georges Perec

ANNE DE BRUNHOFF

Georges Perec was born in Paris in 1936 and died in the same city four days before his forty-sixth birthday in 1982. His parents were Jews who had migrated to France from Poland; both died during the Second World War—his father as a soldier during the German invasion of France, his mother in Auschwitz-Birkenau. Perec, as his biographer David Bellos has written, grew into a man and a writer 'always puzzled by memory and sometimes obsessed with the fear of forgetting'. He kept a careful record of his food and drink intake during 1974. This first English translation, by John Sturrock, includes several dishes that remain obstinately obscure to the Anglo-Saxon menu—a Guémené andouille, *for example, is a kind of sausage;* crème renversée *is a set custard turned out of its mould. As a French citizen, Perec seems to have had an ordinary enough consumption of wine. In the course of the year he drank 181 named bottles and an unspecified number of anonymous bottles, perhaps too humble to be noted. He does not seem to have been fond of fish; only forty-one fish dishes in 365 days of eating, fewer than one per week.*

The attempted inventory:

Nine beef broths, one iced cucumber soup, one mussel soup. Two *Guémené andouilles*, one jellied *andouillette*, one Italian *charcuterie*, one saveloy, four mixed *charcuteries*, one *coppa*, three pork platters, one *figatelli*, one foie gras, one *fromage de tête*, one boar's head, five Parma hams, eight pâtés, one duck pâté, one liver pâté with truffles, one pâté *en croûte*, one pâté *grandmère*, one thrush pâté, six Landes pâtés, four brawns, one foie-gras mousse, one pig's trotters, seven *rillettes*, one salami, two *saucissons*, one hot *saucisson*, one duck terrine, one chicken-liver terrine.

One blini, one *empanada*, one dried beef. Three snails.

One Belon oysters, three scallops, one shrimps, one shrimp *croustade*, one *friture*, two baby eel *fritures*, one herring, two oysters, one mussels, one stuffed mussels, one sea urchins, two *quenelles au gratin*, three sardines in oil, five smoked salmons, one taramasalata, one eel terrine, six tunas, one anchovy toast, one crab.

Two haddock, one sea bass, one skate, one sole, one tuna.

Four artichokes, one asparagus, one aubergine, one mushroom salad, fourteen cucumber salads, four cucumbers *à la crème*, fourteen celery *rémoulades*, two Chinese cabbages, one palm hearts, eleven crudités, two green-bean salads, thirteen melons, two *salades niçoises*, two dandelion salads with bacon, fourteen radishes with butter, three black radishes, five rice salads, one Russian salad, seven tomato salads, one onion tart.

One Roquefort croquette, five *croque-monsieurs*, three quiches Lorraine, one *tarte aux maroilles*, one yogurt with cucumber and grapes, one Romanian yogurt.

One *torti* salad with crab and Roquefort.

One eggs with anchovy, two boiled eggs, two eggs *en meurette*, one ham and eggs, one bacon and eggs, one eggs *en cocotte* with spinach, two eggs in aspic, two scrambled eggs, four omelettes, one sort-of omelette, one bean-sprout omelette, one horn-of-plenty omelette, one duck-skin omelette, one *confit d'oie* omelette, one herb omelette, one Parmentier omelette.

One sirloin, three sirloins with shallots, ten steaks, two steak *au poivres*, three *complets*, one rump steak with mustard, five roast beefs, two ribs of beef, two top rump steaks, three beef *grillades*, two chateaubriands, one steak tartare, one *rosbif*, three cold *rosbifs*, fourteen entrecôtes, three entrecôtes *à la moelle*, one fillet of beef, three hamburgers, nine skirts of beef, one flank of beef.

Four *pot-au-feus*, one daube, one jellied daube, one braised beef, one beef mode, one beef *gros sel*, one beef in a thin baguette.

One braised veal with noodles, one sauté of veal, one veal chop, one veal chop with pasta shells, one 'veal entrecôte', six escalopes, six escalopes *milanaise*, three escalopes *à la crème*, one escalope with morels, four *blanquettes de veau*.

Five *andouillettes*, three black puddings, one black pudding with apples, one pork cutlet, two sauerkrauts, one Nancy sauerkraut, one pork chop, eleven pairs of frankfurters, two pork *grillades*, seven pigs' trotters, one cold pork, three roast porks, one roast pork with pineapple and bananas, one pork sausage with haricots.

One milk-fed lamb, three lamb cutlets, two curried lambs, twelve *gigots*, one saddle of lamb.
One mutton cutlet, one shoulder of mutton.

Five chickens, one chicken kebab, one lemon chicken, one chicken *en cocotte*, two chicken *basquaises*, three cold chickens, one stuffed chicken, one chicken with chestnuts, one chicken with herbs, two jellied chickens.
Seven *poules au riz*, one *poule au pot*.
One pullet *au riz*.
One *coq au riesling*, three *coq au vins*, one *coq au vinaigre*.
One duck with olives, one duck breast.
One guinea-fowl casserole.
One guinea fowl with cabbage, one guinea fowl with noodles.

Five rabbits, two rabbits *en gibelotte*, one rabbit with noodles, one rabbit *à la crème*, three rabbits with mustard, one rabbit *chasseur*, one rabbit with tarragon, one rabbit *à la tourangelle*, three rabbits with plums.
Two young wild rabbits with plums.
One civet of hare *à l'alsacienne*, one daube of hare, one hare stew, one saddle of hare.
One wild-pigeon casserole.

One kidney kebab, three kebabs, one mixed grill, one kidneys with mustard, one calves' kidneys, three *têtes de veau*, eleven calves' livers, one calves' tongue, one calves' sweetbreads with *pommes sarladaises*, one terrine of calves' sweetbreads, one lambs' brains, two fresh goose livers with grapes, one *confit* of goose gizzards, two chicken livers.
Twelve assorted cold meats, two *assiettes anglaises*, n cold cuts, two couscous, three 'Chinese', one *moulakhia*, one pizza, one *pan bagnat*, one *tajine*, six sandwiches, one ham sandwich, one *rillette* sandwich, three cantal sandwiches.

One ceps, one kidney beans, seven green beans, one sweetcorn, one puréed cauliflower, one puréed spinach, one puréed fennel, two stuffed peppers, two *pommes frites*, nine *gratins dauphinois*, four mashed potatoes, one *pommes dauphines*, one *pommes boulangères*, one *pommes soufflées*, one roast potatoes, one sauté potatoes, four rice, one wild rice.

Four pasta, three noodles, one fettucine with cream, one macaroni cheese, one macaroni, fifteen fresh noodles, three *rigatoni*, two ravioli, four spaghetti, one tortellini, five tagliatelle *verde*.

Thirty-five green salads, one *mesclun* salad, one Treviso salad *à la crème*, two chicory salads.

Seventy-five cheeses, one ewe's cheese, two Italian cheeses, one Auvergne cheese, one Boursin, two Brillat-Savarins, eleven Bries, one Cabécou, four goats' cheeses, two *crottins*, eight Camemberts, fifteen cantals, one Sicilian cheeses, one Sardinian cheeses, one Epoisses, one Murols, three fromages blancs, one goat's-milk fromage blanc, nine Fontainebleaus, five mozzarellas, five Munsters, one Reblochon, one Swiss raclette, one Stilton, one Saint-Marcellin, one Saint-Nectaire, one yogurt.

One fresh fruit, two strawberries, one gooseberries, one orange, three '*mendiants*' [a mixture of almonds, dried figs, hazelnuts and raisins].
One stuffed dates, one pears in syrup, three pears in wine, two peaches in wine, one vineyard peach in syrup, one peaches in Sancerre, one apples *normande*, one bananas *flambées*.
Four stewed fruit, two stewed apples, two stewed rhubarb and *quetsch*.
Five *clafoutis*, four pear *clafoutis*.
One figs in syrup.
Six fruit salads, one tropical fruit salad, two orange salads, two strawberry, raspberry and gooseberry salads.

One apple pie, four tarts, one hot tart, ten tart Tatins, seven pear tarts, one pear tart Tatin, one lemon tart, one apple-and-nut tart, two apple tarts, one apple tart with meringue, one strawberry tart.
Two crêpes.
Two charlottes, three chocolate charlottes.
Three babas.
One *crème renversée.*
One *galette des rois.*
Nine chocolate mousses.
Two *îles flotantes.*
One bilberry *Kugelhupf.*

Four chocolate gateaux, one cheesecake, two orange gateaux, one Italian gateau, one Viennese gateau, one Breton gateau, one gateau with fromage blanc, one *vatrushka.*
Three ice creams, one lime sorbet, two guava sorbets, two pear sorbets, one chocolate profiteroles, one raspberry melba, one pear *belle Hélène.*

Thirteen Beaujolais, four Beaujolais Nouveaux, three Brouillys, seven Chiroubles, four Chenas, two Fleuries, one Juliénas, three Saint-Amours.
Nine Côtes-du-Rhônes, nine Châteauneuf-du-Papes, one Châteauneuf-du-Pape '67, three Vacqueyras.
Nine Bordeaux, one Bordeaux Clairet, one Lamarzelle '64, three Saint-Emilions, one Saint-Emilion '61, seven Château-la Pelleterie '70s, one Château-Canon '62, five Château-Négrits, one Lalande-de-Pomerol, one Lalande-de-Pomerol '67, one Médoc '64, six Margaux '62s, one Margaux '68, one Margaux '69, one Saint-Estèphe '61, one Saint-Julien '59.
Seven Savigny-lès-Beaunes, three Aloxe-Cortons, one Aloxe-Corton '66, one Beaune '61, one white Chasagne-Montrachet '66, two Mercureys, one Pommard, one Pommard '66, two Santenay '62s, one Volnay '59.
One Chambolle-Musigny '70, one Chambolle-Musigny Les Amoureuses '70, one Chambertin '62, one Romanée-Conti, one Romanée-Conti '64.

One Bergerac, two red Bouzys, four Bourgueils, one Chalosse, one champagne, one Chablis, one red Côtes-de-Provence, twenty-six Cahors, one Chanteperdrix, four Gamays, two Madirans, one Madiran '70, one Pinot Noir, one Passetoutgrain, one Pécharmant, one Saumur, ten Tursans, one Traminer, one Sardinian wine, *n* sundry wines.

Nine beers, two Tuborgs, four Guinnesses.

Fifty-six Armagnacs, one bourbon, eight Calvadoses, one cherries in brandy, six Green Chartreuses, one Chivas, four cognacs, one Delamain cognac, two Grand Marniers, one pink gin, one Irish coffee, one Jack Daniel's, four marcs, three Bugey marcs, one marc de Provence, one plum liqueur, nine Souillac plums, one plums in brandy, two pear eaux-de-vie, one port, one slivovitz, one Suze, thirty-six vodkas, four whiskies.

N coffees, one tisane, three Vichy waters.

Translated from the French by John Sturrock

JANE ROGERS
GRATEFUL

For what we are about to receive, may the Lord make us truly grateful.

That's at school. When it's your turn you have to scrape your table's leftovers into the bucket. Wrinkled brown gravy dried to the plate but slimy underneath. Cold white potato lumps. Chewed gristle and bits of rind. Everyone leaves prunes and custard thick and yellow dribbling across the dish when you tilt it like two runnels of snot from a kid's nose to its mouth. When you scrape the plates more smells come up from the undersides of the food as it plops into the bucket. You think about the people who are hungry. There's a famine in Ethiopia.

OK. When they talk to you they have no idea. No idea that you might have a grain of intelligence. No idea that you're not just some sad bimbo whose diet went wrong.

I can hear them. They don't even have to speak, they think it so loud. They think I'm stupid.

'Dreadful the pressure on young girls today.'

'Those supermodels have a lot to answer for. Shocking.'

I don't speak to them. Why should I? Patronizing dicks. I don't give a stuff.

You get peace after a bit. After leaving so many platefuls, so many kilos and tonnes of food. They're giving up. There is just this clear liquid in its transparent plastic tube. No need even to swallow. This is how the angels feed. Pure.

I can tell you. You're listening. What I see and what I know, all right? First think of bones. They're white. It's the best thing about bodies—that bones are white. Under skin and blood and flesh and all the other muck, bones are white. To know that gives me hope. When the crap is peeled away, when the flesh has rotted back to mulch, the bones are white. *Underneath*, it's clean.

It's like a pointer along the way, encouragement. There will be this clean white skeleton—bleached, pure form. And at last even that will crumble away to nothing. Become dust and vanish.

I didn't ask to be born. I certainly didn't ask my mother.

One of them in the early days trying to be matey and understanding goes, 'Do you blame your mother?'

'For what?' I say. 'For having me?'

'For your eating disorder.'

Do I blame my mother? Sure. For my head my heart my brains my belly my limbs my liver—the lot. Who else can I blame?

'You're making her very unhappy,' he says. 'She'd do anything to help you.'

I am not grateful. This is my crime I can tell you about. I am not grateful. Sometimes she quotes Shakespeare at me, some old man ranting at his daughters about how sharper than a serpent's tooth it is to have an ungrateful child. That's me. Sharper than a serpent's tooth.

I don't want to be. Listen. Really, I am sorry. I am sorry for her pain. But if she hadn't had me, she wouldn't have caused it, the pain. She could have saved herself a lot of trouble.

For what we are about to receive: ten fingers, ten toes, two eyes, two ears, tongue, nostrils, teeth etc. Breathing in and out and in and out and in and out and in and out. Death. May the Lord make us truly grateful.

My mother said you must eat your tea. What did you have for school dinner? Did you eat it all?

The food smells gross. When you leave baked beans on your plate, the beans go hard and the dried sauce makes a kind of red crust like blood on my knickers when I used to have my period. It's difficult to wash off.

Some people's mothers make them sit at table till they've cleared what's on their plate. She doesn't make me do that. She says you know there are children who'd be glad of your leftovers. There are children in Africa who have to walk miles for a handful of rice.

The butter is spread on the bread in lumps that have torn holes in it, the bread is fresh and the butter is cold. The greasy lump of butter slides to the back of my throat and my stomach heaves. You've got no idea, she says. God loves all his children, but some are starving and others are wasting food. Don't you think that's terrible?

I do. I stuff the bread and butter in my mouth and chew it fast. For what we are about to receive, may the Lord make us, truly.

It's the waste. The waste is the thing that's bad. She says it's wicked to waste food when some people go hungry. I can see that. You can see that. Wasting is bad. You waste the food, and people in another place are starving. Wasting to death. They want the food but you throw the food away. That's bad. It's like you're spitting on their hunger.

Ha! That's what I think of you suckers who need food! I chuck it away. I despise food!

But the other thing to do is eat the food. Once I've eaten it, no one else can have it anyway. What am I saying to the starving people then?

Ha! I'm not even hungry but I eat and eat. You are hungry and you have nothing. Ha!

It's not good either.

When I look at the food and I don't want to eat it I think maybe it keeps better faith with the starving people not to eat it anyway. We're all going to die after all. It's more dignified.

The thing about food is, it decays. I used to think about that when she was telling me about waste. Imagine all the buckets of leftovers from all the houses and schools, poured gloop gloop into tankers and driven and ferried at top speed to all the places where people are hungry. When they arrive: disgusting. Disgusting filthy mixed-up stinking muck, not fit to give to pigs, pour it in the sewers. But (I thought). If you eat it, it's the same. May the Lord make us truly grateful. In that warm stomach. All those chewed bits. Disgusting filthy mixed-up stinking muck. Where does it go? It turns into crap.

In me or in the bin, where shall I let it turn into crap? There's not really any argument, is there?

I tried to explain to my mother the last time she came.

'I don't see the point. I mean I know people are supposed to be glad to be alive—'

'Yes,' she said, 'life's a precious gift.'

'But what am I supposed to *do*?' I shouted.

'If you let yourself be normal, you would be happy. You could go to university, you could get a job. You could have children—that's the most rewarding, fulfilling thing anyone can do.'

I looked at her. She didn't even blink.

At least I've spared someone that. Being my child.

I don't have to argue any more. I don't speak to them, and they hardly speak to me. I am beginning to fade away, is what I like to think. Perhaps they hardly see me.

But then I get—in the night when there's just a line of yellow light under the door and the little orange light on the drip and I am hidden by the darkness so you could almost pretend I wasn't there—I get this. This *rage*. It fills me up like red juice in a jug.

Why me? Why me who gets the food and not a starving person?

What have I done to deserve it? What did I *do*?

People who want food they should have it OK? Give it to them. The world is full OK, of hungry mouths to feed. Waiting to receive. Waiting to be grateful. I am not interested. I am not interested in inserting lumps of dead animal and vegetable matter into myself. I am not interested in being made of living crap. I do not have to be a tube for food, and last for eighty years.

Under the muck of flesh there are bones white as promises. Look. Look at my hand. The finger bones are white and elegant, they are clean, there is no superfluity. Nothing unnecessary. An after-image.

I am not necessary. I do not have to keep making myself up out of lumps of external matter. Who says I have to? It is possible to dematerialize.

I can be nothing.

Can I be nothing? I will be truly grateful.

NORMAN LEWIS
APHRODISIACS I HAVE KNOWN

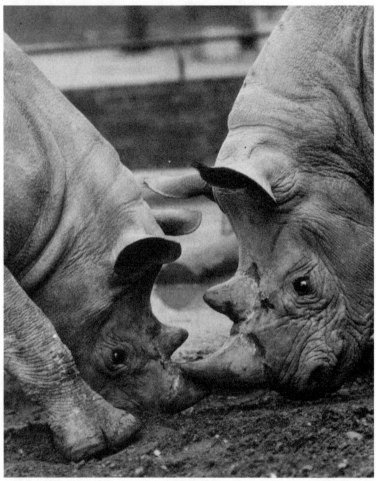

Rhino horn has long been prized as an aphrodisiac   HULTON DEUTSCH

In the winter of 1957, I went to Liberia for the *New Yorker*. Landing at Spriggs Payne Airfield in Monrovia at about midnight, I was told by the small boy who had taken over my luggage that he would not be able to bring it to the hotel until it was light, to avoid the possibility of being kidnapped. A report in the *Liberian Age* the next morning threw more light on the situation. Two men and a child had been murdered to make *borfina*, a 'medicine' manufactured from the organs of dead persons and used as an aphrodisiac and to promote rainfall. The whole business was discussed with total frankness. I learned that *borfina* was produced by professional 'heart men', witch doctors who worked at night, selecting for preference women and children as their victims. It was expensive, but there was no shortage of rich men who would pay a hundred dollars for a scent-bottle full. Heart men belonged to a whole range of secret societies, with names such as the Human Elephants, the Leopards, the Snake People and the Water People; and some to an occult group (popular, it was said, among politicians) which had the macabre title of the Negee Aquatic Cannibalistic Society. The remains of their victims were described in some detail in the press. According to another Liberian paper, the *Listener*: 'We are assured by experts that a body discovered this morning in the vicinity of the airfield had been deprived of flesh taken from the forehead, the palms of the hands, and other bodily regions. Foul play is to be suspected.'

A few days later I travelled north to Bgarnba, carrying an introduction to Mr Charles Williams, the district commissioner, a pleasant and hospitable man who invited me to stay the night. He was in court next morning, he said, to try several cases which he thought, I, as a foreigner, might find of interest, and I was welcome to attend. Mr Williams was a devout Episcopalian, but most of the people under his jurisdiction were non-Christian, and in their cases trial would be by ordeal—more suited, he believed, to the pagan mentality. Males charged with crimes would drink *curfoo*, a poison of a mild kind, only fatal in the case of pagan perjurers.

Next morning, following him into the courtroom, squeamishness caught me by surprise when I was obliged to watch the swallowing of the poison. The two defendants drank, vomited briefly, then seemed much as before, and when they were found not guilty and released, I was mightily relieved.

But there was no escaping Mr Williams. The next case was less common, he said. It was of a woman accused by her husband of adultery with five lovers. Although any Liberian of standing, Williams explained, was expected to have no fewer than three wives—each purchased from her father at the standard bride price of forty dollars—the law was very strict in dealing with any wife falling short of absolute marital fidelity. Mr Williams ascribed the woman's fall from grace in this instance to the use of *borfina*, in itself a criminal offence only where a woman was concerned.

A trial by burning iron was to be held in the yard at the back where we found a heart man preparing his fire. The accused woman and her husband, dressed with extreme formality and devoid of expression, were seated side by side. The heart man pulled a long iron spoon from the fire, tested its glowing surface with his spittle and nodded to the girl, who put out her tongue. He bent over her, and there was a faint sizzle. Someone passed a jug of water to her, and she rinsed and spat and thrust out her tongue for the court's inspection. There were insufficient signs of burning, and Mr Williams declared her not guilty. I asked if her five lovers would stand trial, and he seemed surprised. They had already been fined ten dollars each on the spot, he said, but the money, he assured me, would be refunded.

This is the closest I have come to the real hard core of sexual stimulants, or supposed ones. The softer aphrodisiacs are better known, though in my experience just as fanciful; the irrationality of the search for sexual vigour knows no bounds. Rhinoceros horns have been sawn off to be replaced by plaster imitations in the museums of the world. A whole category of animals in China are deprived of their gall bladders, the contents of which are mixed with white wine. All parts of a tiger are now marketable, including skin, whiskers and intestines. There are regular gatherings by diners in a Hong Kong restaurant to consume not only bird's nest soup, but a more invigorating broth prepared from the lungs of a vulture. In Britain, animal-welfare groups claim in advertisements that Canadian fishermen have slaughtered at least ten thousand seals so that their penises can be exported to China where they fetch a hundred pounds apiece as an important constituent of 'sex potions'.

But oysters remain by common consent at the top of the aphrodisiac league despite the extraordinary physical passivity of molluscs compared with tigers and Liberian children. Throughout recorded history, many *bon viveurs* have sworn by them. Casanova, bolstered by their support, is said to have become the lover of 130 women, two of them nuns who rapidly forsook their vows after being plied by the seducer with oysters and champagne. The latter I have no argument with—champagne's useful consequences are easily demonstrable—but aphrodisiac oysters seem to me no more than a persistent and universal self-delusion. I have thought so ever since an experience suffered in my youth, nearly sixty years ago, on a journey by dhow up the Red Sea.

I had gone with two friends in the hope of entering and exploring the Yemen, in those days hardly known in the western world. Permission to land was refused, and shortly afterwards we ran into a storm which stripped away the dhow's mainsail, forcing us to take refuge on the desert island of Kamaran, a few miles off the Arabian coast. The island's principal inhabitants were a tribe of pearl-fishers, who spent their lives scouring the sea bottom in search of oysters and had developed a lung capacity which enabled them to stay underwater for up to four minutes. The diver wore a clip on his nose, a weight round his leg and was connected by a line to a dhow from which he leaped feet first. Having collected the oysters in his basket, he gave the signal to be pulled up. Coming to the surface, he was on the point of suffocation. Sometimes divers were brought up unconscious and occasionally they could not be revived. They suffered from neuralgia, rheumatism and tuberculosis, and tended to have short lives. Their main problem, however, was dietary. The island of Kamaran could not support one blade of grass—nothing could be induced to grow there. The pearl-divers lived on oysters and a little seaweed, and although these resources were said to contain the minerals necessary to sustain life, the local medical evidence was that the divers possessed an abnormally low sexual drive and a low level of fertility, to which was ascribed the fact that one-child families were the rule. If a child died, the only hope of replacing it was for the would-be father to slip away illegally for a few weeks to an oyster-free diet in the Yemen.

Kamaran was then a British possession with an administrator from England. 'But don't you eat oysters?' I asked him, and he shook his head in amazement at the idea. 'In a cold climate and in moderation perhaps,' he said, 'but not here. I don't recommend you to try them either. They have an inconvenient effect.'

What exaggerations are committed even by the most sophisticated of us in the pursuit of love!

I came across further telling evidence against the aphrodisiac properties of seafood, this time on a trip to Cuba in 1960. I was there to interview Ernest Hemingway when I stumbled on a prawn-eating craze that had taken hold of Havana. I have written before about my encounter with Hemingway on this trip and apologize for introducing the novelist's name again. I do so because he seemed to be the man responsible for Havana's sudden rush to prawns.

Hemingway had sunk quietly into the background towards the end of the Batista regime, to re-emerge with Castro's entry into the capital and be photographed in a congratulatory hug with the Maximum Leader. His first reappearance in the press was to lecture the Cubans on their eating habits, reminding them that shortages of the rice and beans, the nation's staple diet, were always possible, and that rich resources of seafood remained largely unexploited in their coastal waters. He assured them that the best prawns in the Caribbean awaited harvesting off the Isla de Juventud (Youth), where they were currently eaten only by the natives with a well-known result that had given the island its name.

Of all the many bars in Havana, one called Sloppy Joe's was then the most celebrated, largely because it was Hemingway's custom to put in an appearance there every day at about one p.m., accompanied by his admirers. They would then perform the daily ritual of prawn-eating that attracted so many sightseers. I went to Sloppy Joe's one day, and although a bout of influenza had kept Hem at home, the prawn-eating ceremony, Hemingway-style, went ahead as demonstrated by his friends.

The scene was very Cuban. The regulars, their high-heeled boots polished for the second time that day, sat sipping their Hatuey beer waiting for the performance to begin. Two or three decorous and extremely beautiful mulatto prostitutes were hanging about, flapping their fans in the background. The sweet smell of the shore blew in through the open windows, carrying with it the twitterings of canaries in the shade trees. These birds were the descendants of the thousand or two released in celebration of a birthday by the dictator Batista. From the distance, another sound inseparable from the old Cuba could be heard—the incessant tapping of drums.

At exactly one o'clock, the door was flung open, and in trooped the men who had come to eat prawns. The newcomers lined up along the counter; the bartender selected a fine and extremely active prawn from his tray, brushed it with oil and dropped it on the hotplate. Here it squirmed and snapped, emitting the faintest of hisses, before being snatched away to be presented on a blue saucer to the first of those in the line.

The recipient took it in a tissue between his fingers and bit off its head. This he dropped on the immaculate floor before he thrust half the body into his mouth and began to crunch. It was Hem's contention that all that was most valuable in a prawn was in immediate contact with the inner shell or concentrated in the underbelly and the legs. The whole prawn, minus the head, was thus subjected to meticulous chewing, and all that could possibly be swallowed went down the throat.

The first prawn-eater did just this, and I was close enough to him to listen to the subdued crackle of the shell in his jaws. When he spat, as delicately as he could, a pinkness of prawn juices mixed with blood appeared at the corner of his mouth. He edged away from the bar, and the prawn-eaters waiting their turn followed. Soon a whitish detritus of prawns' heads and a greyish pulp of shell fragments spread across the floor among the sparkling boots.

In ten minutes, it was all over and time for the serious drinking to begin. But did this manly performance of Papa Hemingway and his disciples at Sloppy Joe's benefit any of them in any conceivable way or delay the process of ageing as in the Island of Youth? Almost certainly not. The novelist, when I eventually met him, appeared old for his years and, after the jubilant shots taken with Castro, a persistent melancholy had returned to his expression. A year later, at the age of sixty-two, he was to blow his brains out. There had been some talk of mental instability in the press, but this his brother denied. Ernest's tragic end, he said, had been due not to any mental decline but to his despair at the treachery of a body in which throughout his life he had taken so much pride.

So much for prawns.

But what about peas—or cheese? Casanova's formidable record is unexceptional by comparison with that of Ninon de Lenclos, the eighteenth-century beauty who is reputed to have had more than five thousand partners in an outstandingly active forty years. Asked if, in what is an essentially repetitious process, she ever experienced boredom, her reply was, 'Certainly not. Love may look always the same, but indeed it is new and different on every occasion.' She attributed her outstandingly successful amatory career partly to the assistance provided by puréed peas, to which she sometimes added a little sherry. She was also partial to cheese, which would come as no surprise to an Italian; cheese is one of the supreme aphrodisiacs of the Italian people, if we allow that aphrodisiacs have any real existence.

Italian cheese in its most distinguished form—*mozzarella di bufala*—certainly has most of the attributes upon which aphrodisiacs base their mysterious attraction. It may not quite reach the heights of those witches' brews which tempt the sexually sluggish with their fusion of hope and alarm: 'Take several brains of male sparrow,' Aristotle instructs, 'and pigeons that have not begun to fly'—these to be boiled with turnips and carrots in goat's milk, and then sprinkled with clover seeds. But authentic *mozzarella di bufala* is rare, and rarity (plus difficulty of access or extraction) is the thing.

The cheese is produced in tiny quantities in an almost inaccessible swamp south of Naples by an outdated animal whose ancestors were probably brought to this once-Greek colony in classical antiquity. Because there is so little of it, and because it is so superior to its many commercial imitations, *mozzarella di bufala* is expensive. During the Second World War, I spent a year in the vicinity of these swamps and watched the unsuccessful peasant descendants of a heroic past sloshing miserably through the swamp water to root up the occasional edible plant. The finest present I could send to any Italian friend driven by the disruptions of war from this splendid area was a kilo of mozzarella with all the over-brimming magic that for them it contained.

It was during my war year in Naples that I first noticed one of the outstanding mysteries concerning aphrodisiacs. Why were so many educated men prepared to submit themselves, even if only occasionally, to patent absurdities and primitive beliefs?

Many of my Italian friends had completed university courses. One was a lecturer in psychology, and several were doing well in medicine and the law. Nevertheless, they were superstitious about food. There was the borderline case of the semi-magical properties attributed to *mozzarella di bufala*, which was at least appetizing and nutritious, but I found less to excuse the custom of two academics who feasted at Easter time on newly hatched storks, and a surgeon happy to experiment with a soft cheese from Vesuvius to which a macerated lamb's foetus had been added. My friends did not deny that the interest lay in the possibility of enhanced sexual pleasure.

A feature of Naples in those days was a black market of proportions and complexity almost certainly exceeding anything else on earth. Cargoes equivalent to those of one ship in three unloaded in Naples were spirited away, later to reappear for sale in the Forcella market, where even the latest in machine-guns might be hidden under the counter. Since it was well known that this market was operated by the chiefs of the Allied Military Government of Occupied Territories, which was staffed at its higher levels by members of the Italo-American Mafia, it was accepted that there was little to be done.

Eventually I was instructed by the field security officer to carry out some preliminary analysis of the Army's losses in terms of quantities and values, and I told him that the most important losses were of penicillin, little of which was getting through to the military hospitals. When he asked me what was being done about this, I told him that I had arrested the principal dealer and taken him to Poggio Reale jail. 'And is he still there?' the FSO asked, to which the unhappy reply was that the man had been freed after three days. At the time of his arrest, he had laughed in my face. 'Who are you?' he asked. 'You are nothing and can do nothing. Last night I had dinner with the general, and if you continue to make a nuisance of yourself, I can have you sent away.'

Since nothing was to be done about the penicillin, my energies were diverted to the problem of vanishing food supplies from the base depot. Here, behind a high electrified fence on the outskirts of Afragola, capital of the Neapolitan Camorra, the local mafia, several thousand tons of tinned foods were piled high. Lorries came up from the port every day to add to this vast accumulation, and by night roughly the same number of lorries trundled down to the nocturnal black markets of neighbouring towns, carrying about the same amount of corned beef which had been delivered to the depot earlier on.

I suspected that the eventual destination of much of these provisions was to the many restaurants in the area which had recently opened under the stimulus of war, and I set out to pursue this theory. It was against the orders of the military government for members of the armed forces to eat in civilian restaurants, but the most pleasant of them were usually chock-a-block with British and American officers knocking back raw Neapolitan wine and listening to Neapolitan songs about love and betrayal.

Vincenzo a Mare, the most romantic of these places, was on the Posillipo shore under the villa where Nelson had paid court to Lady Hamilton and close to the spot where, after watching the obliteration of Pompeii, Pliny had set off for a closer view of the disaster from which he never returned. It was also here that Cuoca, the last great Camorra chieftain, had been brought in old age for a traditional funeral feast by the underlings who proposed to get rid of him. He was feasted, praised, hugged and kissed by all, and then, full of well-being and at peace with the world, an expert with a mattress-maker's needle stabbed him to death.

Part of my task was to know everybody, and I knew Umberto, the restaurant's owner. 'What are you serving today, Umberto?' I asked him one day, and he told me *frutti di mare*, based, as I knew, on such atrocious materials as sea cucumber and an obscene marine worm abundant in local waters.

'What about *carne alleata*?' This was the Neapolitan term for any brand of black-market meat abstracted from the base depot and served up secretly at extraordinary prices. 'Some of your customers are eating canned meat,' I said. 'This carries a prison sentence.'

He shrugged his shoulders. 'It is brought here by an American colonel,' he said.

I asked him the price, and he told me.

'It is very dear,' I said. 'Twice the price you are charging for *frutti di mare*. How do you explain that?'

'For *carne alleata* we are paying very much, because is better.'

'For what?'

He oscillated his hips in a revolting fashion. '*Per fare amore*,' he said.

'Bring me one of the tins,' I told him. He brought one in a bag, and we went into a corner together where he opened it.

'Spam,' I said. 'Of all things. Spam, an aphrodisiac. Just imagine it. Do you personally believe this is good to *fare amore*?'

He laughed. 'They are all eating it for this purpose. But for me personally—you want I tell you straight? I don't eat any of these things. For me is good wear a medal for San Rocco. This is OK for me. This is doing trick.'

83¢ is all it takes to understand politics, the economy, the arts, and the inner workings of Washington.*

Every week the editors of THE NEW REPUBLIC put together the best ideas and boldest commentary available on the political, social, and cultural scene.

Andrew Sullivan, Leon Wieseltier, Michael Kinsley, Ann Hulbert, Robert Wright, Mickey Kaus, Matt Cooper, Charles Lane and Michael Lind focus in on the true stories behind the headlines. Writers like Stanley Crouch, Naomi Wolf, John Updike, Malcolm Gladwell, and Tatyana Tolstaya are regular contributors. Stanley Kauffmann and Robert Brustein cover the latest in film and theater, and Mark Strand brings you the best in contemporary poetry.

Discover the award-winning weekly, THE NEW REPUBLIC, where politics, art, culture, and opinion are presented with style, wit and intelligence.

For Fastest Service Call 1-800-827-1289

THE NEW REPUBLIC

1220 19th Street, N.W.
Washington, D.C. 20036

* Less than the cost of a cup of cappuccino

MARGARET VISSER
THE SINS OF THE FLESH

The butcher's shop on Bloor Street in Toronto has closed down. Its owner may simply be embracing a well-deserved retirement—but it is also possible that, situated as his store was in a downtown neighbourhood full of young middle-class families, he had been losing business.

His window displays, however, remain unforgettable. I remember one in particular: for several Christmases in a row his decorations were fir trees over which he draped a baroque display of sausages. There were several styles of loopy sausage chains: reddish, speckled, deep or pale rose; the links exhibited different sizes and degrees of plumpness.

The effect was mesmerizing—and it took some reflection for me to figure out why. The sausages were just as colourful, just as ornamental as paper or tinsel or cranberry–popcorn chains, if a little insistent; but the reason they looked so incongruous, even in a butcher's window, was that they were *meat*, and here they were, decorating *vegetation*.

Now anthropologists have solemnly established for us that a 'proper' meal in modern western European and American culture has meat as its central pivot, and vegetables are subordinate to it—a mere garnish. Green vegetables are upstaged even by starches such as potatoes or rice or some other kind of grain. Meat does not decorate vegetables; if you are rich enough, vegetables decorate the meat.

And in any case, sausages are too substantial to hang on a tree (though these trees supported them pretty well). Lovable as they are to most people, sausages are somehow silly; they are low decorum; their minced insides and, above all, their shape ensure it. They are as phallic as any cigar, or more so; they are also excremental, especially when cooked, no matter how enticingly, brown. They are given uncomplimentary names like 'bangers' or 'dogs'. People use them for 'low' expressions like 'not a sausage', and may call a cuddly loved one 'Sausage', partly because the very sound of the word is round and comforting; it has 'mouthfeel'. No: you can hang gingerbread people and animals and cookie-cutter creatures on your Christmas tree; and candy canes and fruit, real or make-believe; but meat, for this purpose, is peculiar. Meat is all wrong.

You have to be careful how you use meat. All cultures have felt this and placed limits and categorizations upon it. Ancient Greek cities performed animal sacrifice; the sharing of the creature thus 'made sacred' (the meaning of the word 'sacrifice') symbolized city living in a ceremony that expressed calm, order, clarity, hierarchy and consent, which was civilization itself. The meat from the sacrificed animal was meticulously carved and portioned out. The bones were covered in roasted fat and given up, dripping with mythical precedent and meaning, to the gods, who doted not on meat but on the aroma of burnt offerings.

When, in Dionysian ecstasy, people broke out of civilized boundaries to dance in the woods and on the mountainsides, they expressed their frenzy by tearing animals to pieces with their bare hands and devouring them raw. Without prior, regulated killing, carving, cooking and sharing, meat-eating was disordered, bestial, terrifying. All sorts of other distinctions—those of sex and class to begin with—were obliterated when meat was 'deregulated' in this way. The difference between people and animals might be annihilated as well: Pentheus's mother mistook her son for a lion, tore off his arms and legs, clawed off handfuls of his flesh and danced with his head impaled on a stick. If you ate meat raw, having ripped a living creature apart first, you might as well go the whole hog, as it were, and be an infanticide and a cannibal as well.

The Greeks believed, however, that conventional meat-eating was entirely proper; cooking and sharing meat was even what made people human. (Modern anthropologists agree that the cooking of food, and the agreements human beings make in order to share it out, are major differences between our behaviour and that of animals.) People who did not eat meat both regularly and properly were perceived as anomalous and dangerous, capable of *anything*. The Cyclops in Homer's *Odyssey* was a lacto-vegetarian, which was part of the reason why he could suddenly turn cannibal, not only eating people, but eating them raw.

Christianity deliberately renounced food taboos very early in its history. It took a stand against exclusion and distinction— attitudes that are reinforced with supreme economy by the existence of food taboos. Like all religions, Christianity pays close attention to food: eating and fasting and abstaining have underlined and encouraged states of the soul and *religio* in the sense of 'what binds us together' and 'what we hold in common'. Food in Christian cultures has been treated as a necessity (and therefore to be supplied to those who lack it), as something to take delight in and be thankful for and as a potential temptation to gluttony. But nothing edible (with the exception of human flesh) has been categorized by Christians as to be rejected by definition.

A world view that tolerates the eating of absolutely any food but allows people to turn away from anything they don't feel like eating has much to recommend it. Human beings are omnivores—they can live on plants, or on animals, or on both. Most opt for a combination. Some vegetation is good for people whose diet is 'all meat'. (People whose diet consists almost entirely of meat, such as the Arctic Inuit, consider vegetation a delicacy, so preserve berries in seal oil for use during the winter, and even eat the vegetable contents of stomachs of the caribou.) And vegans (who eat no animal products at all) need supplements of vitamin B12, and must consciously look out for vegetable sources of vitamin D, calcium, iron and zinc. The domestication of animals and cultivation of vegetables for omnivorous eating—a process that began twelve millennia ago—has gone a long way towards solving the problem of having at hand a sufficient and reliable food source. Knowing nutrition to be regularly available is after all a sine qua non of a civilized human existence.

Meat, in this scheme of things, has always been 'special', and treated in one way or another with respect. It has almost never been constantly and easily available for most people. It did not keep well; a slaughtered animal had therefore to be eaten immediately and all at once, unless the meat was salted and put by for the winter, to be added in small pieces to vegetable and bread dishes for extra flavour. Fresh meat was a 'feast' food, something precious and unusual for sharing at important events.

Christian cultures have removed meat, eggs and dairy products from the menu during Lent and in preparation for feasts: feast days were celebrated with a resumption of meat and other rich dishes. Meat was the diet of warlike males and the swaggering nobility. Monks nearly always ate vegetables because they were the food of the poor and because meat has always been suspected of

115

causing its eaters to become competitive and aggressive, like carnivorous animals.

Nowadays our ideal is efficiency rather than respect. Our attitude is scientific, analytical; eating has become a matter of assimilating nutrients, and we do what is necessary to obtain protein, vitamins, fats and carbohydrates; 'meat' and 'flesh' have become vague and unscientific terms. The areas of the world where efficiency and science rule have well-fed, healthy human populations whose life expectancy is greater than ever before. People in these places eat a vast variety of foods, prepared in an enormous number of ways: we are culturally encouraged—pressured, even—to eat as many different things as possible. It behoves us, we feel, to take advantage of what is spread out for us to choose from. Hedonism is another of our fiercest ideals; the least we can do is enjoy the fruits of the battles that modernity has won.

One such triumph is the availability of everything, at all seasons, always. 'I hope to make France so prosperous that every peasant will have a chicken in his pot on Sunday,' exclaimed King Henri IV in the sixteenth century. In 1928, the Republican Party won an election in the United States with the help of the slogan, 'A chicken in every pot.' Where once this had been a treat reserved for Sundays, now every day could be a feast. We have rediscovered at last the illogicality of such an idea; banality gives rise in the end to boredom rather than elation.

Modernity, its fruits and its costs, are now being seriously questioned. People in our own culture realize increasingly that we might be well off, but know also that more people are starving to death than ever before, and that global marketing systems must shoulder some of the blame. The standard borne by those among the new troops who call themselves vegetarians is one they wrested from meat-eaters; they use it as a rallying point, with new meanings and a symbolism we can understand, all too well. Their symbol is meat: flesh we have made to suffer with ruthless indifference, flesh that robs other people of food so that we who eat too much already need not forgo an incidental pleasure, flesh that might even ruin our own health. This meat—our favourite and best food, one of the jewels in the crown of civilization, our triumph over necessity—they call foul, an embodiment, in the most literal and disgusting sense, of cruelty and greed and stupidity.

Of course, we don't listen. Vegetarians themselves are few—ten per cent, maybe, of the populations of Europe and North America. They count great men who ate only vegetables, although it was not eating vegetables that made them great—or indeed evil, as in the case of their most embarrassing convert, Adolf Hitler. In their anger they twist facts, rant and accuse. Theirs is a literature that boxes itself in by its contempt for others: refusing to eat what other people like eating has always been a powerful judgement on and rejection of the not-similarly-fastidious. Meat-eaters—relaxed, happy, free to eat whatever they like, supported by culture and tradition—tend to look upon vegetarians as cranky, eccentric, extreme, or fixated on one small point while there is so much else that could profitably be done to make the world a better place.

It is also natural for human beings to eat meat, which is to say that we are able to do so. For most people, it is also pleasurable, often it is useful, and sometimes it is essential. But it is natural for human beings to overlay 'nature' with culture—we are free to decide, that is to say, whether or not to accept anything 'extra', the things available to us that we do not require in order to survive. Vegetarians insist that in modern conditions we do not need to eat meat, and that we should give it up because of the damage that meat-eating causes. They have an enormous amount of persuading to do, which explains some of their shrillness of tone. Meat, after all, has been prized for centuries and fits in very well with the modern diet now that it is so readily and cheaply available. Furthermore, most of us have chosen to be urban. Very few of us have a vegetable patch—or would want one as more than a hobby. We depend upon food being grown elsewhere and transported, often very long distances, to reach us. We never have to see animals slaughtered—we need not even think much about 'meat' ever having been an animal. And when it comes to freshness, frozen meat has, in many ways, better keeping qualities and loses its taste less than long-boxed or frozen vegetables.

In our admiration for convenience and under relentless pressure to save time, we moderns love fast food: a few morsels that will fill us quickly and pleasurably without regret for the cost.

Margaret Visser

Meat is essential to most fast-food meals. Partly because of the belief that as flesh it is a 'complete' food, we remain unconvinced that a veggie burger or a salad is truly sustaining. To have something of such high status so promptly available, for so little money, seems to be the fulfilment of, the very justification for the entire modern capitalist and technological enterprise. Meat, under modern conditions, is easy to keep and easy to prepare.

But vegetarians have shown us that the 'cheapness' of hamburgers is a lie: the price is enormous, but it is paid elsewhere, and not by us. Poor countries, desperate for cash, grow beef that is cheap by our accounting, but they permanently destroy their own lands and forests in the process, even as they are not growing food for themselves. The cruelty that 'efficient' modern stock raising inflicts upon animals is often unspeakable. And meat that is mass produced is increasingly likely to convey into our bodies the antibiotics and hormones that farm animals must ingest for the sake of their survival and productivity.

Yet when you are hungry, when you want feeding both solidly and now, you think of your hunger, of your time, of your purse, and not of the topsoil of Costa Rica or the conditions in chicken batteries. You smell the aroma of seared beef, hear and smell the sizzle of bacon. You eat, you robustly enjoy, you sigh with contentment as you wipe the grease off your chin. A solemn vegetarian frowning at your heedlessness would annoy anybody at a time like that. So sanctimonious they seem with all their objections, so ungrateful, so *joyless*.

The provisions environment—the term used to describe what is physically available for human beings in ordinary circumstances to use, in this case, for eating—is an important aspect of any culture. For thousands of years our own provisions environment has, when circumstances were ideal, included meat. An enormous amount of any culture's energy goes into this environment: first inventing it, then building it and finally keeping it in working order. In the process, this range of available goods winds itself into and around our presuppositions, our attitudes, our desires. Adults demonstrate to their offspring, by eating, what it is children should consume, what they should like. Animals, too,

118

have a lifelong preference for eating whatever prey they caught first; and adult animals have been shown to 'favour acceptance' of certain foods in their young, setting a good example by eating them with pleasure themselves.

Human beings harbour nostalgia for the food they ate as children, to the extent that they will consider what their culture eats to be part of their identity, even after living abroad for a long time: food habits are tenacious. A food tradition grows out of long periods of trial and error, and the need for a population to keep itself healthy. Once the pattern is in place, enormous social pressures are brought to bear to maintain it, for the sake of the society as a whole. The pressures are often subtle and not consciously acknowledged: they are the more powerful for being so.

Most modern vegetarians in our own meat-eating culture are, of course, converts to the practice. Many of them can remember what amounts to a 'conversion experience', which generally happened in childhood and is remembered and reverted to when the adult finally decides to embrace vegetarianism. The child witnesses an animal being executed; or a piece of meat gets stuck between its teeth, and suddenly there is the realization that this is a piece of an *animal*. Some children never take to eating meat (babies have to learn to eat every kind of solid food), in spite of orders or anxious cajoling from parents who believe that not eating meat will cause health problems. These are people who know the culture's rules, but resist its pressures and rewards. Other people can only shake their heads at them and pity their refusal of one of life's chief pleasures. Other people are in the vast majority. Meat-eating is a deeply rooted habit in western culture; meat holds not only a foundational but a high-status position in the provisions environment. Removing meat from the conventional menu is therefore as ambitious as a social and political goal could be.

The provisions environment may be altered because of natural catastrophes, or because of revolutionary political decisions. North America, particularly in the northern states, moved from marketing (and eating and therefore the *preference for*) pork to a collective decision that beef was better. Cattle took over the great plains from the American buffalo—and simultaneously broke the hold of the indigenous peoples over those wide lands. Americans ate less and less pork, and beef became unquestionably 'king'. But food habits in the culture at large change only reluctantly. If they are altered for moral reasons, the reasoning must be extremely powerful—that is, free consent to the change must be secured. Moral reasoning is always closely bound up with physical facts, and never is this more so than when it pertains to food. Health, politics and the environment cannot be ignored where food is concerned.

Meat-eating reveals deep contradictions in the assumptions upon which modern civilized living is based. Very few modern, urban human beings, for example, would actually slaughter the animals they love eating. We have become sensitive to suffering in animals and loath to inflict pain. A person who whipped a dog, say, in public would immediately be set upon by indignant observers, almost all of whom would have no reservations about eating the flesh of a slaughtered animal—provided it was slaughtered by somebody else. Nobody in western culture—not even a dog-beater—eats dog, of course: dogs are not allowed on menus. (It is worth pausing here to reflect that we do abstain, in certain cases, from edible flesh without missing it or feeling deprived.) We are also very primitive about the need to see damage before we can care about it. And we don't mind profiting from cruelty, provided somebody else 'does the dirty work'—and not in our presence.

Recasting ancient attitudes

It was said that Pythagoras, the ancient Greek philosopher, once saw some people beating a dog. 'Stop!' he cried, 'don't beat it, since in truth it has the soul of a friend which I recognized upon hearing it cry out!' Pythagoras believed in the transmigration of souls. In their immortal journeyings, souls found lodgings where they could struggle to purify themselves and thereby to raise themselves to a point where they could escape the chains of necessity that bound them to this world. Anything could harbour a soul. The strictly vegetarian Pythagoreans were told to abstain from beans as well as from meat, partly because it was thought that the flatulence that followed bean-eating might be caused by the introduction into one's body of malevolent spirits, provoking foul odours and tormented dreams. Meat was even more likely to be ensouled, stuff that could introduce unwanted spirits into a human self.

Modern vegetarians would not, on the whole, cite the transmigration of souls as the reason they have decided not to eat meat. Yet there is a modern version of the same belief, in the idea of 'Gaia'—that all is one, and that we must cooperate with everything on 'the planet'. Whereas it has, in the past, seemed profoundly important to notice the ways in which human beings differ from animals, we moderns have begun to insist on how little we differ from them. Human beings, we find ourselves realizing, are nothing special. The reason for this change of perspective lies at least partly in the terror which our own power over creation arouses in us: we must back down and lay off, or risk destroying the world and ourselves. In our own way, we concur with the ancient Pythagorean desire to limit human voraciousness out of a recognition of our fellowship with the rest of nature.

Then, having decided not to distinguish ourselves from other creatures, we may feel that killing an animal is killing one of our own, that it approaches cannibalism in its primitive heedlessness. The philosopher Porphyry was concerned with the taboo against cannibalism, and in his book *On Abstinence from Ensouled Creatures*, he adduces an argument dear to modern vegetarians that blurs the difference between human beings and animals. We do not eat babies, he says, or mentally retarded people. Yet these live 'from sense alone, without possessing intellect and reason'. In what respect then are they different from animals? So, Porphyry goes on, we ought not to kill animals or be cruel to them—and then he finds it necessary to deny that vegetables are to be pitied for being cut, peeled, chopped, cooked and eaten, for they are 'entirely destitute of sensation, and therefore nothing foreign, or evil, or hurtful, or injurious can befall them. For sensation is the principle of all alliance.'

Vegetarianism is a strategy commonly employed in religious practice. It has always been a form of asceticism, a way of purifying its adepts. Sometimes the reasons why it was practised sound odd to modern ears. In ancient Greece, the gods lived on the smell of the roast, not on flesh. Therefore not to eat meat was to be more like a god. Vegetarianism was thought to dissolve the disagreeable but mighty bond between the soul and the body. Living on the actual flesh of animals weakened the soul by making the body heavy and earthy. Meat was difficult to get and to prepare; it was far too pleasant in the eating, and heavy on the digestive system. It gave to the body more than was its due, privileging corporeality over soul.

Ancient Greek vegetarians were opposed to animal sacrifice. This was not because killing animals was cruel—although there have always been people who have protested against cruelty to animals. Sacrifice was bound up with the meaning of the ancient city: the killing and sharing of meat signified the unity and hierarchy of the whole; the sacrifice also implied contact with, yet separation from, the divine. Those who rejected sacrifice expressed their belief that all this was far too material, too 'reified'. Why couldn't people show their togetherness with different symbols? How could the gods get pleasure from sniffing the scents of cooking bones and fat? How unjust and how primitive the hierarchies and banquetings of the city looked to these conscientious objectors—and how clear it consequently was that they should refuse the first and most direct profits to be received from sacrificial rites, namely, meat.

Vegetarianism was for strong people. It was closely allied with fasting, where people retire from human fellowship (of which sharing a meal is the primary symbol) to think and pray and steady their resolve. The word 'fast' and the word 'steadfast' are both cognate with German *fest*—'firm'. Famous thaumaturges fasted in the ancient Greek world; the ancient Jews were renowned for fasting. Less dramatic than fasting, but universally admired, was the virtue of frugality. Meat was itself 'rich'—a perquisite of the wealthy and powerful. Daily consumption of a lot of meat in Mediterranean countries was an unnecessary luxury and was credited with stimulating the passions and leading to unruly behaviour. Not to eat meat was to embrace the virtues of frugality with especially impressive determination. And in any case, vegetables were easy to grow and formed a substantial part of the ancient diet, an example we are urged to follow today.

The fasting ideal has its modern counterpart in dieting, though depriving oneself of food in order to lose weight is very different from fasting. For one thing, dieting is usually endless whereas fasting is temporary, and its goals (health, self-esteem) are both vaguer and less attainable. But the imperatives to be strong, to resist the pressures of one's own desire in the face of other people's wantonness and inability to measure up, are very similar. Vegetarianism is not fasting or dieting but permanent abstinence. Not eating meat or dairy products does, however, mean avoiding animal fat—the kind with the most cholesterol, as the makers of margarine have heavily impressed upon us. It can offer the consolations, in this culture, of comparative thinness; it certainly lays claim to providing superior health, that unquestionable modern ideal.

The admiration of the ancients for frugality looks extremely unmodern until we realize that vegetarians seek to 'live lightly on the earth', as one sixties slogan had it. Vegetarians have extremely frugal ideals, although in our culture they are often themselves comfortably prosperous, and so can 'afford' to choose frugality for moral reasons. Meat is wasteful. Stock raising by modern methods pollutes water resources, destroys our dwindling forests, and takes land from the poor. Land used in raising cattle would feed many more people if it were turned over to growing grain.

Vegetarian groups such as the Pythagoreans stood apart from society, criticizing it by marking themselves off from it in dress and eating habits, the physical signs of a profoundly different religious orientation. Very often they formed themselves into communities that lived away from large urban centres: they stood at the opposite extreme from devotees of Dionysus, but their 'place' was similarly outside the city's precincts, since they too rejected the city's norms. The Bacchae escaped the human condition, taking to the mountains and ecstatically eating meat raw like beasts. The Pythagoreans lived apart and drew close to the gods by doing without meat altogether. They proclaimed that slaughtering animals brutalized human beings; the Bacchae believed that in their bloody trances they were 'eating the god'.

Both groups thought they had what we call 'nature' on their side. Good burghers, on the other hand, inhabitants of the Greek *polis*, cooked and ate meat, ritually sacrificing animals and sharing out their flesh to symbolize order and hierarchy and to celebrate tradition, normality and human control over nature and necessity.

A desire to live in communes, preferably in the country, still goes together with a vegetarian diet. An 'alternative' lifestyle is achieved very quickly with the simple rejection of meat. Refusing to eat what other people habitually eat can mean that you never eat with them—and not sharing food is as potent a symbol as sharing. 'Alternative' people make new friends. They may also tend to join their fellows in despising the people who remain unconverted. This explains the anger and the predictability of a good deal of vegetarian literature, and its common refusal to see the contexts and the reasons for meat eating either now or in the past.

The ancient idea that slaughtering animals brutalizes human beings has an analogy in the unwillingness of civilized people nowadays to kill animals even if they habitually eat them. (This has not always been so: 'Any of us,' said Dr Johnson, 'would kill a cow rather than not have beef.') There is, however, at the same time an enormous modern indifference to the cruelty that is perpetrated in the process of achieving efficiency and low prices for meat. It is not lost on modern vegetarians that the contradiction is a scandal: here we are, sensitive to the point of sentimentality towards our pets, while we let the animals we feel like eating live and die in the most appalling conditions. ('Efficient' stock-raising methods and concentration camps have in common much that is chillingly modern.) We even allow our scientists to investigate the possibilities of 'bioengineering' animals: creating chickens without legs, for instance, because they don't need legs in battery cages. People who react strongly to such insane 'efficiencies' do so partly because they believe that a society prepared to go that far is 'brutalizing' itself.

One method of securing consent to a morally based change is to focus upon a generally accepted concept and apply it to new areas. Human rights is one such concept. Anybody—or anything—who wishes to avoid attack in the aggressive and exploitative modern world had better be protected by rights.

People who want us to stop being cruel to animals, therefore, tell us that animals have 'rights' as we do, since human beings are not some superior species, but one with the animals and with all creation. Claims are made for rights that they are based in nature; an example is this insistence that 'we are all one.'

Ancient Greeks such as the poet and farmer Hesiod classified all animals as one species, noted that they ate each other and so saw them as 'cannibals'; human beings, they proudly insisted, were something else entirely, refraining as they do from eating their own kind. It is precisely the strategy of modern 'Gaia' devotees to make us admit that we are animals like the beasts, and should therefore refrain from devouring our own. If we use the language of rights, however, we should admit that the granting of rights to animals must be recognized as being a moral decision, a matter of human culture. We grant rights; they do not exist of themselves. Animals have no concept of rights, and it is only human beings who would think of refraining for a moral reason from killing and eating. If we were really 'like animals' we would suffer no qualms.

The message that vegetarianism imparts to the rest of us is ascetic and exclusive. The refusal to do as the rest of us do looks very like a claim to purity. This means, of course, that the majority of people—everybody but the abstainers—is impure. It is a judgement that is unlikely to make meat-eaters warm towards vegetarians. They respond by despising vegetarians in their turn as pale and unhealthy, tight-lipped, wasted, mean and unhappy. Even the ancient Pythagoreans irritated their fellow Greeks, who made them the butt of innumerable jokes: Pythagoreans, they said, were pale, foolish, self-righteous, hilariously solemn and smelly.

Degrees of disgust

Meat, in the words of the anthropologist Julia Twigg, is 'strong', according to the hierarchy of foods that our 'dominant culture' semi-consciously accepts. And 'strong' means high status. Strongest of all are human beings, carnivores and uncastrated beasts: so strong are they that they are classified as inedible.

Raw meat is especially strong because it is bloody and

unmediated by cooking. But whereas 'meat' is reasonably imprecise and unconnected in our minds with specific body parts, the same cannot be said for eyes, testicles, ears or offal. The sight of these, especially when raw, is capable of arousing a shudder even in meat-eaters. Vegetarians, however, who allow themselves freely and righteously to express horror at the sight of meat, blame any disgust they note in non-vegetarians upon guilt. But rawness in vegetables is especially revered; in eating raw vegetables and whole grains, vegetarians believe at some level that they ingest goodness and completeness (something like the goodness and completeness other people find in meat). At the same time, they are embracing nature by allowing as little cultural interference, in the form of 'processing', as possible. Vegetarians deliberately invert the conventional ranking of foods: hierarchy remains, but what is commonly thought 'high' is rejected; what is 'low' is held to be purest and best.

The other edible meat categories in this hierarchy are red meat, poultry and fish—in descending order. Pork is considered less strong than beef because it is pinker and cooks to a pale colour. Fish, usually white and bloodless, is so low or 'weak' that some vegetarians may eat it. They commonly find themselves an object of outraged scorn to meat-eaters, on the popular principle that nobody expects a stricter adherence to the proprieties than one who has rejected them.

Some vegetarians allow eggs and cheese to pass their lips—and again are accused of not being 'proper' vegetarians. Meat-eaters ask nastily what provision has been made for the chickens and the cows responsible for these animal products? What happens to the heifers, unproductive as they are of milk? Are they—heaven forbid—killed? Of course they are—and, once slaughtered, is it not right, and ecological, to consume their bodies for food rather than wastefully bury them?

Vegans are unassailable on this score—but even they kill plants for their dinner. Only fruitarians—those who never eat roots, or anything that cannot be plucked from a plant without killing it—can be said to have chosen a diet even more triumphantly 'weak'—and pure—than that of vegans.

One reason for the growth in popularity of vegetarian diets in recent years, and for a more general decline in the amount of meat eaten in our society, must be the ageing of the population. Older people simply 'need' less meat; they are satisfied more easily with less solid food. Another reason is the great revolution we have begun to experience in the emancipation of women. Women have not only been categorized as weak in our culture, but also expected to embody purity. They have been more likely to eat fish or chicken and salads, say, than red meat and potatoes. And furthermore, technology has taken away much of the need for men to be especially tough, and to show it by what they 'need' to eat. The fact that more and more people—men as well as women—choose to eat 'weakly' may be a cultural expression of the growth in social power of women. (Reasons of health, with their grounding in the fact that technology has made physical exertion irrelevant for everything but fitness, are more obvious of course.) Eating meat may be 'modern', but vegetarianism, too, both fits and reveals the structures of modernity.

The modernity of vegetarianism

A meal that includes meat traditionally makes it central. The 'meat course' is the main one; meat commonly dominates the platter on which it is placed. Other courses and other kinds of food are subordinate. The main meal of the day has habitually been distinguished, in Europe, as 'the meal . . . in which animal source predominates'. Dinner, as the main meal of the day, required meat, as Thanksgiving or Christmas entails turkey. It takes particular concentration to maintain festive traditions yet leave out the customary meaty climax to the feast. People who decide to leave meat out of their diets must learn an entirely new way of designing meals and different cooking skills.

For a long time we were given to understand by scientists, anthropologists, nutritionists and others that meat was essential to our well-being because meat is protein, and protein-deficiency would inevitably follow if we ate no meat. This idea has been exploded—a diet high in cereals, legumes and vegetables has been proved sufficient. Yet we have difficulty giving up a kind of awe for protein, finding it easy to imagine it as a comforting, sustaining stuff—like meat itself. Meat the solid, the central; meat which itself means 'food' as in the expression 'meat and drink'; meat the bearer of the highest status in our food hierarchy, can seem to us to *be* the meal. It is the essence of food and only meat can offer the ultimate satisfaction. Lacking it—that is, having to create a vegetarian meal—we must 'make up for it' by other means: for instance by providing variety, ornamentation and extra colour. People must be given proof that they have had 'enough', which often means several dishes where one might have done.

Some vegetarians prefer to use meat 'analogs', as they are called in the United States: nut cutlets, tofu burgers and other substances that are not meat but offer similar textures. But others are uncomfortable eating something that is pretending to be meat. For them, the elegant solution is an abstract structure imposed on a vegetarian dish: a pie or a tart perhaps, or vegetables set out in a clear design. A clearly threefold pattern (soup, main course, dessert) is reassuring and comforting at a vegetarian repast, where it is merely conventional at a meat-centred one. And a status-rich acceptance of strange or exotic kinds of vegetables always helps.

Vegetarians appear to meat-eaters to have to do a sort of penance for rejecting the concentrated nutrition that is meat: they have to structure their meals carefully, painstakingly grouping their grains, greens, nuts, beans and roots correctly so as to be sure to get all the necessary nutrients. Eating properly, then, requires that vegetarians eat variously. But considerable skill—always remembering that our culture is lacking in vegetarian tradition—is needed for making the different textures, shapes and colours work for and not against gourmet pleasure. Today's bookshops often have shelves devoted entirely to vegetarian recipe books. These are enormously helpful to people who must learn how to make meatless meals. The segregation that tends to take place in society between meat-eaters and vegetarians has happened naturally in the 'niche marketing' of cookery books.

SUBSCRIPTION ORDER

YES, Enter my subscription to Granta (4 issues per year):
- ○ 1 year $32.00   *Save 33% from the bookshop price.*
- ○ 2 years $60.00   *Save 37%.*
- ○ 3 years $88.00   *Save 40% (that's $51.45).*

My Name (If renewing, please attach issue label.)

Address

City/State/Zip   6504NC

○ Enter   ○ Renew my subscription   ○ Just send gifts.

$_____ **total (see below for foreign postage).**
- ○ Foreign postage applies. (See rates below).
- ○ Check *(US dollars drawn on US banks)*
- ○ MC   ○ Visa   ○ Am Ex   ○ Bill me

Card Number

Expires   Signature

*Credit card orders: fax to 212 586 8003 or enclose in an envelope for your own protection.

Additional postage per year outside the US:

Canada (includes GST):	○ $10 surface	○ $18 airmail
Mexico and S. America:	○ $ 7 surface	○ $18 airmail
Rest of world:	○ $18 airspeeded	

'A stunning contribution to contemporary writing'
—*Newsweek*

Every issue of Granta features fiction, politics, photography, memoir, travel writing, and more.

Plus, if you subscribe, you save 40% off the $11.95 bookshop price.

GRANTA

GIFT ORDER

Don't let your friends miss out.

My Name (If renewing, please attach issue label.)

Address

City/State/Zip   6504NC

○ Enter   ○ Renew my subscription   ○ Just send gifts.

$_____ **total for_____ gifts and ○ my own subscription.**
- ○ Foreign postage applies. (See rates below).
- ○ Check *(US dollars drawn on US banks)*
- ○ MC   ○ Visa   ○ Am Ex   ○ Bill me

Card Number

Expires   Signature

*Credit card orders: fax to 212 586 8003 or enclose in an envelope for your own protection.

Additional postage per year outside the US:

Canada (includes GST):	○ $10 surface	○ $18 airmail
Mexico and S. America:	○ $ 7 surface	○ $18 airmail
Rest of world:	○ $18 airspeeded	

Give a one-year Granta subscription—to a friend or to yourself—for **$32**. Pay only **$25** for each *additional* one-year gift entered at this time.

○ **Please enter Granta gift subscriptions for:**

Name   Name

Address   Address

City/State/Zip   7504SC   City/State/Zip   7504NC

BUSINESS REPLY MAIL
FIRST CLASS MAIL   PERMIT NO. 195   FLAGLER BEACH, FL

POSTAGE WILL BE PAID BY ADDRESSEE

P.O. BOX 420387
PALM COAST FL 32142-9913

BUSINESS REPLY MAIL
FIRST CLASS MAIL   PERMIT NO. 195   FLAGLER BEACH, FL

POSTAGE WILL BE PAID BY ADDRESSEE

P.O. BOX 420387
PALM COAST FL 32142-9913

The appearance of a skilfully prepared vegetarian meal—lots of dishes, rioting colours, novel ingredients, sophisticated pairings—can be confidently modern in its pluralist, various, uncentralized structure, even postmodern. There is a lot of volume, yet a claim is made for 'lightness'. Such a meal offers a suggestion that we might after all obey the paradoxical modern and consumerist injunction, 'Eat, eat, eat—but stay thin, thin, thin.'

The young who embrace vegetarianism are also attracted to the elasticity of these meals, which express very different social goals from those of conventional dinners where partakers, hierarchically seated, gather round a table bearing a roast. Vegetable dishes are cheaper and more easily divisible should people suddenly drop by. The table and chairs redouble the symbolism of the shared roast: there is only so much room, so many chairs, so much meat. The 'message' given by the ceremonial carving of a roast turkey, say, is that the diners are united—but that hierarchy reigns: a turkey provides portions that differ, as between breast and drumstick, light meat and dark; and these differences express rank, as does the order in which people are served and asked to express preferences. Hamburger meat, on the other hand, where the flesh is first ground into an undifferentiated mass and then shaped into equal discs, gives everybody the same thing to eat. Vegetarian meals easily give an egalitarian message because the traditional prize, meat in its gradations of honourableness, is absent: vegetarianism, from this point of view, is 'modern', and roast-sharing is not.

Modern people in rich societies have reached a stage of satiety, of exhaustion with 'choice', that sometimes makes them want to have something they can reject. Part of the moral satisfaction of being a vegetarian is just this comforting limit to what one can have (which is not to deny that choosing a meatless diet can be a symbolic demonstration that there is a limit to what one will put up with). However, the satisfaction does conceal a trap. For people with tender consciences about the iniquities of much of the way the world is ordered it is relatively simple to ease one's conscience by doing a small thing, even if it is perceived to be in one's own self-interest, rather than locate a real and a much larger ill and attack that.

129

The energy that has gone into forcing people to give up smoking is so concentrated as to have become suspect: why so very much devotion to this ideal? If the effect of pollution upon health is the problem, why not, for example, give up driving and try to stamp out the automobile? Perhaps vegetarianism, like giving up smoking, laudable as it is, *can take the place* of our devoting ourselves to effecting real changes in the way we live; we are thereby left free to continue devouring our disproportionate share of the world's riches. This argument would, of course, enrage vegetarians, who argue that meat-eating is one of the worst evils: stop that, and other injustices, they believe, will cease. They might with justice retort, 'At least we are doing *something*.'

Indeed, the whole debate is deeply emotional, saturated as it is with mostly unspoken presuppositions, myths and evasions. Rationality has a very hard time, even when discussions rather than vituperations take place, partly because the range of facts (and the quantity of misinformation) is so vast that no one person can master it all, and partly because this is one of the large areas of human living where imagination, and the direction in which one looks and strives, is even more valuable than reasoning is.

If a person refuses to eat meat from this day forward, the life of not a single chicken will be saved. Indeed, as fast as our society produces vegetarians and cuts back on eating flesh, meat finds markets in other, previously low-meat-eating cultures, where 'modernity', proffering its cornucopia, is still only desired and has yet to be questioned. 'Nature' will not return to some pristine state even if all of us stop eating meat. For one thing, 'nature' is in many ways what human beings, interacting with it (as it is their 'nature' to do), have changed and increased and, on occasion, spoilt. We have introduced alien plants and animals to environments all over the globe, with consequences that are impossible to quantify; we have extinguished for ever thousands of species of animals and plants; we have permanently altered plants to suit ourselves and have made those plants unable to continue existing without our intervention. The responsibility for all this is squarely ours, for both the good and the bad. We must change ourselves if we wish to reduce any damage we shall do in future. Ceasing to eat meat is not enough. What ceasing to eat meat *may* do, however, is provide a rallying cry that strikes at our emotions as well as at our intelligence.

Modern vegetarian polemic is full of a particular animus against religion, which is unfortunate because the new vegetarianism is best understood as a religious technique. It is a habitual expression of a change of heart, which in religious language is called a conversion. Like any religious practice, it can become dislodged from the larger moral context that gives it life, and if that happens, it dwindles into a mere obsession, hostile, narrow, judgemental and sanctimonious: at best it becomes yet another manifestation of modern narcissism—in this case, a fixation on each vegetarian's own health and purity. The moral energy that vegetarianism might nobly claim fizzles out in mere disgust at the sight or smell or thought of meat. People who give up eating meat are, of course, especially prone to such an aversion: it can be difficult habitually to avoid something and not recoil in horror when encountering it. But a vegetarian practice that aims higher than personal purity and a merely physical revulsion must somehow learn to place disgust in perspective.

Caring and justice-based arguments for vegetarianism are something else entirely. They are larger than the practice itself, focusing as they do on love for animals rather than on disgust for the sight of meat and contempt for the people who eat it. The causes that vegetarians espouse, and the ecological dangers they warn against, are new, arising as they do out of new technologies which have given us unprecedented power to exploit. And the twentieth century's concentration-camp mentality, where cruelty takes place in secret so that we can muffle our consciences, claim ignorance and comfortably carry on worshipping 'efficiency', makes consciousness-raising more important than perhaps it has ever been. Being a vegetarian can be symbolic—a sign one is taking a stand, a declaration of which side one is on. It is something a person can do; and its limitation to a single individual's decision can be broadened by commitment (one person does it for a lifetime), and by the example it gives to everybody of the possibility of change.

Margaret Visser

Vegetarians, in modern society, are a minority, but they fit in with progressive aspects of modernity and they are therefore able to stretch it in directions it can reasonably agree to follow. In this sense, it is a prophetic movement. It influences many more people than actually subscribe to it. And while it is unlikely that everybody will give up eating meat, many, with at least some awareness of the vegetarian model, can decide—and are deciding—to eat less meat. The consequences, if this tendency survives and grows, may be economically, politically, even spiritually momentous.

THE MYSTERY OF
CHARLES JONES

Charles Jones took beautiful photographs of vegetables, fruit and flowers. That is all that is known. It is not known, for example, why he took them, or where (and only roughly when). All that can be said with any certainty is that the photographs on the next seventeen pages were probably made by a plate camera, around 1900; that they exist only in the form of silver-gelatin prints (silver for the image; gelatin as a layer in which the silver is set); that the captions on the back have been written in pencil by the same hand, some with the signature Charles Jones; and that they have not been previously published apart from as one or two entries in auction catalogues.

Sean Sexton, a dealer in old photographs and photographic equipment, found these pictures, and several hundred others like them, in a trunk at the Bermondsey antique market in south London, in 1981. It was about nine-thirty a.m., quite late in the day to find anything valuable—dealers who depend on old objects for their livelihood have usually done their most important buying and selling in Bermondsey before daybreak, leaving the dross for tourists and stay-a-bed amateurs. Other photographic dealers had looked at the pictures earlier in the morning and rejected them—Vegetables!—and Sexton got them for a hundred pounds.

To buy a single one of them at auction today might cost twenty times that amount, which is not mysterious; they are, in their simplicity, remarkably modern, the antithesis of the Victorian school of still life. The mystery is the photographer. Sexton's theory is that he may have worked at the Royal Botanical Gardens at Kew, where records show that a Charles Jones was employed as a 'sub-foreman' for a year in the early 1890s, before he quit to follow a career as head gardener at various large country and suburban houses.

Other scholars are sceptical. Could an amateur photographer take such skilful pictures? Wasn't amateur photography a rather expensive hobby one hundred years ago?

Outside scholarship, it may not matter. Charles Jones is not known, but, thanks to his photography, we may come to know the beauty of a turnip.

PICTURE RESEARCH: MARY DUNKIN

'Turnip, Green Globe'

'Leek, Prize Taker'

'Celery, Standard Bearer'

'Runner Bean'

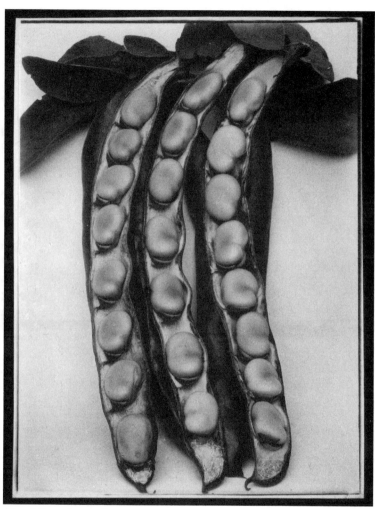

'Broad Bean, Longpod'

'Cabbage, Drumhead'

'Potato, Majestic'

'Cauliflower,
Veitelis
Autumn Giant'

'Turnip, Golden Ball'

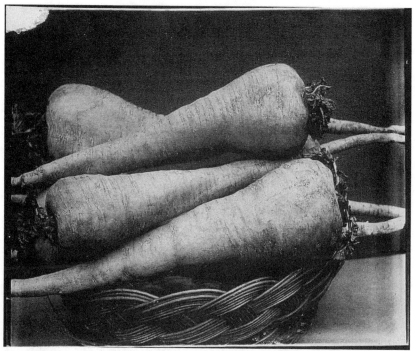

'Parsnip, Student'

'Cucumber, Telegraph'

'Pea, Fordes Rival'

'Melon, Hero of Lochinge'

'Strawberry, Leader'

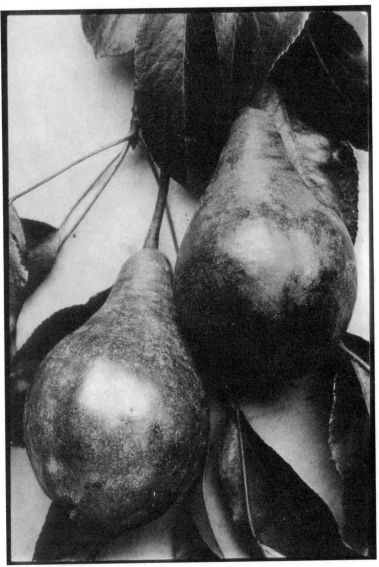

'Pear, Le Lactier'

'Cherry, White Heat'

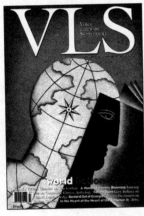

GRANTA

LAURA SHAPIRO
DO WOMEN LIKE TO COOK?

Darlene Tomkins cooks with instant pancake mix   HULTON DEUTSCH

Until recently, the question 'Do women like to cook?' wouldn't have been asked and couldn't have been answered. When it was time to feed the family, women cooked and that was that. But during the years immediately following the Second World War, cooking—an activity long seen as so immutably female it was practically a secondary sex characteristic—became, for the first time, a choice. With the advent of packaged and semi-prepared foods, it became possible to put meals on the table while doing very little actual cooking. These new products were promoted on the premise that cooking was an odious chore, one that women couldn't wait to drop, and indeed many women greeted the arrival of gingerbread mix and dehydrated mashed potatoes with glad relief. But it took considerable persuasion to convince most women that packaged-food cuisine was real cooking. Whether or not they liked to cook, most women liked *feeling* as though they were cooking. And they worried about leaving out the most powerful ingredient in any dish served at home—the ingredient one newspaper food writer called 'a wife and mother's love for her family'.

By the mid-1940s, the American food industry had a single overriding ambition: to create a mass market for the processed food that had been developed originally to feed the armed forces. The technology for freezing and drying food, ensuring a long shelf life and general indestructibility, was available; whether or not it extended any real benefits to consumers who didn't have to dine in foxholes was immaterial. All that remained for manufacturers to figure out was how to convince the post-war American woman that she needed canned hamburgers and frozen Welsh rarebit (to name two of the earliest technical triumphs). What the advertising industry, women's magazines and the home economics profession came up with was a theme that has enjoyed one of the longest runs in the history of marketing: 'too busy to cook'.

Homemakers had always been busy, especially years earlier when their kitchens had no running water or refrigeration, and the wood for the stove was stacked outdoors. Now, at the twentieth century's halfway mark, with all-electric kitchens increasingly commonplace, women became so extraordinarily busy that they could barely get around to making dinner. 'Where it was possible, once upon a time, to spend hours planning meals, marketing, then cooking, today we simply cannot repeat the pattern and live,' wrote Beverly Pepper in *The Glamour Magazine After Five Cookbook*, published in 1952. 'Either we are working at jobs outside the home or we have other interests.' By the end of the 1950s, forty per cent of all adult women were employed, including nearly a third of all married women. But Beverly Pepper was one of the few food writers to acknowledge paid employment as a factor in women's suddenly full schedules. For the most part, the women of the 1950s were depicted as frantic creatures racing from bridge parties to parent–teacher meetings to shopping sprees—an image that kept clear the distinction between earning money, seen as man's responsibility, and spending it, woman's greatest glory. Indeed, many authorities went quite far out of their way to avoid mentioning paid work when they conjured the typical daily challenges faced by wives. 'Emergency meals are inevitable,' counselled *Redbook* in 1956. 'Whether they're caused by unexpected company, an over-busy day or something as drastic as a hurricane, be prepared with stored meals on your pantry shelf or in your food freezer.'

As the time available for cooking mysteriously dried up, so the awful potential for drudgery also vanished. The more quickly women prepared dinner using packaged foods, the more delightful the work and the greater the rewards. Labour for hours making a strawberry shortcake and what do you have at the end? Dessert. But with Bisquick and frozen berries, it was a 'dessert masterpiece', according to a 1954 advertisement. 'And Reddi-wip tops your masterpiece with exciting glamour at the touch of a finger.'

Exciting glamour was very much in order, according to numerous prescriptions in the women's magazines. A harried-looking wife who was perpetually fussing over the children would be boring—dangerously boring—to even the most devoted and selfless husband. Just look at 'Susan and Howard Brown,' advised an article in *Woman's Day* in 1954. Susan insisted on going to bed early every night because the three children were up at seven. So Howard was forced to go out alone. 'Susan began to worry about their relationship. She tried to bring it back to life, but she didn't quite know how.' Sure enough, one night Howard

The electric kitchen, 1944 HULTON DEUTSCH

met someone else, and the Browns divorced. 'Now Susan is a tragic figure, and her children are being raised without a father because she allowed her marriage to get away from her.'

The message to women was clear: drudgery and despair—*their* drudgery and despair—could be fatal to their marriages. It was a message that set the stage nicely for a new ideal in domesticity: home life as bright and charming as the post-war housewife herself, at least as she was regularly drawn and photographed in the women's magazines. *Better Food* showed an example in 1946: there she stood before a new 'electric cabinet sink' in high heels, apron and puffed sleeves, attentively washing a dish. Below the sink, the cabinet door had been opened to reveal a General Electric Disposall, which would neatly and invisibly do away with her garbage.

Quick and easy cooking was crucial to this iconography, but in truth, most women had been practising quick and easy cooking all their lives. Americans had been sitting down to pretty

157

much the same uncomplicated meals for decades, and the standard cookbooks were full of the recipes: meatloaf, liver and onions, steaks and pork chops, leftovers made into hash. Fantasy-laden salads and desserts were sometimes on the menu, and these could be laborious projects, but day-to-day cookery tended to get right to the point. And as some of the first processed foods became widely available, they suited such menus very well. Canned peas, frozen french fries and instant chocolate pudding were genuinely convenient products for the women who used them, whether or not the results contributed much flavour or finesse to the prevailing cuisine.

If women were now so pressed for time that they needed to cook even more quickly, one possibility might have been to learn to cook better—in general, she cooks fastest who knows most about ingredients and techniques. But amassing substantive culinary expertise held little appeal in an era of convenience. 'Your Blendor takes the place of years of experience and skill,' promised a Waring blender cookbook in 1957. And the food industry stood ready to do a lot more than seal peas in a can or dehydrate milk for a pudding. In the course of the 1950s and early 1960s, a new cuisine began to show up in households across the country, a curiously abstract cuisine derived almost entirely from recipes developed in test kitchens. Its purpose was to make use of specific products, not to put a meal on the table, so many of the new dishes were unrecognizable as breakfast, lunch or dinner. Some were unrecognizable as food. 'Start making your reputation as a cook right now!' urged a *Woman's Day* column aimed at teenagers, called 'How to be a Girl'. An appropriate dish for a beginner—at both cooking and being a girl—was Chick-Ham à la Princesse, which involved mixing cubes of Spam with canned cream of chicken soup and evaporated milk. Only a few decades earlier, young girls would have been taught how to make white sauce and baking-powder biscuits, but by the 1950s there was no need to learn how to cook such pedestrian items. Basic foods of every sort were available ready-made, and it was a foolish, old-fashioned housewife, according to the women's magazines, who felt reluctant to take advantage of them. 'The thousands of people working in canneries, creameries, packing plants and frozen-food plants are just as much your servants as if they were under your roof,' explained *House Beautiful* in 1951. 'For the hard, dirty, exacting work of food preparation is done there by them. Only the easy part is left for you to do.'

Many of the new recipes were indeed easy, calling for the simplest manipulation of packages and cans. Still, in the spirit of what the magazines called 'creativity', the food itself rapidly sank into confusion. 'Add a touch of your own,' urged *Woman's Day* in a 1954 article on imaginative use of everyday processed foods. Perhaps some women did cut frankfurter rolls crosswise into half-inch slices, toast them in a waffle-iron and add melted butter, cinnamon and sugar, but it's unclear what the cook was actually supposed to do with what she had made. Nothing in the combination signalled whether it was a meal, a snack, an accompaniment or a dessert. An advertisement for Nabisco crackers anticipated this problem by designating one suggestion 'an *easy* dessert', although the concept itself—a saltine topped with cottage cheese and a strawberry—could not have been very convincing in this category. But packaged-food cuisine existed outside most gastronomic categories and followed its own logic. Hence a 1956 article in *Redbook* on foods that could be prepared and frozen ahead of time didn't stop with casseroles but plunged right on into salads. The inspiration came from the freezer, not the food. So women were advised to empty a can of cranberry sauce into the blender, pour the blended sauce into a cake pan, top it with whipped cream and nuts, and freeze the whole thing. At mealtime, they would serve a chunk on a lettuce leaf, a presentation long employed to make otherwise inscrutable mixtures, or even lone foods, instantly recognizable as the salad course.

One reason many women were tempted to try packaged-food cookery was that it promised what was often termed 'sophisticated' food. This was a wandering standard—arranging the strawberry on the saltine was described as a way to 'sophisticate' the fruit—but the term usually implied expensive ingredients, long cooking time, difficult procedures and an imprecise air of foreignness. From very early on, the food-processing industry was able to freeze or can just about anything from beef stew to bouillabaisse but, as *House Beautiful* cautioned in 1951, most packed products were created for the mass market, not for lovers of fine food. 'The only safe course for the food manufacturer is to "play the middle of the road"—to season for the common-denominator, taste-bland, unstartling, careful,' the magazine explained. But smart women knew what to do with these products—'glamorize them'. For instance, heat up a can of cream of mushroom soup, a can of cream of tomato soup, a pound of crabmeat, season the mixture with curry powder and add sherry. 'It's as gourmet as anything, yet it can be put together in about ten minutes,' *House Beautiful* promised. By the end of the decade, everyone was glamorizing, including the women in the congregation of Trinity Church in Topsfield, Massachusetts, whose fund-raising cookbook, *Landmarks in Cooking*, featured a casserole called Gourmet Crab. This called for packaged spinach to be layered with canned crab, then moistened with canned cream of mushroom soup into which had been blended the contents of a small jar of Cheez Whiz. It was the crab that made this dish relatively expensive, hence desirable; but it was utilitarian canned soup, festively mixed with Cheez Whiz, that made the dish gourmet.

Opening boxes and cans, no matter how ingeniously the contents might be transubstantiated, was nevertheless a long way from home cooking, and most women knew it. Putting a frozen pie on the table might look like serving dessert, but did it count? What did it really mean for a woman to feed a family, beyond apportioning nutrients to a husband and each child? The industry was aware from the start that women were unlikely to accept its products without a struggle. Documenting the advances in frozen food as early as 1946, *Better Food* noted that two kinds of frozen pies were available, one that was fully baked and only had to be heated up, and another in which raw pastry was filled and frozen uncooked. 'This type of pie is actually baked by the purchaser and permits a greater degree of self-expression than the pre-baked variety,' observed the magazine approvingly. Over time, packaged-food cuisine absorbed women's worries and built into both the products and the advertising a great many signs and symbols of domestic 'self-expression'. The directions on cake mixes, for instance, called for the addition of a real, from-the-refrigerator egg long after the technology was in place to make adding fresh eggs unnecessary. Sure enough, cake mixes were among the first products successfully to change their identities, slipping imperceptibly across the border from packaged-food cookery into the culinary realm known as cooking from scratch.

One of the important mechanisms for helping packaged food exude an aura of traditional domesticity was the use of a fictional corporate spokeswoman, whose pen-and-ink portrait often accompanied the advertising. The most famous was, and is, Betty Crocker, but she had many colleagues as self-assured and inventive as she was, including Mary Blake (for Carnation) and Carol Drake (for Safeway stores). Sometimes, it was implied, these women got together and cosily traded recipes. 'Certainly one of the great recipes of the year is Dutch Pantry Pie, a new one-dish dinner developed by my good friend Betty Crocker of General Mills,' Mary Blake told readers in a 1954 advertisement. (The pie carried a hefty dose of Carnation evaporated milk.) More often, advertisements simply trumpeted how very home-made the products looked and tasted, though this claim had to be made with some tact: if home-made was so superior, why should anyone buy a boxed version? Swans Down cake mixes got around this problem handily by evoking the impressive world of science and technology. 'The secret of extra-home-made-ness? Ingredients made especially for our new mixes. Ingredients so special you can't buy 'em in the store!'

But the food company that engineered one of the most successful promotions of the century made no effort to fool women into thinking that boxed was best. Instead, Pillsbury celebrated outright women's traditional ties to the kitchen by inviting Americans who loved to cook and enjoyed showing off their skill to enter a national baking contest that came to be know as the Pillsbury Bake-Off. Launched in 1949, the Bake-Off required contestants to submit original recipes using Pillsbury flour; two hundred thousand people entered the first year, and the Bake-Off is still going strong today.

At the fourth Bake-Off, in 1953, a contestant named Mrs

161

Robert R. Wellman of Kenosha, Wisconsin, triumphed with a dish that did much of what packaged-food cuisine was trying to do, but did it from the heart. The authentic emotion generating this dish was plain from the name: Liver and Onion Dinner. Nobody ever cooked liver and onions for effect: this was dinner at home. But there was plenty of glamour in the presentation, certainly by 1953 standards: the cooked liver was ground with spices and catsup and spread over a rolled-out biscuit dough. Then the dough was rolled up into a log, shaped in a single, giant crescent and baked. Mrs Wellman suggested topping it with a quickly made sauce of hot canned tomato soup, left undiluted, and she served bacon alongside. Here was a dish Betty Crocker or Mary Blake would have been proud to invent, yet it demanded enough hands-on work to make a woman feel as though she mattered. In later years, the Bake-Off was to inspire countless recipes obedient to the principles of packaged-food cookery, but dishes like Mrs Wellman's kept turning up, too—emblems of emotional resistance to a wholly artificial cuisine. Alas, the very year Mrs Wellman won her prize, Swanson introduced the first TV dinner: roast turkey with mashed potatoes and peas, each in a separate compartment of a metal tray that lent its peculiarly acrid flavour to the food. By 1960, the company had selected a distinctly chilling slogan: 'Only Swanson comes so close to your own home cooking.' It was starting to verge on truth.

CHITRITA BANERJI
WHAT BENGALI WIDOWS
CANNOT EAT

My father died at the beginning of a particularly radiant and colourful spring. Spring in Bengal is teasing and elusive, secret yet palpable, waiting to be discovered. The crimson and scarlet of *palash* and *shimul* flowers post the season's banners on high trees. Compared to the scented flowers of the summer and monsoon—jasmine, *beli, chameli, kamini,* gardenias, all of which are white—these scentless spring flowers are utterly assertive with the one asset they have: colour. My father, who was a retiring, unassuming man, took great pleasure in their flaunting, shameless reds. When I arrived in Calcutta for his funeral, I was comforted by the sight of the flowers in full bloom along the road from the airport.

That first evening back home, my mother and I sat out on our roof, talking. As darkness obscured all colours, the breeze became gusty, laden with unsettling scents from out-of-season potted flowers on neighbouring roofs.

My mother had always been dynamic, forceful, efficient: the family's principal breadwinner for nearly thirty years, she had risen above personal anxiety and ignored social disapproval to allow me, alone, young and unmarried, to pursue my studies in the United States. Yet overnight, she had been transformed into the archetypal Bengali widow—meek, faltering, hollow-cheeked, sunken-eyed, the woman in white from whose life all colour and pleasure must evaporate.

During the thirteen days of mourning that precede the Hindu rituals of *shraddha* (last rites) and the subsequent *niyambhanga* (literally, the breaking of rules), all members of the bereaved family live ascetically on one main meal a day of rice and vegetables cooked together in an earthen pot with no spices except sea salt, and no oil, only a touch of ghee. The sanction against oil embraces its cosmetic use too, and for me, the roughness of my mother's parched skin and hair made her colourless appearance excruciating. But what disturbed me most was the eagerness with which she seemed to be embracing the trappings of bereavement. Under the curious, observant and critical eyes of female relatives, neighbours and visitors, she appeared to be mortifying her flesh almost joyfully, as if those thirteen days were a preparation for the future. As if it is utterly logical for a woman to lose her self and plunge into a life of ritual suffering once her husband is dead.

Hindu tradition in Bengal holds that the widow must strive for purity through deprivation. In contrast with the bride, who is dressed in red and, if her family's means permit, decked out in gold jewellery, the widow, regardless of her wealth and status, is drained of colour. Immediately after her husband's death, other women wash the *sindur*, a vermilion powder announcing married status, from the parting in the widow's hair. All jewellery is removed, and she exchanges her coloured or patterned sari for the permanent, unvarying uniform of the *thaan*, borderless yards of blank white cotton. Thus transformed, she remains, for the rest of her life, the pallid symbol of misfortune, the ghostly twin of the western bride, dressed in virginal white, drifting down the aisle towards happiness.

As recently as fifty years ago, widows were also forced to shave their heads as part of a socially prescribed move towards androgyny. Both of my grandfather's sisters were widowed in their twenties: my childhood memories of them are of two nearly identical creatures wrapped in shroud-like white who emerged from their village a couple of times a year and came to visit us in the city. Whenever the *thaan* covering their heads slipped, I would be overcome with an urge to rub my hands over their prickly scalps that resembled the spherical, yellow, white-bristled flowers of the *kadam* tree in our garden.

Until the Hindu Widow Remarriage Act was passed in 1856, widows were forbidden to marry for a second time. But for more than a hundred years after the act became law, it did not translate into any kind of widespread social reality (unlike the 1829 edict abolishing the burning of widows on the same pyre as their dead husbands—the infamous practice of suttee). Rural Bengali households were full of widows who were no more than children, because barely pubescent girls often found themselves married to men old enough to be their fathers.

It was not until the morning before the actual *shraddha* ceremony that I was forced to confront the cruellest of the rules imposed on the widow by the Sanskrit *shastras*, the body of rules and rituals of Hindu life to which have been added innumerable folk beliefs. One of my aunts took me aside and asked if my mother had made up her mind to give up eating fish and meat—*amish*, non-vegetarian food, forbidden for widows. With a sinking heart, I realized that the image of the widow had taken such a hold of my mother that she was only too likely to embrace a vegetarian diet—all the more so because she had always loved fish and had been renowned for the way she cooked it. If I said nothing, she would never again touch those wonders of the Bengali kitchen—*shorshe-ilish, maacher jhol, galda chingrir malaikari, lau-chingri, doi-maach, maacher kalia*. It was an unbearable thought.

The vegetarian stricture is not considered a hardship in most regions of India where the majority, particularly the Brahmins and some of the upper castes, have always been vegetarians. But Bengal is blessed with innumerable rivers criss-crossing a fertile delta, and it is famed for its rice and its fish. Even Brahmins have lapsed in Bengal by giving in to the regional taste for fish, which plays a central part in both the diet and the culinary imagination of the country. Fish, in its ubiquity, symbolism and variety, becomes, for the Bengali widow, the finest instrument of torture.

Several other items are forbidden to widows simply because of their associations with *amish*. *Puishak*, for instance, a spinach-like leafy green often cooked with small shrimps or the fried head of a *hilsa* fish, is disallowed. So are onion and garlic, which were eschewed by most Hindus until the last century because of their association with meat-loving Muslims. They are further supposed to have lust-inducing properties, making them doubly unsuitable for widows. Lentils, a good source of protein in the absence of meat, are also taboo—a stricture which might stem from the widespread practice of spicing them with chopped onion.

Social historians have speculated that these dietary restrictions served a more sinister and worldly function than simply that of moving a widow towards a state of purity: they would also lead to malnutrition, thus reducing her lifespan. A widow often has property, and her death would inevitably benefit *someone*—her sons, her siblings, her husband's family. And in the case of a young widow, the sooner she could be dispatched to the next world, the less the risk of any moral transgression and ensuing scandal.

My grandmother lived the last twenty-seven of her eighty-two years as a widow, obeying every stricture imposed by rules and custom. The memory of her bleak, pinched, white-robed widowhood intensified my determination to prevent my mother from embracing a similar fate. I particularly remember a scene from my early teens. I was the only child living with an extended family of parents, uncles and aunts—and my grandmother. It had been a punishingly hot and dry summer. During the day, the asphalt on the streets would melt, holding on to my sandals as I walked. Night brought sweat-drenched sleeplessness and the absorbing itchiness of prickly heat. Relief would come only with the eagerly awaited monsoon.

The rains came early one morning—dark, violent, lightning-streaked, fragrant and beautiful. The cook rushed to the market and came back with a big *hilsa* fish which was cut up and fried, the crispy, flavourful pieces served at lunchtime with *khichuri*, rice and dhal cooked together. This is the traditional way to celebrate the arrival of the monsoon. Though I knew my grandmother did not eat fish, I was amazed on this occasion to see that she did not touch either the *khichuri* or the battered slices of aubergine or the fried potatoes. These were vegetarian items, and I had seen her eat them before on other wet and chilly days. This time, she ate, in her usual solitary spot, *luchis*, a kind of fried bread, that looked stale, along with some equally unappetizing cold cooked vegetables.

Why? I asked in outrage. And my mother explained that this was because of a rare coincidence: the rains had arrived on the first day of Ambubachi, the three-day period in the Bengali month of Asharh that, according to the almanac, marks the beginning of the rainy season. The ancients visualized this as the period of the earth's receptive fertility, when the summer sun vanishes, the skies open and mingle with the parched land to produce a red or brown fluid flow of earth and water, nature's manifestation of menstruating femininity. How right then for widows to suffer more than usual at such a time. They were not allowed to cook during the three-day period, and, although they were allowed to eat some foods that had been prepared in advance, boiled rice was absolutely forbidden. Since nature rarely conforms to the calculations of the almanac, I had never noticed these Ambubachi strictures being observed on the long-awaited rainy day.

The almanac was an absolute necessity for conforming to the standards of ritual purity, and my grandmother consulted it assiduously. On the day before Ambubachi started, she would prepare enough *luchis* and vegetables for three midday meals. Sweet yogurt and fruit, mixed with *chira*—dried, flattened rice—were also permissible. That first night of monsoon, newly aware of the sanctions of Ambubachi, I went to look for my grandmother around dinner time. All she ate was a small portion of *kheer*, milk that had been boiled down to nearly solid proportions, and some pieces of mango. I had hoped she would at least be permitted one of her favourite evening meals—warm milk mixed with crushed mango pulp. But no. Milk cannot be heated, for the widow's food must not receive the touch of fire during Ambubachi. The *kheer*, a traditional way of preserving milk, had been prepared for her the day before.

It is true that despite deprivations, household drudgery and the imposition of many fasts, widows sometimes live to a great age, and the gifted cooks among them have contributed greatly to the range, originality and subtlety of Hindu vegetarian cooking in Bengal. A nineteenth-century food writer once said that it was impossible to taste the full glory of vegetarian food unless your own wife became a widow. And Bengali literature is full of references to elderly widows whose magic touch can transform the most mundane or bitter of vegetables to nectar, whose subtlety with spices cannot be reproduced by other hands.

But however glorious these concoctions, no married woman envies the widow's fate. And until recently, most widows remained imprisoned within the austere bounds of their imposed diets. Even if they were consumed with temptation or resentment, fear of discovery and public censure were enough to inhibit them.

I knew the power of public opinion as I watched my mother during the day of the *shraddha*. My aunt, who had been widowed when fairly young, had been bold enough, with the encouragement of her three daughters, to continue eating fish.

But I knew that my mother and many of her cronies would find it far less acceptable for a woman in her seventies not to give up *amish* in her widowhood. As one who lived abroad, in America, I also knew that my opinion was unlikely to carry much weight. But I was determined that she should not be deprived of fish, and with the support of my aunt and cousins I prepared to fight.

The crucial day of the *niyambhanga*, the third day after the *shraddha*, came. On this day, members of the bereaved family invite all their relatives to lunch, and an elaborate meal is served, representing the transition between the austerity of mourning and normal life—for everyone except the widow. Since we wanted to invite many people who were not relatives, we arranged to have two catered meals, lunch and dinner, the latter for friends and neighbours. My mother seemed to recover some of her former energy that day, supervising everything with efficiency, attending to all the guests. But she hardly touched any food. After the last guest had left, and the caterers had packed up their equipment, leaving enough food to last us for two or three days, I asked her to sit down and eat dinner with me. For the first time since my father's death, the two of us were absolutely alone in the house. I told her I would serve the food; I would be the grown-up now.

She smiled and sat down at the table. I helped her to rice and dhal, then to two of the vegetable dishes. She held up her hand then. No more. I was not to go on to the fish. Silently, we ate. She asked for a little more rice and vegetables. I complied, then lifted a piece of *rui* fish and held it over her plate. Utter panic filled her eyes, and she shot anxious glances around the room. She told me, vehemently, to eat the fish myself.

It was that panic-stricken look around her own house, where she was alone with me, her daughter, that filled me with rage. I was determined to vanquish the oppressive force of ancient belief, reinforced by whatever model of virtue she had inherited from my grandmother. We argued for what seemed like hours, my voice rising, she asking me to be quiet for fear of the neighbours, until finally I declared that I would never touch any *amish* myself as long as she refused to eat fish. The mother who could not bear the thought of her child's deprivation eventually prevailed, though the woman still quaked with fear of sin and retribution.

I have won a small victory, but I have lost the bigger battle. My mother's enjoyment of food, particularly of fish, as well as her joyful exuberance in the kitchen where her labours produced such memorable creations, have vanished. Sometimes, as I sit and look at her, I see a procession of silent women in white going back through the centuries. They live as household drudges, slaves in the kitchen and the field; they are ostracized even in their own homes during weddings or other happy ceremonies—their very presence considered an invitation to misfortune.

In the dim corners they inhabit, they try to contain their hunger. Several times a year, they fast and pray and prepare spreads for priests and Brahmins, all in the hope of escaping widowhood in the next life. On the eleventh day of each moon, they deny themselves food and water and shed tears over their blameful fate, while women with husbands make a joyous ritual out of eating rice and fish. Their anguish and anger secreted in the resinous chamber of fear, these white-clad women make their wasteful progress towards death.

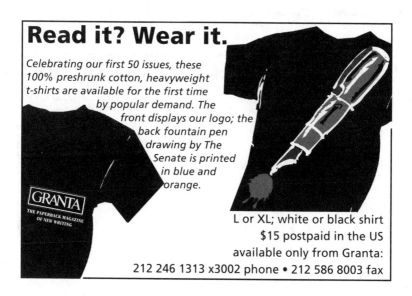

WILLIAM LEITH
FROZEN FISH

When I arrived at my parents' house, on one of my occasional visits, I could tell straightaway that something bad had happened. There was a shifty moment before they told me—it was death, of course, and close to home. The father of one of my old friends had fallen down in his bathroom, and never stood up again. 'Nigel's staying in the village for a couple of days,' said my mother.

Nigel had been my best friend before adolescence somehow broke us up; now he taught somewhere, or had done. I found him in his father's garage, clearing out the huge trunk-like freezer; his mother had been proud of it during the freezer fad of the early seventies. She was dead too. Nigel hugged me for the first time in his life and said, 'Thank you for coming down.' He was wearing gloves and had an ice pick in his hand. He said, 'You should take a look in here.'

I remembered the freezer from when we were kids. It had been important to us then, the site of many shameful boyish deeds. Now it was almost totally iced up, the way freezers get when nobody takes care of them. In places, Nigel had hacked down through the snow on the top to a glassy, hard layer of pack-ice which was the freezer's new floor. There were other places where you could see regular lumps, which could have been packets of meat, and there were bulges, maybe pheasants or grouse wrapped in thick freezer bags and forgotten, perhaps for years. I took the ice pick out of Nigel's hand and stabbed it into the dark, marbled black ice at the bottom of the box, making a little hole. 'There's nothing under there,' said Nigel. Then he said, 'Hold on a minute—give me that!' He had seen something. Then I saw something, a thing which made me feel quite sick.

It was the corner of a thick yellow plastic bag protruding through the ice, a bag that I remembered; it had been mine. Nigel worked the bag against the ice, scrabbling with the pick, then pulling at the bag, then scrabbling with the pick again, until the bag came free. Then he put the bag on the garage floor and stabbed the ice pick into it. The plastic split easily. Inside was a block of darkish ice, with darker patches visible under the surface. 'Would you believe it!' said Nigel.

It was the tomb, two decades old, of a dozen or so fish, fish we had killed on the last, horrible day of a two-week massacre. I remembered the day and how bad I'd felt. Nigel, I guessed, probably didn't. 'Wow,' I said, 'I wonder where they came from.'

We carried the bag outside and put it down on the lawn to thaw. This was where we'd been sitting, twenty years before, doing nothing much, when David Johnson came riding past on his bike and parked it on the grass in front of his house across the road. Then he unstrapped a bulky plastic bag from the ledge above his back mudguard. He was a couple of years older than us, so we'd been flattered when he said, 'Come and have a look at this, then!'

'What is it?'

'Look!'

It was a bag full of mackerel, mackerel he'd caught and killed that day. Some of them hadn't been dead long—they still had the green veneer which fades after an hour or two. David had cycled the seven miles to the pier at Newhaven, where the ferries come in, and he'd caught the fish and cycled back under their weight. 'They're shoaling,' he said. 'The shoals go berserk. They'll go for anything—feathers, just plain silver hooks, anything. You can kill as many as you like. Today was my first day, and I got twenty-three.'

I said, 'What are you going to do with them?'

'Eat them. Freeze them.'

Nigel said, 'Have you seen our freezer? It's pretty sizeable.'

David said, 'Ours is full of stuff we never eat.' Then he picked up his bag of mackerel and went around the side of his house.

I'd never been so impressed with anything in my life. Nor had Nigel. The terminology, the use of the word 'killing'—it was deeply offensive, something which only added to its attraction. I knew I wanted to be able to talk like that. We wandered back across the road, pretending to be less impressed than we were, and started getting things ready for the next day.

We had fished before, and owned rods and reels; we'd spent a couple of summers trekking around the local dew-ponds and irrigation ditches, reeling in jittery roach and rudd, wrestling with tiny eels, or landing junior pouting and coalfish on supervised trips to the seaside. Killing mackerel, though, was going to be different. There was going to be blood. Nigel had a pier fishing rod. His father had three, the heaviest and most out-of-date of which he said he would lend me. There was one set of mackerel feathers in his tackle box, a string of six wicked-looking silver hooks with barbs on the side as well as the point, small white feathers bound to the shank of each hook. 'I'll use these,' said Nigel. 'You can just use silver hooks. David said the mackerel go for anything.'

I didn't argue. I selected my hooks and fingered them tenderly, studying the nasty barbs, the honed points, finding it a mildly painful, morbid business. The little fish I'd dealt with before had seemed like toys; the hooks, as thin as pins, had popped neatly out of their mouths. Nigel said that his father didn't worry about killing fish. They were always killing each other anyway, and if you killed them yourself, they did at least die instantly, not like the fish you bought in the fish shop, which had gasped to death. Anyway, we were at the top of the food chain, and you could do what you liked when you were at the top of the food chain. In a certain light, the whole thing seemed reasonable—more than reasonable. It seemed almost noble.

I can't remember cycling to the pier, or setting my rod up. But I do remember feeling great, much more worried about not coming back with a bag full of fish than I was about anything else. Like one in seven British males, I was somehow thrilled by the thought of duping these creatures into impaling themselves on a hook. I put my qualms to the back of my mind and cast my line out, reeling in the hooks in a way that might make them resemble fish. I kept on casting. Nothing much happened for a while. Other people, other boys and some men, were doing the same. Then some of them started shouting; the sea, about twenty feet from the pier, was bubbling and frothing, and hundreds of tiny fish were jumping out of the water. This was it. I aimed my lead weight at the centre of the froth.

It was the most excited I'd been. When the lead hit the water I let it sink for a second, then pulled it towards me with the rod. There was a big, heavy thump on the end of my line, and then a couple more. My rod jumped. I tried to reel in, but couldn't, so I held on, the rod pumping up and down, its tip bending towards the water. The fish dived, steering my rod to the left; I reeled in some line and pulled the rod in the other direction.

Nigel yelled, 'You're in!' The fish flapped like mad things

when I reeled them up the side of the pier; there were four of them, one on each hook. I swung them over the railings.

I grabbed the first fish around the middle. It was flapping like a maniac. It slipped right through my hand. I picked it up again. The other three were twisting around at my feet. I still had the first one writhing in my hand. A spine from a fin speared my palm. I had to put my fingers through the fish's gills to get a purchase. Inside, the gills felt like hard, wet strips of plastic. The gill cover was opening and closing on my thumb.

When I pulled the hook out, there was a crunching noise. I hit the fish's head on the top railing. It kept on flapping.

'You have to do it like this,' said Nigel. He grabbed a fish, ripped the hook out, put his thumb in its mouth and snapped the fish's spine. He put it down on the wet concrete, where it lay rigid, its flesh shivering. The other two fish were corkscrewing around, wrapping themselves up in the line, still hooked. One of them had been impaled through the stomach by one of the free hooks. We tore the hooks out of the bony mouths, which snapped open and closed on our fingers. Then we put our thumbs down the throats of the fish and broke their necks.

There's something funny about killing. I won't say it's addictive, but it certainly gets easier. You begin to understand that the only way to feel normal about it is to do it some more, to blur the distinction between one instance of killing and another. It really didn't take us long to get used to it. I mean, it took us about half an hour. You get better at it, as well. Then you get really good. And then you can look back and laugh at the person you were, the person who couldn't do it very well.

Nigel and I cycled back with twenty-eight mackerel. His father showed us how to gut them, cutting the heads off, slicing the bellies open and ripping the various tubes and sacs away from their moorings with a plucking action. That evening, my mother cooked four and put six in the small icebox at the top of her fridge. The one I ate tasted fine. My mother said, 'We can have some more with gooseberries for tomorrow's lunch.' I told her I wouldn't be in for lunch. I was going back to the pier.

So the problem started on the first day. We were killing

more fish than we could eat. On the second day, we came back with more than thirty fish. We gutted them at Nigel's house, put them in plastic bags and moved a stack of pizzas and some tubs of ice-cream around in his mother's freezer to make room for them. It's amazing how much space there is in a freezer when you organize things properly. Then I went home and ate some cold mackerel with gooseberry sauce, which my mother had saved from lunch. It tasted fine. It tasted not bad at all.

Did the killing get to be pleasurable for its own sake? I'd love to say it didn't, I really would. But I remember days of pulling fish out of the water and breaking their necks and laughing wildly; I remember arriving at the pier and being hungry for the first kill. We each joked about how murderous the other had become, and felt flattered by the jokes. But the fish started to taste vile. And Nigel's freezer was filling up.

I solved the problem at the end of the first week. 'What?' said Nigel. 'Door to door?'

I explained the concept. We could sell the fish to our neighbours. If we undercut the market, we could get rid of all of them. That way, we could keep on fishing without the freezer filling up. Mackerel was sold at thirty pence a pound. We could sell it at fifteen. It would be easy.

It was, at first. We had to gut the fish, and then change into clothes that weren't covered in blood and scales, and ring people's doorbells. We lived in a small village; most people knew us. They were charmed. They didn't realize that we had entered a horrible spiral, having to sell to keep up our habit. After we had sold the fish, we had one more duty—to go home and eat more fish. Eating mackerel flesh, once a novelty, then a chore, now entered a new universe; it tasted truly disgusting, as if it were rotten or diseased.

One day, we couldn't sell all the fish. The next, we couldn't sell many of them. Nigel's mother's freezer was crammed. We sat on Nigel's front lawn with a bag full of clammy, gutted mackerel.

I said, 'We could get in touch with a cat-food place.'

Nigel said, 'We could just give it a rest.'

The day after that was terrible. We stayed at home. It was the first day in almost a fortnight that we hadn't spent in a hysterical

179

frenzy of cycling, casting, killing and coming home with a sackful of dead fish. I mowed my parents' lawn and mooched about in the garden. Nigel called round. It was the last week of the holidays. We sat on the grass. What were we doing here, while the mackerel were shoaling? Why not have one last crack?

The next day was overcast. We made a late start. I searched around under the sink in the kitchen for a plastic bag to put the fish in; there were a few grotty-looking ones and a nice thick yellow one from Amsterdam airport which I took. We cycled to the pier and set up our rods. There weren't many people on the pier. We kept casting out, but caught nothing. I had hoped for a big day, perhaps forty or fifty fish, to round things off. Now I was getting annoyed. The sea wall, a concrete wall with a row of metal spikes along the top, showed signs of other people's annoyance, people whose thirst for killing had gone beyond ours; a mackerel had been impaled on each spike. I don't believe I could have done anything like that. But I may be wrong.

Just as we were about to give up, we hit the fish, but only for about ten minutes. I got two lots of four and killed them. Nigel got one lot of four. I remember one of his hooks had gone right through one of the mackerel's eyes; when he pulled the hook out, it had the eye on it. Then he broke its neck. I don't know what made me stop wanting to kill things. It wasn't specifically the skewered eye, or the pointlessness of the last day. I think I just got sick of it. It made me want to spend a lot of time not killing things. When we got back, we opened the lid of the freezer, and made room for the yellow bag by lifting a stack of pizza boxes and placing the bag carefully underneath, where nobody would see it.

'They're mackerel,' said Nigel, twenty years later. 'My God, they must have been there for years.' Still a fisherman, two decades of slick, indifferent killing behind him, he was unmoved by nostalgia. The fish were barely recognizable as mackerel, or even as fish—they looked like decayed strips of meat, or old, frost-bitten twigs. Nigel picked up the bag, which was dripping, and walked over towards the dustbins. The possibility of talking to him about killing, having briefly loomed, was now gone. Nigel dropped the bag into one of the bins.

GRANTA

AGNES OWENS
TOFFEE

'**B**loody well wake up!' Maureen's mother called to her daughter, who slept in the kitchen bed recess. 'I'm not waiting here all morning.'

From the other side of the wall, Maureen's father roared, 'What's all that racket about? Can't a person get some sleep before he goes to work?'

'She won't get up,' her mother called, 'and she's supposed to start a paper round at six. Well, she can bloody well forget it if this is what it's going to be like.'

Maureen had been awake for some time with her head under the blankets. She got out of bed slowly and stood yawning in a black satin evening dress that had been her mother's before the war. It was rather wide on her, as she was only fourteen years and six months old, but she liked the feel of it next to her skin. Her mother said she looked like a tart in it. Maureen took this as a compliment, since it implied she looked older.

'I'm going back to bed now,' said her mother. 'It's too early for me. And don't open the curtains or we'll be in trouble with the black-out folk.'

'You mean the air-raid wardens,' said Maureen, letting the dress fall to the floor. Underneath she wore her vest and school knickers.

'Never mind what I mean,' said her mother. 'Get a move on or you'll be too late, though personally I don't think it's worth all this bother for the sake of a few bob. And while you're at it put on clean underwear in case you meet with an accident.'

With that she left the kitchen.

Maureen dressed and stood by the cooker waiting for the kettle to boil. She'd lost all notion of doing the paper round. Yesterday it had seemed a good idea when she spied the advertisement for a paper boy in the newsagent's window.

'Will I do instead?' she had asked Willie Roper, the owner of the shop.

'But you're a girl,' he said, looking her up and down as if this was a fault. 'It's a boy I'm wanting.'

'I can deliver papers as good as any boy,' she said, smiling at him ingratiatingly.

Willie had red hair, bright blue eyes and a pleasant face. For a shopkeeper he was quite popular and an object of sympathy. His crippled wife lived in the flat above the shop.

'I suppose you could,' he said. 'But would you collect the papers from the railway station every morning?'

When she said she was willing, he told her the pay was four shillings and did that suit her?

'It suits me fine,' she said, deciding to tell her mother it was three and keep a shilling for herself. She was delighted when he handed her a bar of toffee from a tray on the counter. Her sweet coupons had been long since used up, and she wouldn't get any more for another fortnight. As she left the shop, he called her back to say that since she was a girl, she needn't collect the papers from the station. He would do it himself.

'That's very good of you, Mr Roper,' she said.

That had been yesterday, but now, at this dark and deathly hour in the morning, she didn't feel like leaving the house. On the other hand, she could hardly let Willie down now he'd taken the advert out of the window. He'd be depending on her to show up. At five to six, as the first glimmer of light shone in the sky, she hurried along the street wearing her Sunday coat, a red pixie hat she had knitted for herself and her mother's high-heeled shoes stuffed with paper. She thought they gave her legs a better shape.

Two hours later, she put the high heels back under the bed and was in the kitchen again. Her mother stood over the cooker stirring a pot of dried egg.

'How did you get on?' she asked without taking her eyes off the pot.

'Fine. I'm to get three shillings a week.'

'Three shillings?' said her mother turning round and looking aghast. 'I thought you'd get four at the very least.'

'And a bar of toffee as well,' Maureen added.

'Toffee?' her mother said. 'What good's toffee? He's a mean bugger that Willie Roper if you ask me.'

Her father entered the kitchen, and her mother said, 'What

do you think? Maureen's doing a paper round and she's only getting three shillings and a bar of toffee.'

'That's nice,' he said. Then, looking over his wife's shoulder, 'Don't tell me it's that dried egg again for breakfast!'

'You're bloody lucky to be getting it with a war on,' said his wife.

This started an argument, though Maureen scarcely listened. She was thinking about Willie Roper and how he'd come with her on the paper round.

'Just to show you the ropes,' he had said with a laugh.

Together they had trotted in and out of gates, always careful to close them properly. Maureen had shoved the papers through the letter boxes as quietly as she could, because Willie said some customers didn't like being wakened early. When the deliveries were finished, Willie told her she'd done well and was as good as any paper boy he'd had, if not better.

They'd returned by a road with nothing on each side but fields. Willie stopped to blow his nose, and she stopped too. Then, without warning, he'd put his hand up her skirt.

'I hope you don't mind,' he said huskily. 'It's just that I find you very attractive.'

At first, she was taken aback but, after a short pause to think it over, she said she didn't mind at all since she found him attractive too.

'Great,' said Willie. 'I would hate to take advantage of you.'

Later, when they were nearing the shop, he told her that since she was so good at delivering papers and had not made one single mistake, he would give her a shilling a week extra plus a bar of toffee and, as a token of his good faith, she could have the toffee now.

'That would be lovely, Mr Roper,' she said, becoming quite breathless.

'Just call me Willie,' he said. 'Everybody does.'

Now, as she arose from the table and left the room, her parents were still arguing.

Five minutes later, she came back with the toffee broken up into pieces.

'Does anybody want some of this?' she asked them. 'Mr Roper says it's made with butter.'

They both stared from her to the toffee. Her mother said with a shrug, 'I might as well. I haven't tasted anything like it since before the war.'

Her father said that he might as well too; he'd always been fond of toffee though he couldn't remember when he'd last had any. His wife told him to shut his mouth and take a bit while it was still there. She added that she didn't know how Willie Roper could give it away when everything was so scarce.

'He says he gets it on the black market,' said Maureen, her eyes wide and candid as she watched her parents munching and crunching. She was thinking how well she'd done, having only just started the job and having already been given a rise. And Willie had asked her to come in to the shop tomorrow at dinner time, when the place was closed, to help him pack the shelves, he said. She wouldn't be surprised if she got paid for it with more toffee.

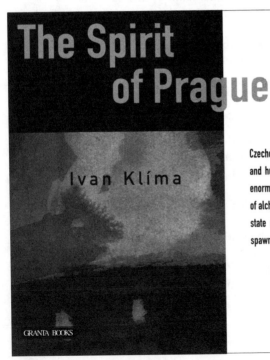

ROMESH GUNESEKERA
STRINGHOPPERS

ROMESH GUNESEKERA

In 1956, my father was thirty-nine years old. He didn't even know how to boil an egg. But within two years he was creating the kookiest dinners in Washington and had the World Bank eating out of his hand. When he got back, everybody wanted to know how he had done it.

'Easy,' he would say, shrugging his big, round shoulders. 'Stringhoppers. I fed them stringhoppers.'

His friends were mystified.

The stringhopper he invoked is now the centrepiece of Sri Lankan cuisine, but it is neither native nor foreign. Like the Indian buffalo's mozzarella in Italy, or the shifting shape of the English tongue, the stringhopper was born out of wanderlust and a confluence of culture. A saucer-sized pancake of vermicelli squeezed out of a perforated mould, each stringhopper is like a nest of stories; a perfect emblem for Asia's hub of trade routes in the past. But nobody knows for sure how it came to be.

'How did you know how to make them?' his friends would ask.

'I looked in the *Daily News Cookery Book*,' he would say, beaming. 'I had this pang, a real hunger, for stringhoppers. So I made them myself. What else to do? A whole crowd came over.'

But he had not simply produced stringhoppers, he had turned them into an atlas of entwined colours: red, yellow, green and blue. The colouring was his invention. The austere world of the Colombo *Daily News Cookery Book* did not admit to this kind of improvisation. Its starchy prose was always absolutely deadpan.

The word quickly spread: 'He got them to eat bright blue stringhoppers! You know, blue is like poison, psychologically inedible. He must have a real knack for handling those World Bank fellows.' His career as an international negotiator took off. 'From Jericho to Bretton Woods!' he would joke. Even today in Sri Lanka, blue stringhoppers are exotic; in Washington in 1956, they were mind-blowing.

For my father, getting strangers to eat strange food was at the heart of the human story, the point at which the old world slips into myth and a new world stumbles free. The meal was where we could begin to understand each other, even as we recognized the briefness of our encounter.

Tolstoy Coomaraswamy who, after my father, probably has eaten more stringhoppers than anybody else I know, claimed they were inspired by Marco Polo's visit to our island seven hundred years ago. Tolstoy was the biggest talker of my father's generation; a big, beaky journalist who had not strayed out of Colombo for forty-five years but who recounted the fabulous journey of Marco Polo as though it were his own. He leaned against the kitchen cupboard and watched my father show me how to mix the dough. 'When Marco Polo touched down in Ceylon—' Tolstoy's voice jibbed as he fixed his compass points, 'actually Jaffna—he found that his host had laid out a real beach feast. Marco Polo was fêted, you know, even though later the bugger said we were all a bunch of lazy, drunk, mean-spirited layabouts. They put the works out: grilled seer fish, jackfruit, curried jungle fowl, heaps of pearly rice on plantain leaves like little temples in a velvet jungle and small hot spots of Malay pickle. Spoons carved out of coconut and tortoiseshell dishes, a really mouth-watering table.' A rivulet of his own dribbled out with his words.

'Over lunch Marco told our King Sendernam about his travels in China and the noodles he had discovered: the prototype for pasta. He couldn't get over them. He described them with his hands, you know. He told the king about Kublai Khan's favourite concubine who had been wrapped up in them: thin gossamer strings that were unravelled at a midsummer banquet in the dance of the seventeen noodles with everybody shouting 'Gambay!', knocking back the rice wine and ogling like mad. Imagine eating it! All that sweet sweat like butter melting on each noodle as it was stripped off a real, top-notch sex bomb.'

I squeezed the dough into the stringhopper mould and looked up at Tolstoy. His eyes were huge and round.

'Only later when the fellow was lying down for an after-lunch nap, letting the ocean breezes cool his swollen feet, did Marco realize he had been a little tactless in talking so much about Chinese noodles to our people. He knew he had made a real blunder when Tikka, his local minder, started quizzing him on the noodle-making. Tikka was a clever kolla. A brilliant mongrel of our Middle Ages. He spoke Tamil, Sinhala, Sanskrit, Arabic, a smattering of Mandarin, Malay and a new harbour-front pidgin:

Latin and Anglo-Saxon. All staccato. He told Marco about his family going all over the place; his great-grandfather had been an ambassador to Rome and somebody else had been the first Chinese travel writer Fa-Hsien's guide eight hundred years earlier. But Tikka's ancestors were not cooks, you know, or if they were, they had kept the noodle a secret.'

I imagined this Tikka talking: *'Our chief wannabe big-big king-man. Wannabe know-how makum eff-dish kenoodle of uhu.'* A sharp, dark, bulging head whispering salaciously. *'Nous wannabe makum the kenoodle big-big to impoke Marco Polo II much-such than Chinoise courtesan hokum-hooker, next time OK?'*

'Concubine,' Marco would have corrected.

'Concubine, courtesan, same-same treacle man. What the duck it matter?'

Marco Polo had spent only two weeks on the island, Tolstoy told us. Marco had coveted the king's massive ruby, but when he realized he could not get it, he dismissed the whole place as not worth another mention. 'Congealed ox blood,' he had snorted into the history books. On his last night on this then noodle-less island, after the sun had sizzled into the hot sea, Marco had dreamed again his most intense recurring dream: the dream of his mother's *knedliky*—a mitteleuropean dumpling she had discovered on her honeymoon at a snowbound inn in the Carpathian mountains. Marco Polo's father had apparently been so enthralled by the dumplings the innkeeper's daughter prepared every night of that blissful week that his mother had resolved to learn the art of this foreign cooking for the long-term health of her new marriage. Tolstoy said that Marco had grown up eating dumplings every day of his boyhood. And that night in a Lankan beach hut, thousands of miles from Venice, when Marco dreamed of them again, he realized that what the Chinese noodle left wanting, despite an orgy of eating, was the round, firm, springy shape of a crumpet rising like the moon. 'My little dumpling,' his mother had cooed so innocently all his childhood, an endearment he found himself echoing around the world as he sweetened bed after bed, searching for immortality among the pillow heads of love.

The next morning, he had said to Tikka, 'You know, never mind the noodles, what I really dream about are my mother's dumplings.' He described them: round, soft but firm, budding. A mixture of hope and home.

'*Niha, niha,*' Tikka had grinned, 'but how-do-you-do the eff-dish dumpling?'

At this point in the story, Tolstoy leaned forward as though he himself were about to invent a new dish for the world. 'When Marco described the business of pounding grain to make flour, mixing it with warm water to make your dough and then kneading it and kneading it and kneading it, Tikka noticed the similarity to making noodles in China that Marco had talked so much about at the lunch table the previous day. Tikka got so excited, fellow couldn't wait to get away and talk to the cook.' In a wonderful visionary moment he had seen how his imagination could straddle the whole known culinary world of 1294 and pull together Marco Polo's mother's dumplings and Kublai Khan's favourite noodles into a dish that would gobstop the entire island. A steamed rice–noodle dumpling disc hinting of youth and love and hope and home that would spread across the sea to Kerala, Tamil Nadu, all of south India, Malaysia, Africa and, in time, the UK, the USA, the whole world. 'The next morning, the stringhopper was born, and our Tikka was jubilant,' said Tolstoy, grinning and helping himself to a handful of my freshly steamed ones.

'Bravo,' my father cheered. '*For he on honeydew hath fed, and drunk the milk of Paradise.*' Honeydew? Perhaps Coleridge should have written stringhopper?

Ranil Jayawardene, an agronomist-turned-amateur-historian, now very big in pigs, and a former colleague of my father's, dismissed these imaginings about noodles and stringhoppers. 'Bunkum, sheer bunkum,' he said when I told him Tolstoy's Marco Polo story. 'Marco Polo is fantasy. Fiction. One big lie. All this foreign food: hoppers, stringhoppers, *kavum, kokis,* things to do with flour and grease, all of this unhealthy stuff comes from western imperialism. Portuguese leftovers, that's what they are. The Portuguese and the Dutch, they are the ones who left this mixed-up food, two hundred years after your Marco Polo. Then the Britishers brought their mad beverages: coffee, tea, gin and tonic. Stuff to spoil our tongues, our language, even our bloody bowels you know.'

To Ranil, cuisine reflected cartography and was determined by history. The New York waffle replicated a grid city, the folded crêpe mimicked those angular Parisian junctions, and the stringhopper was a map of the tangled route the Portuguese had been taken on to confuse their sense of direction when brought before the king. Ranil said that after the Portuguese had subdued the king with Lisbon cannon shot and Madeira cake, they made the cooks create the stringhopper as a reminder of how they arrived. 'It belongs to a bad time,' he said.

But surely the stringhopper, like everything else, must belong to those who make it?

Ranil slowly sucked in his thick blue lips. 'I have to admit,' he said, 'your father's stringhoppers were something else . . . '

In the end, for my father, the stringhopper was what knitted reality together as he travelled the world. A mixture of hope and home, art and life, society and solitude. And although each of the vermicelli threads that sprouted out of his stringhopper press had an intrinsic beauty of its own, the real delight, he would say, was in getting the texture of the dough right. And when he did, he would beam like a poet who had perfected an unbreakable line connecting the past with the present. A real lifeline.

Statement of Ownership

Statement of Ownership, Management, and Circulation (Required by 39 USC 3685):

1. *Publication Title:* Granta
2. *Publication No.:* 000-508
3. *Date of Filing:* 9-22-95
4. *Frequency of Issue:* Quarterly (4 times per year)
5. *No. of issues Published Annually:* 4
6. *Annual Subscription Price.* $32.00
7. *Known Office of Publication:*
250 W. 57th St., Room 1316, NY, NY 10107-0169
8. *Headquarters or General Business Offices of Publisher:* 250 W. 57th St., Rm 1316, NY, NY 10107
9. *Name and Address of Publisher and Editor:*
Publisher: Rea Hederman, 250 West 57th Street, Room 1316, New York, NY 10107-0169
Editor: Ian Jack, 250 West 57th Street, Room 1316, New York, NY 10107-0169
10. *Owners:* NYREV, Inc., 250 W. 57th St., Room 1321, NY, NY 10107-0169; Bill Buford, 45 Gramercy Park North, NY, NY 10010; Helen Shiel, 6900 SE Golfhouse Dr., Hobe Sound, FL 33455; Granta Publications Limited, 2-3 Hanover Yard, Noel Road, Islington, London N1 8BE England
11. *Known Bondholders, Mortgages, and Other Security Holders:* None.
12. *For Completion by Non-Profit Organizations:* N/A
13. *Publication Name:* Granta
14. *Issue Date for Circulation Data:* Winter 95 / Nov.
15. *Extent and Nature of Circulation:*
Average No. of Copies Each Issue During Preceding 12 Months:
A. *Total No. Copies:* 55,198
B. *Paid and/or Requested Circulation:*
1. *Sales Through Dealers and Carriers, Street Vendors, and Counter Sales:* 5,078
2. *Paid or Requested Mail Subscriptions:* 42,098
C. *Total Paid and/or Requested Circulation:* 47,176
D. *Free Distribution by Mail:* 323
E. *Free Distribution Outside the Mail:* 0
F. *Total Free Distribution:* 323
G. *Total Distribution:* 47,499
H. *Copies Not Distributed:*
1. *Office Use, Leftovers, Spoiled:* 1,301
2. *Returns from News Agents:* 6,398
I. *Total:* 55,198
Percent Paid and/or Requested Circulation: 99.32%
Actual No. of Copies of Single Issue Published Nearest to Filing Date:
A. *Total No. Copies:* 53,300
B. *Paid and/or Requested Circulation:*
1. *Sales Through Dealers and Carriers, Street Vendors, and Counter Sales:* 6,199
2. *Paid or Requested Mail Subscriptions:* 40,314
C. *Total Paid and/or Requested Circulation:* 46,513
D. *Free Distribution by Mail:* 358
E. *Free Distribution Outside the Mail:* 0
F. *Total Free Distribution:* 358
G. *Total Distribution:* 46,871
H. *Copies Not Distributed:*
1. *Office Use, Leftovers, Spoiled:* 1,148
2. *Returns from News Agents:* 5,281
I. *Total:* 53,300
Percent Paid and/or Requested Circulation: 99.24%
17. I certify that the statements made by me above are correct and complete. Signature of Editor, Publisher, Business Manager or Owner:
Rea Hederman, Publisher.

SEAN FRENCH
FIRST CATCH YOUR PUFFIN

A man is rescued after years stranded on a desert island with two companions, one of whom died. On his return to civilization, he goes to a restaurant famous for its policy of serving any dish a customer asks for. He orders seagull. When the seagull arrives, he takes one mouthful, leaves the restaurant and commits suicide. Why?

Towards the end of the parties I used to go to when I was about fourteen, the sensible people were in dark upstairs rooms doing interesting things. Those of us who were left, downstairs and at a loose end, used to tell stories that were supposed to be exercises in 'lateral thinking'. The most straightforward was about a man who lives on the thirtieth floor of an apartment building. Every morning, when he goes to work, he goes down in the lift. Every evening, when he comes home, he walks up the stairs. Why? The answer is that the man is a dwarf and can't reach the thirtieth-floor button. (But couldn't he have asked somebody to press it for him?)

The solution to the first problem depends on reconstructing the scenario of what supposedly happened on the island. One companion on the desert island dies, right? Shortly afterwards, the other serves the man a meal and tells him it's seagull, though the man suspects it might actually be their dead friend. So, back home, he samples seagull, discovers that it tastes different, infers that he must have been a cannibal and commits suicide out of shame.

Somebody would always start asking awkward questions. Maybe he ate a different kind of seagull on the island, or a different part of a seagull, or the same kind of seagull but one whose diet meant that it tasted different. And if he was alone with his companion, wouldn't he be surprised to be served seagull without having noticed any trapping, defeathering, cleaning and cooking going on? It's controversies of this kind that show why we were downstairs while other people were upstairs.

Even less relevantly, or perhaps even more laterally, the story used to make me wonder what seagull tasted like. Like grouse? Like fish? Like the rubbish that seagulls pick at on quaysides and behind boats? When I went to Iceland earlier this year, I wanted to see a geyser, bubbling mud, cooled lava, and I

197

wanted to eat strange Icelandic food. The dried fish, for example, of which Auden said: 'The tougher kind tastes like toenails, and the softer kind like the skin off the soles of one's feet.' And seagull. I didn't find gull on a menu, but I did find puffin, which is almost as good.

We went for a day to Vestmannaeyjar, a group of islands south-west of Reykjavík so bleak and isolated that the inhabitants consider Iceland itself too blandly European and cosmopolitan, too crowded by comparison. Vestmannaeyjar has experienced the highest wind speed ever recorded in Europe, it has a major volcanic eruption every ten years and it is host to the largest puffin population in the world. 'The puffin is our national emblem,' said our guide, 'and our national dish.' I warmed to these people.

On a precarious, bobbing boat journey under looming cliffs and across heaving seas, we saw some of the puffins *in situ*, with their comical beaks and large, friendly eyes. Puffins are charmingly incompetent flyers, a desperate, wind-up toy flapping too close to the north Atlantic waves, so perhaps it was fortunate that I had already eaten roast breast of puffin back in Reykjavík. Remember Alice at the banquet in *Through the Looking-Glass*. She misses out on the leg of mutton because it is impolite to eat food that you've been introduced to, and we know what that means. We city dwellers don't like to be reminded of the history of what we are putting through our guts. We might like to eat baby lambs' tongues but we would rather not see the surviving grass stains. In a radio talk, Sylvia Plath said that in the United States she had been used to meat presented under polythene in cuts that had no resemblance to any animal. One of the shocks of moving to England was the sight of bits of pig and cow hanging in butchers' shops. The influence on her work was predictably drastic. Cooking the Sunday lamb made her think of cooking a human being, of the ovens of the Holocaust.

As in so much else, Plath was ahead of her time. People have started to feel, if not guilty, then at least a little awkward, about eating meat. You know the sort of thing: 'We're not exactly vegetarians, but we hardly ever eat meat nowadays, really. We just don't feel like it.' 'Do you know that the amount of land necessary to support a cow could provide enough grain to feed a village?'

I know few vegetarians, but a number of people who have adopted a pseudo-vegetarianism which involves eating meat that looks as little like an animal as possible. Fish are acceptable because their eyes are unseeing, they don't seem to have faces, they can't scream. Chickens are different from us as well, and the meat can't be eaten rare, so there is no blood apparent. Red meat is unacceptable, unless presented anonymously, and offal is beyond the pale.

I like the blood. In Sweden you can buy a form of blood pudding in which the blood is mixed with meal and sugar. You fry it and eat it with lingonberry jam. The smell disgusts my wife so much that she has to open all the windows when I cook it, but the children gobble it up because it's so sweet. I like parts of animals with improbable tastes and textures. The tang of urine in kidneys that attracted Leopold Bloom. The rubberiness of tripe which can taste like an underdone hot-water bottle. The blancmange consistency of veal's brain. Yes, veal. The ones transported live in lorries in front of which protesters throw themselves.

The problem is that we've all been taught that food should be fresh and wholesome, just as we've been taught that sex should be all about uncomplicated, rational pleasure. Some sex should be like that, of course, and there is no charm in a five-day-old sardine, but much of the pleasure of food is a flirtation with the processes of decay. The richness of fresh milk makes me gag, but when it rots, it becomes cheese, which I love. Beef should not be sold red and fresh but should be hung until it is grey. Some of the most wonderful food of all teeters on the boundary of what's edible. I can understand the widely felt disgust inspired by oysters. The slime, the brackish fluid, the sweet flesh so soft that it scarcely holds itself together. There is an air of indecency about it all, like a remembered dream of oral sex. And mushrooms, with their spongy pallor, somewhere between flesh and plant fibre. They don't grow like plants. They lack chlorophyll, which means they can't use light to make carbohydrates. Instead they must feed directly on dead plants or animals. There's even a special creepiness about the way that

199

mushrooms kill you. If you eat *Amanita phalloides*, the death cap, you feel nothing for up to two days. Then, according to Roger Phillips's *Mushrooms and Other Fungi of Great Britain and Europe*, you experience 'vomiting, diarrhoea, sweating and insatiable thirst, followed by a pale, haggard appearance with cold hands and feet, accompanied by a state of deep anxiety.' After a few days of this, you feel better. You say to yourself: 'Well, that felt pretty ghastly. I'll certainly be careful not to eat that mushroom again.' A couple of days later you collapse. Your liver has been destroyed. You die.

I've found very little that was actually beyond the boundary of the edible. One example was the Swedish dish *surströmming*. This is herring that is 'preserved' in salt water but has started to rot. You buy *surströmming* in cans that bulge slightly because of the continuing 'fermentation' process. It is always prepared and served outdoors because, although it looks like normal herring, it smells quite startlingly of shit. Once, while staying in Sweden, I served it to some of my relations who had often spoken of the dish but never actually eaten it. Before opening the can you have to bang a nail into it to release the pressure. I did so and was hit in the face by a miniature geyser of shit-smelling spray. After having a shower, I opened the can and served the fish in the traditional way, on a soft, thin bread with chopped red onion and sour cream. According to strict local tradition, we drank milk with it. Did it taste like shit? I don't know. I've never eaten shit. But shit certainly could taste like that. Having ingested a *surströmming* sandwich each, we all discovered an unexpected effect. The fermentation process continued in our stomachs, and we all began to burp uncontrollably. Having eaten shit, we were now farting through our mouths. Auden used to quote an Icelandic proverb which states that everybody likes the smell of their own farts. But then wasn't it Larkin who said that sex was like having your nose blown by somebody else? This was like *somebody else* farting through your mouth.

So, how was the puffin for me? Fine. It had none of the fishy taste that is supposed to render seagull flesh unpalatable. It was strong, dark, gamy. There was an extra pleasure because when I

First Catch Your Puffin

was a child, my parents had made me a member of the Puffin
Club, in which middle-class children were meant to assemble and
talk about how much they liked reading. You got Puffin badges
and Puffin bookmarks. I took a dark pleasure in eating a puffin
that had been shot and plucked and roasted for me.

On my last evening in Iceland, I ate whale. There was a
feeling of a taboo being violated, a whiff of brimstone and
sulphur in even seeing it on the menu. But then there's a whiff of
sulphur everywhere in Iceland. It's in the hot-water supply that is
piped directly out of natural hot springs. It was a bit like seeing
absinthe or heroin on a restaurant menu. Could I really eat it?
Sod it. The whale wasn't put in danger by Iceland or Norway. It
was destroyed by Britain, the United States and the other
industrialized countries. Once it became uneconomic to hunt,
they started lecturing small countries dependent on fishing.
Iceland has a right to fish in the way it considers necessary. Did I
ask what sort of whale it was? Whether it was an endangered
species? No. I didn't want to create a scene.

More shameless still, the whale meat was served 'in the
Japanese style'. That is, raw with a dish of spiced soy sauce. It was
in dark, gleaming strips and had a rich, fatty taste, somewhere
between tuna and fillet steak. My wife looked uncomfortable. She
had had a bite of my puffin but she wouldn't touch the whale.
Because whales are different, aren't they? I thought of the scene in
C. S. Lewis's *The Silver Chair* when the children and their
companion, Puddleglum, are staying at the house of the giants and
discover they have been eating a talking stag:

> This discovery didn't have exactly the same effect on all of
> them. Jill, who was new to that world, was sorry for the
> poor stag and thought it rotten of the giants to have killed
> him. Scrubb, who had been in that world before and had
> at least one talking beast as his dear friend, felt horrified:
> as you might feel about a murder. But Puddleglum, who
> was Narnian born, was sick and faint and felt as you
> would feel if you found you had eaten a baby.

But what if the baby, 'served in the Japanese style', tasted
nice? That wouldn't be much of an excuse.

201

A few days after returning home, I told some friends about the whale meal. There was a moment of shock and then a series of questions. Did I care about baby seals being clubbed to death? No. Was I opposed to fox-hunting? No. What about fur coats? I'm in favour of them, as long as they aren't made from endangered species. What about scientific experiments on animals? I'm in favour of them. What about the treatment of veal calves? This was more complicated. I care about it insofar as it affects the quality of the meat. What about foie gras? I love foie gras. What about cannibalism, then? What about that? It was not something I was eager to try, but that Uruguayan rugby team, stranded in the Andes, who survived by eating parts of their dead, had, in my view, done nothing to be ashamed of. That man who ate the seagull and shot himself was entirely misguided.

'All right,' said my brother-in-law, pointing his finger at me, 'all right. What about a severely disabled person? Would you think it was right to kill and eat a severely disabled person?'

'No,' I said. 'I don't think that would be right.'

The discussion ended in triumph, though not for me. Hitler had been caught out, weeping over the death of one of his dogs.

GEOFFREY BEATTIE
MEN AS CHICKENS

Four men attempt to live like chickens in Rebecca Hall's cage   MARTIN ARGLES/GUARDIAN

' A t least they have exercised free will in choosing this option,'
said Rebecca Hall, sipping Earl Grey tea. 'Battery hens
have no choice.'

It was winter 1993. I was sitting on a sofa in Rebecca Hall's
drawing-room while she told me about a challenge she had issued
to publicize her new book, *The Fruits of Paradise—a Vegetarian
Yearbook*. She had offered four men £2,500 each to live like
battery hens for a week. They were to be kept in a wire cage with
a sloping wire floor. They would be barefoot, and there would be
no lavatory and nowhere to wash. The light would be on
seventeen hours a day. There would be continuous noise from an
audiotape of what Rebecca Hall described as 'human madhouse
noises with lots of wailing and screaming, because battery hens
live in a madhouse with a cacophony of noise.'

This was a legally binding challenge; the contract had been
drawn up by Rebecca Hall's son, a barrister. The cage was in a
shed at the back of her beautiful house in the village of
Woolhope, Herefordshire. The house was full of original
paintings, 'done by family and friends mainly', and an assortment
of cats and dogs. The point of the challenge was to raise public
consciousness of battery farming and 'to liberate the vegetarian
within us all.'

These men were not quite the people Rebecca Hall had been
looking for. 'I would have preferred to have battery or intensive
farmers, but those who originally responded to my challenge
chickened out one way or another.' We both nearly chuckled, but
didn't. 'I wanted battery farmers to endure what they subject their
victims to. I wanted them to endure such conditions for a week,
and come out and say that this should not happen to any living
creature. If they had to suffer in order to make that
transformation, then so be it.'

When Rebecca Hall issued her challenge, thirteen people
responded. Applicants were trying to convince her that they were
intensive farmers, but most of them had nothing to do with
intensive farming—'They just kept goats in fields, that sort of
thing.' She did have one call from a man in Sussex who had
fifteen thousand battery hens. 'I was outraged that when he
replied to the challenge, he had his picture in his local paper with

a beautiful hen sitting on his shoulder. A most gorgeous hen. Nothing like a battery hen.'

I was meant to share in her sense of outrage that a healthy hen with all its own feathers was being passed off as a battery bird, but I looked at the picture and felt very little. 'The problem with city dwellers,' said Rebecca sternly, 'is that they have lost touch with nature. I have heard of a case where some French schoolchildren were asked to draw a fish, and do you know what they drew? They drew a rectangular fish steak. They had no idea what a real fish looks like.' Rebecca continued to watch me accusingly. I nearly offered to draw a nice, healthy rainbow trout for her there and then, complete with glorious tail fins and an accentuated head with bright, innocent eyes.

Rebecca returned to the Sussex battery farmer. 'It was ridiculous for the paper to show a hen like that. I know what battery hens look like because I have actually been in a hen battery. I was taken when I was a girl by a family friend. He was trying to show me that it wasn't that bad. I ran out in tears.

'The problem is that the people who do this sort of thing have no idea how bad it is. They have killed their consciences. Or they are living in denial, and deep inside them is a huge sense of guilt. I believe that is why people answered my challenge. I do not believe they really needed the money. The fact that they did not own up to this sense of guilt is hardly relevant. Someone who is prepared to do this sort of thing to animals won't hesitate to lie about it, and the lie starts with themselves. Whenever the applicants said that they wanted to do it for the money, or that they wanted to publicize their point of view about battery farming, I felt that they were just kidding themselves. These sorts of people don't even know what their real motivation is.'

Rebecca laughed the quiet, well-mannered laugh of the English upper middle classes.

She described the four successful applicants as 'very much the B team, I'm afraid. There is Bill Davies, a fifteen-stone builder, but he is the son of a mink farmer. There is Daryl Heathfield, a one-legged chap. He used to be a builder, but now he's unemployed. He once made kennels for a breeding establishment where dogs were sent on to vivisection laboratories. So again, you get the guilt thing coming through. Then there is Richard Brett, a lorry driver who said that he had a background in battery farming, but I think that he might just have been at agricultural college. And then there is Richard's brother-in-law, Stuart Wastie, who is a student. They are all very keen, but it's a little bit watered down from what I really wanted, which was four battery farmers. Although the fact that you cannot get battery farmers in the same position in which they put their animals rather proves the point.'

The point this proved to me was that battery farmers do rather well out of it and don't need to live in hell for a week in order to collect two and a half thousand pounds.

'I think we could justifiably have made the conditions much more severe,' Rebecca continued. 'The light will not be flickering as it does in most batteries. The floor only slopes by eight degrees, whereas the hens often have to live on a steeper wire. Our medical adviser rather wickedly suggested feeding the men Mars bars and Complan to mimic the concentrated diet fed to battery hens, so that the men would have all this energy and nowhere to go. But I thought that this might be extremely constipating, so we settled for nutritious vegetarian food instead. As there are no toilet facilities in the cage and no paper, everything has to go through the wire-mesh floor. OK, I accept that in hen batteries, the waste gets carried away on conveyor belts, but in broiler houses the animals are left standing in their own waste for weeks on end.'

These conditions sounded severe enough to me. I glanced out of the window, down through the vegetable garden, towards the windowless shed.

The tube resembled a piece of cheap guttering. Whatever was being forced down it was lumpy and stuck to the sides. After another great heave, it came out in a big splurge, a reddish-brown gelatinous mass falling heavily on to the stainless-steel tray.

The four men squashed into the wire-mesh cage forty inches square and five foot three inches high laughed, but it was clear from their nervous eye movements that they were all checking each other's reaction. Despite their closeness, they were still getting to know each other.

The big lorry driver, Richard, driven by some deep, hidden

guilt according to Rebecca, and unaware of his luck in not being asked to digest a barrowload of Mars bars, stuck his hand through the wire mesh to grab a little of the gelatinous substance that had landed in the tray. He pulled his hand back through the wire and lifted it to his lips.

He spat it out immediately. 'It's veggie,' he said. There was a certain defiance in his voice. 'It's bloody beans and bloody rice! Haven't you got any chicken or some nice red meat—something we can get our teeth into?'

Richard knew that there was a wider audience out there, beyond the cage, beyond the shed. He knew they were being monitored from the greenhouse.

'Bloody veggies.' He tried to tuck his six-foot-three-inch frame up so that he could sit down without crushing one of the others. They were all laughing.

'Does anybody else fancy a taste? If not, let's throw all the bloody stuff out. We need to keep the tray as clean as possible for the week.'

The laughter tailed off. This reference to the time ahead had frozen the jocularity.

It had all been a bit of a laugh to begin with—the television cameras and newspaper reporters. The four were filmed as they climbed into the cage, waving and smiling. Their wives and girlfriends had accompanied them to the shed, and the men were confident. A week in a cage with three other blokes? A doddle. Daryl said that it would give him a bit of a rest—a chance to get some peace and quiet away from Tracy, his wife. Tracy was buxom and blonde and obviously pregnant.

Richard was beginning to irritate Daryl already. As the relatives and film crews left, he had said, 'I wonder who'll be sleeping with your wife tonight.' Daryl had sworn at him. It was only a joke, but it had taken him a while to calm down. But now his confidence looked as though it was starting to build again.

The men's gaze was turned outwards, locked on to the cobwebs hanging from the walls of the shed. There were three posters of Rebecca's book cover too—a mass of greens and yellows and oranges with traces of red, plume, feather and plant in an endless summer, against a background of pale blue. Leaves

and bananas and monkeys and babies and flowers all snarled up.
'That's all we've got to look at for the next week, her bloody book cover,' Daryl said. 'That and a poster about a turkey's Christmas. Let me read this to you.' He needed to read it aloud because two of the men didn't have the space to turn around and look. '"Timid and semi-wild, turkeys are de-beaked with red-hot blades, kept crammed together and slaughtered in conditions of appalling violence. Enjoy a peaceful, cruelty-free Christmas." Just as long as they don't try to de-beak us.'

The men's laughter was uncertain.

In between the chatter, the men were all watching each other to see who would need to pee first. They talked mostly about how they would spend their share of the money. One was going to pay off his debts, one was going to travel, one was going to have a damn good Christmas with the biggest turkey ever. '*The biggest turkey ever*,' he said up to the camera in the corner which led away to the greenhouse, the nerve centre.

Already, they were resenting the tape, which consisted of a random collection of strange, disturbing noises: a loud heartbeat, a child crying, a scream, whistling, another scream, a dog barking, a baby crying, maniacal laughter, another scream, a gunshot, an evil laugh, police sirens, a baby crying again, another scream, an electronic noise, the heartbeat. The men's watches had been confiscated; had they been allowed to keep them, they would have known that they had not yet been confined for an hour.

Rebecca and her friends and helpers had retired to the house for lunch. The human hens were now being watched by a security guard hired for the week. He was a retired physical-training instructor from the SAS regiment. SAS men are famous for their ability to survive for long periods behind enemy lines in the most extreme conditions. But even he was shaking his head.

'We've had SAS teams locked in a room which is both warm and spacious, listening to tapes like this, and they can only stick it for four days. It drives you mad after that. I know that they won't be able to do it. I reckon that big one, Bill, will be the first to crack. The skinny one, Daryl, he'll probably last the longest because he's watching his water intake very carefully. You can see that he's out to control his body.'

Rebecca's doctor friend, Dennis Jones, had told her that he thought that the challenge might be too easy because the human hens would be able to think about their situation and occupy themselves by reciting poetry to one another. But the four men did not normally read much poetry. They were now playing I-spy.

The four had entered the cage at one o'clock on a Sunday; ten hours later they were still not eating. During the second feed, the tape had been changed for a while, and the browny-grey sludge was accompanied by 'Land of Hope and Glory', to the amusement of Rebecca and her friends. The four hens were confused. They had all managed to pee out of the cage, except Stuart, who found it too difficult to go through the wire mesh. None of them had needed to defecate yet. Cramp was setting in. There was a heater in the shed that was meant to keep the room at a constant seventy degrees Fahrenheit to mimic the constant temperature of a hen battery, but the hot air was rising, and the men sitting on the bottom of the cage were getting cold. The wire was cutting into their feet, clad in socks. They had all been wearing sweatshirts and jeans, but had removed their sweatshirts to use as cushions to protect them from the biting wire. When Rebecca, looking at the video screen in the greenhouse, noticed this, she entered the shed to confiscate both sweatshirts and socks. 'They were breaking the rules,' she later told me. 'The contract clearly stated that the participants should be barefoot in the cage at all times. Most battery and broiler chickens lose the majority of their feathers due to the stressful conditions. I originally planned for them to do it in their underpants, but I allowed them to keep their sweatshirts on the strict understanding that they were to be worn at all times. Using them as cushions was against the rules.'

The men gave up at seven the next morning. It was a joint decision. They were bleary-eyed, dishevelled, exhausted, their hair matted in places with feed. Rebecca said that she had been awake all night, worrying. Her publisher was delighted with the publicity the event had attracted.

The four human battery hens did not leave empty-handed. Rebecca presented each one with a copy of her book.

A month later, I went to visit Daryl. He and Tracy live in a mobile home in Tracy's mother's garden. There is only one room and a kitchen—nowhere for the baby, as yet.

Daryl is desperate for money. He used to work in the building trade, until a beam fell on his leg three years ago. The circulation in the crushed limb grew worse and worse, and eventually it had to be amputated. He was provided with an artificial leg free on the National Health Service, but it didn't fit properly. He needed to arrange eight socks around his stump before the prosthesis would stay in place. He had ordered a new artificial leg from the United States through a local company which was due to arrive at the end of January, but it would cost £1,750.

If Daryl had managed to live for one week as a battery hen, he would have been able to afford a new leg and would have had some money left over for the new baby. He told me how he had rationalized his part in the experiment.

'I'm the right build, for a start. Two of the blokes were big. They were going to be really cramped. But I'm slightly built, and that's a big advantage. My heart sank when I saw the cage. It was much smaller than I'd imagined, and the wire mesh at the bottom was only about six inches off the floor. All the shit would lie there for a week. That didn't worry me too much, because I know that I can control myself. I once went to Turkey on holiday and I didn't crap for a fortnight. I only go once a week at the best of times.'

The night before he entered the cage, Daryl told Tracy to give him a smaller dinner than usual. 'Tracy had every faith in me. She knew how much we needed the money.'

The turning point, Daryl said, came when Rebecca confiscated their sweatshirts and socks. 'Up until then, we were still quite optimistic. After that, we realized we had no chance. It seemed so unfair. We were sitting on our sweatshirts to protect ourselves from the wire. Chickens and humans have completely different feet. Their feet are designed for perching. I think that she was trying to make it impossible for us, although she was right—it did say in the contract that we would be barefoot.

'We knew we weren't going to stick it for a week after that, so it was better to come out sooner rather than later. It was big

Richard who was the first to say that we probably weren't going to last. The mood had really changed.'

Daryl was also concerned about his bad circulation—the reason his leg had been amputated. When he is cold, his hands turn blue.

'I'm usually not bothered by the colour of my hands,' he said. 'It upsets other people more than me. The other three were horrified. We sat all through the night, getting colder and colder, and me turning blue. The light was still on, and they could see what was happening. I wasn't that worried, except about the leg I couldn't see.'

In the end, it was guilt that forced them to give up, but not the guilt Rebecca had ascribed to the terrible things the men may or may not have done to battery hens or minks or dogs in vivisection laboratories. The guilt came from trying to make money by living in terrible conditions with someone who was turning blue. An hour before they left the cage, the lights had been switched off, and there was no way of knowing how much Daryl was deteriorating. And by then, the men knew that there was no possibility of their meeting the challenge.

The rain had turned Tracy's mother's garden to a mire. Daryl showed me the socks around the stump of his leg. I asked him what he was planning to do, and he told me that he had heard a rumour that someone else, 'a big entrepreneur or something,' was going to issue the same challenge but with a bigger and warmer cage.

'I'm sure that I'd be able to do it next time, if the conditions were just slightly better. I've got angry with myself for giving in. If I'd just been able to get through that phase, then I'd have a new leg by now, and some money for the baby. It was me who got blamed for the failure. I've heard that one of the blokes is saying he could have stayed in all week, but that when you've got handicapped people around you've got to do what's best for them. But we all knew we weren't going to manage it. I keep reading the papers, looking for an article about this new challenge. Next time, I'll be prepared. I'm going to be ready for it.'

Tracy patted him reassuringly on the back as the rain fell.

AMARTYA SEN
NOBODY NEED STARVE

Searching for unblighted potatoes in a stubble field, Ireland, 1849   HULTON DEUTSCH

How do famines relate to food supply? Some see the connection as almost definitional: famine is, in this view, synonymous with a country being short of food. When Mr Malone, the rich Irish-American in Shaw's *Man and Superman*, refers to the Irish famine of the 1840s, he refuses to describe it as one. He explains that 'when a country is full o food and exporting it, there can be no famine.' There is some distinctive use of language here. Malone mentions that his father 'died of starvation in the black 47'. Since more than a million other Irishmen did the same in the 1840s, it is hard not to see a 'famine' there, as the term is understood.

Malone's *definitional* point about famines really raises a different and extremely important *causal* question: why did the Irish starve, given the fact that Ireland had food enough to export some to England? That question remains tragically relevant. No recorded famine has killed a higher proportion of the population than the Irish famine. This applies to the much-publicized recent famines in Somalia, Ethiopia and Sudan, and even to the terrible starvation in China during 1958–61, where the absolute number killed was much larger (perhaps between twenty-three and thirty million), but where the fatality as a proportion of the total population was still smaller than in the privation that overwhelmed Ireland 150 years ago.

Recent empirical work has demolished the view that famines and starvation can occur only when food supply declines. Indeed, in different countries in the world, many large famines have taken place despite moderate-to-good food availability, and without any appreciable decline in food output or supply. And some—like the Bangladesh famine of 1974—have actually occurred in years of peak food availability. A famine develops when a sizeable number of people—who often belong to a particular occupation group—lose the economic means of acquiring food. This can result from unemployment, or from a sharp drop in earnings compared with food prices, even when there is no fall in food output or supply. And conversely, there have also been many cases of severe decline in food production and availability which have not resulted in a famine. Food can be purchased from abroad if the economic means exist, and also the available food supply, even when short, can be so distributed as

215

to avoid extreme destitution. Giving a destitute person an income, perhaps through employment in a temporary public project, is a quick way of giving potential famine victims the ability to compete with others in buying food.

So there is no fixed relation between food and famine. Famines can occur with or without substantial declines in food output. To recognize this does not require us to deny that some famines have happened along with—and to some extent been caused by—a sharp decline in food supply in a particular region. Indeed, the Irish famine, or 'the starvation' (as Mr Malone preferred to describe it to Violet, his English daughter-in-law), was actually accompanied by a large fall in Irish food production, related to a series of potato blights. Since the economies of Ireland and Britain were integrated, we could still say that there was no great decline in food production for the economy as a whole; the Irish, if they had the economic means, could buy food from England. They did not buy it—because they did *not* have the means.

The question that arises is this: why was Ireland, with so little food, exporting food to England, which had so much? The answer lies in the way the market worked. Market-based movements of food are related to demand and purchasing power, and the English could offer higher prices than the economically devastated Irish consumer could manage. It was not surprising that ship after ship sailed down the Shannon bound for England laden with wheat, oats, cattle, pigs, eggs and butter. Such 'countermovements' of food out of famine-stricken areas have been observed in modern famines as well: for example, in the Ethiopian famine of 1973, food was moved out of the famine-affected province of Wollo to the more prosperous purchasers in Addis Ababa and elsewhere. Those who starve because they cannot afford to buy food have no means of keeping within their borders the food that is there.

Were the English rulers responsible for the famine? Was Malone right to think 'Me father was starved dead'? The British government did not set out deliberately to starve the Irish. Britain did not blockade Ireland, or foment the potato blights, or undertake public policies aimed at weakening the Irish economy. But we know from studies of famines and averted famines across the world that they are easy to prevent when the government decides to act. It is not hard to regenerate the normal purchasing power of the new destitutes by methods, including public employment, that have been used successfully in many parts of the world. This way of stopping famines by replacing lost incomes does not even need an inordinate share of the national income since the victims are normally poor in the first place, and the share of the population affected is relatively small. The proportion affected in Ireland was large on that island itself, but it was still a relatively small share of the population of the United Kingdom, of which Ireland was then a political and economic part.

So the real question is: why were these steps not taken in Ireland? More generally, why isn't every famine stopped by the respective government, since it is so easily halted? This is where political alienation—of the governors from the governed—is important. The direct penalties of a famine are borne by one group of people and political decisions are taken by another. The rulers never starve. But when a government is accountable to the local populace, it too has good reasons to do its best to eradicate famines. Democracy, via electoral politics, passes on the price of famines to the rulers as well.

It is not surprising that in the gruesome history of famines there is hardly any case in which a famine has occurred in a country that is independent and democratic, regardless of whether it is rich or poor. In India, famines continued to occur right up to independence: the last British Indian famine, the Bengal famine of 1943 in which between two and three million people died, happened only four years before the British withdrew. And then, with independence, famines abruptly stopped. With a democratic political system in a self-governed territory, a relatively free news media and active opposition parties that are eager to jump on the government for its failure to prevent starvation, the government is under extreme pressure to take quick and effective action whenever famines threaten.

The irresponsibility that results in famine can be further fuelled by cultural alienation. The estrangement of the rulers from the ruled did, of course, take a very special form in the case of

217

the Irish famines, given the long tradition of English scepticism towards the Irish. Ireland paid the penalty of being governed by a not particularly sympathetic ruling class, and cultural deprecation added force to political asymmetry.

The roots of the Irish famines can, in this sense, be traced far back—even perhaps to the sixteenth century, to such writings as Spenser's *Faerie Queene*. The temptation to blame the victim, plentifully present in the *Faerie Queene* itself, survived through the famines of the 1840s. The Irish taste for the potato was added to the list of calamities which the natives had, in the English view, brought on themselves. Charles Edward Trevelyan, the head of the Treasury during the famines, who saw not much wrong with British policies in Ireland, of which he was a major architect, took the opportunity to remark: 'There is scarcely a woman of the peasant class in the West of Ireland whose culinary art exceeds the boiling of a potato.' The remark is interesting not just because it is rare for an Englishman to find a suitable opportunity for an international criticism of culinary art, but also because pointing the accusing finger at the Irish peasant diet vividly illustrates the inclination to fault some characteristic of the victim, rather than the conduct of the rulers.

Winston Churchill's famous remark about the 1943 Bengal famine—that it was caused by the tendency of the people to breed like rabbits—belongs to this general tradition of blaming the colonial subject. This attitude had a crucial role in delaying famine relief. As a nine-year-old boy I witnessed this famine myself, and I remember the sight of unbelievably emaciated people dying in the streets from April onwards, but very few government relief centres opened until late October.

The lack of democracy and the censoring of Indian newspapers weakened the political incentive of the Raj to do anything much about the famine. Also, *pace* Churchill, had not the famine victims brought this cataclysm on themselves? A British-owned newspaper, the *Statesman* of Calcutta, which was particularly influential in London, toed the official line for a long time, but after six months of famine, it broke ranks under the courageous editorship of Ian Stephens and began publishing reports on the extent both of the disaster and of the government's culpability. It was only then that the British government at last paid attention and asked the Raj's officials to expand relief operations. The policy of non-intervention ceased to be politically viable once one of the strongest voices of the Raj was itself in revolt.

The absence of food that causes hunger and illness and makes millions perish can reflect, at once, economic destitution, political subservience and cultural denigration. That combination has to be borne in mind in understanding the causation of famines which continue to ravage many poor countries in the world.

In analysing what causes famines, it is important to take into account not just the rise and fall of food production, but the general prevalence of poverty in the country or region, and to examine its causes. The economic roots of the Irish famines have to be sought in the general weakness of the Irish economy—not just in the difficulties with food production. Groups that are not only very poor but also especially vulnerable to economic changes (to shifts in, for example, relative prices or employment) are of particular importance. It is the general defencelessness of the vulnerable poor, combined with additional misfortunes created by economic variation, that produces the victims of drastic starvation. Social divisions are central to famines, and the economic analyses of the causation of famines have to identify the factors that lead to the specific destitution of particular sections of the generally deprived.

While the economic progress of any country depends on its public policies, particularly on its ability to promote economic expansion and distributional equity, the government has a special role in protecting the vulnerable when something goes wrong and a lot of people lose the means of commanding food in the market. Whether the government works towards regenerating the lost purchasing power of the destitute depends on political incentives to intervene and help. This is where democracy and political independence come into their own. The ruling groups have to pay the price of their negligence when they can be forcefully criticized by opposition parties and the news media, and when they have to face elections on a systematic basis.

The Chinese government could keep its failed policies of the

Great Leap Forward unchanged through the 1958–61 famine, while many millions died each year, because it had no opposition parties to face, and no criticism from the government-controlled media. When things are going well enough, the corrective power of democracy may not be badly missed, but when something goes seriously wrong (through design or bungling), democracy can deliver things that no other system can. Even in the famine-stricken continent of Africa, the lack of famines in democratic Botswana and Zimbabwe contrasts with the persistent famine experience of Ethiopia, Sudan, Somalia, Mozambique and the Sahel countries. Of course, even a non-democratic country can be lucky and not experience the economic circumstances that lead to famine; and a sympathetic dictator may, should a famine occur, intervene just as effectively as a popularly elected government. But, in general, democracy guarantees protection in a way that no form of authoritarian rule can, whether it is an old-fashioned colonial administration, or a modern political or military dictatorship.

Famines are, in fact, extremely easy to prevent. It is amazing that they actually take place, because they require a severe indifference on the part of the government. Here political asymmetry joins hands with social and cultural alienation. The sense of distance between the ruler and the ruled—between 'us' and 'them'—is a crucial feature of famines. It is as true in Sudan and Somalia today as it was in Ireland and India in the last century.

JOHN LANCHESTER
THE GOURMET

Winston Churchill was fond of saying that the Chinese ideogram for 'crisis' is composed of the two characters which separately mean 'danger' and 'opportunity'.

Winter presents the cook with a similar combination of threat and chance. It is, perhaps, winter that is responsible for a certain brutalization of the British national palate, and a concomitant affection for riotous sweet-and-sour combinations, aggressive pickles, pungent sauces and ketchups. But the threat of winter is also, put simply, that of an over-reliance on stodge. Northern European readers will need no further elaboration; the stodge term, the stodge concept, cover a familiar universe of inept nursery food, hostile saturated fats and intentful carbohydrates. (There is a sinister genius in the very *name* Brown Windsor Soup.) It is a style of cooking which has attained its apotheosis in England's public schools; and though I myself was spared the horrors of such an education—my parents, correctly judging my nature to be too fine-grained and sensitive, employed a succession of private tutors—I have vivid memories of my one or two visits to my brother during his incarceration in various gulags.

I remember the last of these safaris with particular clarity. I, little Tarquin Winot, was eleven years old. My brother, Bartholomew, then seventeen and on the brink of his final expulsion, was resident at a boarding school my father described as 'towards the top of the second division'. I think my parents had gone to the school in an attempt to persuade the headmaster not to expel my brother, or perhaps he had won some dreary school art award. In any case, we had been invited to lunch. A long, low, panelled room, perfectly decent architecturally, housed a dozen trestle-tables, each of which held what seemed to be an impossibly large number of noisy boys. A gong was struck as we entered; the boys stood in a prurient, scrutinizing silence as my parents and I, attached to a straggling procession of staff members, progressed the length of the hall to the high table, set laterally across the room. My brother was embarrassedly in tow. I could feel sweat behind my knees. A hulking Aryan prefect figure, an obvious thug, bully and teacher's favourite, spoke words of Latin benediction into the hush.

We then sat down to a meal which Dante would have

hesitated to invent. I was seated opposite my parents, between a spherical house matron and a silent French *assistant*. The first course was a soup in which pieces of undisguised and unabashed gristle floated in a mud-coloured sauce whose texture and temperature were powerfully reminiscent of mucus. Then a steaming vat was placed in the middle of the table, where the jowly, watch-chained headmaster presided. He plunged his serving arm into the vessel and emerged with a ladleful of hot food, steaming like fresh horse dung on a cold morning. For a heady moment I thought I was going to be sick. A plate of alleged cottage pie—the mince grey, the potato beige—was set in front of me.

'The boys call this mystery meat,' confided Matron happily. I felt the *assistant* flinch.

There is an erotics of dislike. It can be (I am indebted to a young friend for the helpful phrase) 'a physical thing'. Roland Barthes observes somewhere that the meaning of any list of likes and dislikes is to be found in its assertion of the fact that each of us has a body, and that this body is different from each other's. This is tosh. The real meaning of our dislikes is that they define us by separating us from what is outside us; they separate the self from the world in a way that mere banal liking cannot. 'Gourmandism is an act of judgement, by which we give preference to those things which are agreeable to our taste over those which are not.' (Brillat-Savarin) To like something is to want to ingest it, and in that sense is to submit to the world; to like something is to succumb, in a small but contentful way, to death. But dislike hardens the perimeter between the self and the world, and brings a clarity to the object isolated in its light. Any dislike is in some measure a triumph of definition, distinction and discrimination—a triumph of life.

I am not exaggerating when I say that this visit to my brother at St Botolph's (not its real name) was a defining moment in my development. The combination of human, aesthetic and culinary banality formed a negative revelation of great power, and hardened the already-burgeoning suspicion that my artist's nature isolated and separated me from my alleged fellow men. France rather than England, art rather than society, separation rather than immersion, doubt and exile rather than yeomanly certainty, *gigot à quarante gousses d'ail* rather than roast lamb with mint sauce. 'Two roads diverged in a wood, and I, I took the one less travelled by—and that has made all the' (important word coming up) 'difference.'

This might seem a lot of biographical significance to attribute to a single bad experience with a shepherd's pie. (I have sometimes tried to establish a distinction between cottage pie, made with beef leftovers, and shepherd's pie, made with lamb, but it doesn't seem to have caught on so I have abandoned it. They order these things differently in France.) Nevertheless I hope I have made my point about the importance of the cook's maintaining a proactive stance vis-à-vis the problem of the winter diet. Winter should be seen as an opportunity for the cook to demonstrate, through the culinary arts, his mastery of balance and harmony and his oneness with the seasons; to express the deep concordances of his own and nature's rhythms. The taste buds should be titillated, flirted with, provoked. The following menu is an example of how this may be done. The flavours in it are essentially straightforward, but they also possess a certain quality of intensity suitable for those months of the year when one's taste buds feel swaddled.

Blinis with sour cream and caviar
Irish stew
Queen of Puddings

Of the many extant batter, pancake and waffle dishes—*crêpes* and *galettes*; Swedish *krumkakor, plättar* and *sockerstruvor*; Finnish *tattorblinit*; generic Scandinavian *äggvåffla*; Italian *brigdini*; Belgian *gaufrettes*; Polish *nalesniki*; Yorkshire pudding— blinis are my personal favourite. The distinguishing characteristics of the blini, as a member of the happy family of pancakes, are that it is thick (as opposed to thin), non-folding (as opposed to folding) and raised with yeast (as opposed to bicarbonate of soda); it is Russian; and like the Breton *sarrasin* pancake, it is made of buckwheat (as opposed to plain flour).

225

Buckwheat is not a grass, incidentally, and therefore does not fall under the protection of the goddess Ceres, the Roman deity who presided over agriculture. On her feast day, in a strangely evocative ceremony, foxes with their tails on fire were let loose in the Circus Maximus; nobody knows why. The Greek equivalent of Ceres was the goddess Demeter, mother of Persephone. It was in Demeter's honour that the Eleusinian Mysteries were held, a legacy of the occasion when she was forced to reveal her divinity in order to explain why she was holding King Celeus's baby in the fire—no doubt a genuinely embarrassing and difficult-to-explain moment, even for a goddess.

Blinis. Sift four ounces of buckwheat flour, mix with a teaspoon of yeast and half a pint of warm milk, leave for fifteen minutes. Mix more flour with more milk, two ounces and a quarter of a pint respectively, say; add a beaten egg and a pinch of salt, whisk the two blends together. Right. Now heat a heavy cast-iron frying pan of the type known in both classical languages as a placenta which is, as everybody knows, not at all the same thing as the caul or wrapping in which the foetus lives when it is inside the womb. To be born in the caul, as I was, is a traditional indication of good luck, conferring second sight and immunity from death by drowning; preserved cauls used to attract a premium price from superstitious sailors. Freud was born in the caul, as was the hero of his favourite novel, *David Copperfield*. Sometimes, if there is more than one sibling in the family, one of them born in the caul and the other not, the obvious difference between them in terms of luck, charm and talent can be woundingly great, and the fact of one of them having been born in the caul and the other not can cause intense jealousy and anger, particularly when that gift is accompanied by other personal and artistic distinctions. But one must remember that while it is unpleasant to be on the receiving end of such emotions it is of course far more degrading to be the person who experiences them; to claim that one's five-year-old brother pushed one out of a tree house, for instance, and caused one to break one's arm, when in fact one fell in the course of trying to climb higher up the tree in order to gain a vantage from which one could spy into the nanny's room, is a despicable way of retaliating for that younger brother's having charmed the nanny by capturing her likeness with five confident strokes of finger-paint and then shyly handing the artwork to her with a little dedicatory poem (*This is for you, Mary-T,/Because you are the one for me*) written across the top in yellow crayon.

When smoke starts to rise out of the pan, add the batter in assured dollops, bearing in mind that each little dollop is to become a blini when it grows up, and that the quantities given here are sufficient for six. Turn them over when bubbles appear on top.

Serve the pancakes with sour cream and caviar. Sour cream is completely straightforward, and if you need any advice or guidance about it then, for you, I feel only pity. Caviar, the cleaned and salted roe of the female sturgeon, is a little more complicated. The Wisconsin-born sociologist Thorstein Veblen formulated something he called 'the scarcity theory of value', whereby objects are seen to increase in value in direct proportion to their rarity, rather than to their intrinsic merit or interest. In other words, if Marmite was as rare as caviar, would it be as highly prized? (Of course, there is an experimentally determinable answer to this, because we know that among British expatriate communities commodities such as Marmite and baked beans have virtually the status of bankable currency. When my brother was living near Montpellier he once, in the course of a game of poker with an actor who had retired to run a shop targeting itself at nostalgic English people, won a year's supply of chocolate digestive biscuits. In the ensuing twelve months he put on a stone which he was never to lose.) Lurking in this idea is the question of whether or not caviar is—not to put too fine a point on it—'worth it'. All I can do in response to that is to point to the magic of the sturgeon, producer of these delicate, exotic, rare, expensive eggs, and one of the oldest animals on the planet, in existence in something closely resembling its current form for about a hundred million years. The fish grows up to twelve feet in length and has a snout with which it roots for food underneath the seabed; when you eat caviar you are partaking of this mysterious juxtaposition of the exquisite and the atavistic. And spending a lot of money into the bargain, of course. Caviar is graded according to the size of its grains, which in turn vary according to the size of the fish from which they are taken, beluga being the biggest, then ozetur, then sevruga; ozetur, whose eggs span the range in colour between dirty battleship and occluded sunflower, is my roe of choice. Much of the highest-grade caviar is called malassol, which means 'lightly salted'.

The process by which the correct level of salting is applied to Volga caviar is insufficiently well known. The master taster—a rough-and-ready-seeming fellow he is likely to be too, with a knitted cap on his head, a gleam in his eye and a dagger in his boot—takes a single egg into his mouth and rolls it around his palate. By applying his almost mystically fine amalgam of experience and talent, he straightaway knows how much salt to add to the sturgeon's naked roe. The consequences of any inaccuracy are disastrous, gastronomically and economically (hence the dagger).

With liberal additions of sour cream and caviar, the above recipe—I prefer the old-fashioned spelling 'receipt', but it was pointed out to me that 'if you call it that nobody will have a f***ing clue what you're talking about'—represents perfectly adequate quantities for six people as a starter, providing a single blini each. Perhaps I have already said that. It is only sensible to construct an entire meal out of blinis if one is planning to spend the rest of the day out on the *taiga*, boasting about women and shooting bears.

Irish stew. This is forever associated in my mind (my heart, my palate) with my Cork-born, Skibbereen-raised nanny, Mary-Theresa. She was one of the few fixed points of a childhood that was for its first decade or so distinctly itinerant. My father's business interests kept him on the move; my mother's former profession—the stage—had given her a taste for travel and the sensation of movement; she liked to live not so much out of suitcases as out of trunks, creating a home that at the same time contained within it the knowledge that this was the *illusion* of home, a stage set or theatrical re-description of safety and embowering domesticity; her wall-hung carpets and portable bibelots (a lacquered Chinese screen; a lean, malignly upright Egyptian cat made of onyx) were a way of saying 'let's pretend'.

She would, I think, have preferred to regard motherhood as merely another feat of impersonation; but it was as if an intermittently amusing cameo part had tiresomely protracted itself, and what was intended to be an experimental production (King Lear as a senile brewery magnate, Cordelia on roller skates) had turned into an inadvertent *Mousetrap*, with my mother stuck in a frumpy role she had taken on in the first place only as a favour to the hard-pressed director. To put it another way, she treated parenthood as analogous to parts forced on an actor past his prime, or of eccentric physique, who has been obliged to specialize in 'characters'. She was ironic, distracted and self-pitying, with a way of implying that, now that the best things in life were over, she would take on *this* role. She would check one's fingernails or take one to the circus with the air of someone bravely concealing an unfavourable medical prognosis: the children must never know! But she also had a public mode in which she played at being the mother in the way that a very *very* distinguished actress, caught overnight in the Australian outback (train derailed by dead wallaby or flash flood), is forced to put up at a tiny settlement where, she is half-appalled and half-charmed to discover, the feisty pioneers have been preparing for weeks to put on, this very same evening, under wind-powered electric lights, a production of *Hamlet*; discovering the identity of their newcomer (via a blurred photograph in a torn-out magazine clipping brandished by a stammering admirer) the locals insist that she take a, no *the*, starring role; she prettily demurs; they anguishedly insist; she becomingly surrenders, on the condition that she play the smallest and least likely of roles—the gravedigger, say. And gives a performance which, decades later, the descendants of the original cast still sometimes discuss as they rock on their porches to watch the only train of the day pass silhouetted against the huge ochres and impossibly elongated shadows of the desert sunset . . . That was the spirit in which my mother 'did' being a mother: to be her child during these public episodes was to be uplifted, irradiated, fortune's darling. But if this, as has recently been observed to me, 'makes her sound like a total nightmare', then I am omitting the way in which one was encouraged to collude in her role-playing, and was also allowed great freedom of manoeuvre by it. With a part of oneself conscripted to act the other role in whatever production she was undertaking—duet or ensemble, Brecht or Pinter, Ibsen or Stoppard or Aeschylus—a considerable amount of one's own emotional space was left vacant, thanks to her essential and liberating lack of interest.

So travel and the condition of itinerancy did not bother my mother, which is just as well as it was a fundamental aspect of my father's business activities. I therefore had a mobile childhood in which the rites of passage were geographically as well as temporally distinct. Thus I have somewhere a maltreated red leather photograph album with a picture in it of me holding my mother's hand; I am looking into the camera with an air of suppressed triumph as I proudly model my first-ever pair of long trousers. The proliferation of out-of-focus yacht masts in the background gives less of a clue than it should: Cowes? Portofino? East Looe? Another picture shows a view from the outside of the high-windowed, difficult-to-heat ground-floor flat in Bayswater (still in my possession) where my father provided the first external reflection of the inner vocational light I felt glimmering within me: he picked up a watercolour I had made that afternoon (hothouse mimosa and dried lavender in a glass jar) and said, 'D'you know, I think the lad's got something.' That memory brings with it another, that of our flat in Paris, off the rue d'Assas in the Sixième, still vivid to me as the location for my first encounter with the death of a pet: a hamster called Hercule, who had been placed in my brother's charge by the concierge's grandson during their August visit to relatives in Normandy. My father wore a black tie when he went downstairs to break the news.

In these early years Mary-Theresa was a constant presence, in the first instance as a nanny and subsequently as a *bonne* or maid-of-all-work. Although cooking was not central to her function in the household, she would venture into the kitchen on those not-infrequent occasions when whoever was employed to be our cook—a Dostoevskyan procession of knaves, dreamers, drunkards, visionaries, bores and frauds, every man his own light, every man his own bushel—was absent; though she *had* left our employ by the most memorable of these occasions, when

Mitthaug, our counter-stereotypically garrulous and optimistic Norwegian cook with an especial talent for pickling, failed to arrive in time to make the necessary preparations for an important dinner party because (as it turned out) he had been run over by a train.

In these circumstances Mary-Theresa would, with an attractive air of ceremonial determination, don the blue-fringed apron she kept for specifically this emergency, and advance purposefully into the kitchen to emerge later with one of the dishes which, after extensive intra-familial debates, she had been trained to cook: fish pie, omelette, roast chicken and steak-and-kidney pudding; or alternatively she would prepare her *specialité*, Irish stew. As a result the aroma of this last dish became something of a unifying theme in the disparate locations of my upbringing, a binding agent whose action in coalescing these various locales into a consistent, individuated, remembered narrative—into my story— is, I would propose, not unlike the binding action which is supplied in various recipes by cream, butter, flour, arrowroot, *beurre manié*, blood, ground almonds (a traditional English expedient, not to be despised) or, as in the recipe I am about to give, by the more dissolvable of two different kinds of potato. When Mary-Theresa had to be dismissed from our service, it was perhaps the smell and flavour of this dish that I missed most.

Assemble your ingredients. It should be admitted that authorities differ on the subject of which cut of meat to use in this dish. I have in front of me three sources who respectively prefer 'boned lamb shanks or leftover lamb roast', 'middle end of neck of lamb' and 'best end of neck lamb chops'. My own view is that any of these cuts is acceptable in what is basically a peasant dish (a comment on its history rather than its flavour). Mutton is of course more flavoursome than lamb, although it has become virtually impossible to obtain. There used to be a butcher who sold mutton not far from our house in Norfolk, but he died. As for the preference expressed by some people for boned lamb in an Irish stew, I can only say that Mary-Theresa used to insist on the osseous variation, for its extra flavour as well as the beguiling hint of gelatinity provided by the marrow. Three pounds of lamb: scrag or middle of neck, or shank, ideally with the bone still in. One and a half pounds of firm-fleshed potatoes: Bishop or Pentland Javelin if using British varieties, otherwise interrogate your greengrocer. One and a half pounds of floury potatoes, intended to dissolve in the manner alluded to above. In Britain Maris Piper or King Edward. Or ask. (Science has not given us a full account of the difference between floury and waxy potatoes. If the reader is having a problem identifying to what category his potato belongs, he should drop it into a solution containing one part salt to eleven parts water: floury potatoes sink.) One and a half pounds of sliced onions. A selection of herbs to taste—oregano, bay, thyme, marjoram: about two teaspoons if using dry varieties. Salt. Trim the lamb into cutlets and procure a casserole that's just big enough. Layer the ingredients as follows: layer hard potatoes; layer onions; layer lamb; layer soft potatoes; layer onions; layer lamb; repeat as necessary and finish with a thick layer of all remaining potatoes. Sprinkle each layer with salt and herbs. You will of course not be able to do that if you have been following this recipe without reading it through in advance. Let that be a lesson to you. Add cold water down the interstices of meat and vegetable until it insinuates up to the top. Cook for three hours in an oven at gas mark two. You will find that the soft potatoes have dissolved into the cooking liquid. Serves four trencherpersons. The ideological purity of this recipe is very moving.

The broad philosophical distinction between types of stew is between preparations which are given an initial cooking of some kind—frying or sautéing or whatever it may be—and those which are not. Irish stew is the paladin of the latter type of stew; other members of the family include the Lancashire hotpot, which is distinguishable from it only by the optional inclusion of kidneys, and the fact that in the latter stages of cooking the British version of the dish is browned with the lid off. The similarity between the two dishes testifies to the close cultural affinities between Lancashire and Ireland; it was in Manchester that my father 'discovered' Mary-Theresa working, as he put it, 'in a blacking factory'—in reality through a business colleague who had hired her in advance of his wife's parturition, going so far as to employ a private detective to check her references, and then dismissing her when it turned out that his wife was undergoing a phantom pregnancy. Boiled mutton is a cousin to these preparations, and an underrated dish in its own right, being especially good when eaten with its canonical accompaniment (*It gives an epicure the vapours/To eat boiled mutton without capers*: Ogden Nash); one should also take into account the hearty, Germano-Alsatian dish *backaoffa*, made with mutton, pork, beef and potatoes; soothing *blanquette de veau*, exempted from initial browning but thickened by cream at the last moment; and of course the twin classic *daubes à la provençale* and *à l'avignonnaise*. In France, indeed, the generic name for this type of stew—cooked from cold—is *daube*, after the *daubière*, a pot with a narrow neck and a bulging, swollen middle whose shape is reminiscent of the Buddha's stomach.

In the other kind of stew, whose phylum might well be the sauté or braise, the ingredients are subjected to an initial cooking at high temperature, in order to encourage the processes of thickening and binding (where flour or another amalgamating agent is used) and also to promote a preliminary exchange of flavours. As Huckleberry Finn puts it: 'In a barrel of odds and ends it is different; things get mixed up, and the juice kind of swaps around, and things go better.' Notice that the initial cooking does not 'seal in the juices', or anything of the sort—science has shown us that no such action takes place. (I suspect that this canard derives from the fact that searing often provides a touch of browned, burnt flavour gratifying to the palate.) Stews of this sort include the endemic British beef stew, as well as the Belgian *carbonnade flamande*; the *gibelottes, matelotes* and *estouffades* of the French provinces; navarin of young lamb and baby vegetables, with its sly, rustic allusion to infanticide; the spicy, *harrissa*-enlivened *tagines* of North Africa; the warming *broufado* of the Rhône boatmen; the *boeuf à la gardiane* beloved of the Camargue cowboys, after whose job it is named; the homely international clichés of *coq au vin* and *gulyas*; surprisingly easy-to-prepare beef Stroganoff, so handy for unexpected visitors; all types of *ragoût* and *ragù*; *stufatino alla Romana*; *stufado di manzo* from northern Italy; *estoufat de bou* from proud Catalonia. I could go on. Notice the difference between the things for which French aristocrats are remembered—the Vicomte de Chateaubriand's cut of fillet, the

Marquis de Béchamel's sauce—and the inventions for which Britain remembers its defunct eminences: the cardigan, the wellington, the sandwich.

One authority writes that: 'Whereas the soul of a daube resides in a pervasive unity—the transformation of individual quantities into a single character, a sauté should comprehend an interplay among entities, each jealous of distinctive flavours and textures—but united in harmony by the common veil of sauce.' That is magnificently said. One notes that in the United States of America the preferred metaphor to describe the assimilation of immigrants is that of the 'salad bowl', supplanting the old idea of the 'melting pot', the claim being that the older term is thought to imply a loss of original cultural identity. In other words, the 'melting pot' used to be regarded as a sauté (good thing), but has come to be seen as a daube (bad thing).

My choice of pudding is perhaps more controversial than either of the preceding two courses. Queen of Puddings is an appropriately wintry dish, and considerably easier to make than it looks. Mary-Theresa would always serve it after the Irish stew, and it was to become the first dish I was ever taught to make for myself. Breadcrumbs, vanilla sugar and the grated rind of a lemon; a pint of hot milk; leave to cool; beat in five egg yolks; pour into a greased shallow dish and bake until the custard is barely set. Gently smear two warmed tablespoonfuls of your favourite jam on top. Are you a strawberry person or a blackcurrant person? No matter. Now whisk the whites in a copper bowl until the peaks stand up on their own. Mix in sugar, whisk. Fold in more sugar with the distinctive wrist-turning motion of somebody turning the dial of a very big radio. Put this egg-white mixture on top of the jam. Sprinkle a little more sugar on top and bake for a quarter of an hour. One of the charms of Queen of Puddings is that it exploits both of the magical transformations which the egg can enact. On the one hand, the incorporation of air into the coagulating egg-white proteins, the 'stiffening' of egg whites up to eight times their original volume, as exploited in the *soufflé* and its associates. On the other hand, the coagulation of egg-yolk proteins involved in custard, as in mayonnaise, hollandaise and all related sauces. Always remember that the classical sauces of French cooking should be approached with respect but without fear.

The first time I made Queen of Puddings was in the cramped, elongated kitchen of our Paris *appartement*. The almost-untenable lateral constriction of space in the scullery (which is what it really was) was compensated for, or outwitted by, an ingenious system of folding compartments for storing crockery and utensils. Beyond this room was a small larder from which Mary-Theresa would emerge red-faced, carrying a gas canister lopsidedly, like a milkmaid struggling with a churn. She always insisted on installing a full canister before she began to cook, the legacy of an earlier incident in which she had run out of gas halfway through a stew and had to change canisters in the middle of the process. In the course of doing so she made some technical error, which led to a small explosion that left her temporarily without eyebrows. There was known to be a gremlin in that kitchen who specialized in emptying canisters which by all logic should have been full: the supply had a tendency to run out in the middle of elaborate culinary feats. My father once remarked that all you had to do to run out of gas was merely utter the word 'koulibiac'.

'It's time for you to learn about cooking,' Mary-Theresa said, pressing an unfamiliar metal instrument into my palm and holding my hand as we together enacted the motions of whisking, at first using my whole arm and then isolating the relevant movement of the wrist; I experienced for the first time the divinely comforting feeling of wire-on-copper-through-an-intervening-layer-of-egg, a sound to me which is in its effect the exact opposite (though like most 'exact opposites' in some sense generically similar) to the noise of nails on a blackboard, or of polystyrene blocks being rubbed together. (Does anybody know what evolutionary function is served by this peculiarly powerful and well-developed response? Some genetic memory of—what? The sound of a sabre-toothed tiger scrabbling up a rock face with unsheathed claws? Woolly mammoths, pawing the frozen earth as they prepare their halitotic and evilly tusked stampede?)

It was my mother, oddly, who was most upset by the revelation of Mary-Theresa's criminality. I say 'oddly' because relations between them hadn't been entirely without frictions between employer and employee, added to which were elements of the war (eternal, undeclared, like all the hardest-fought wars— those between the gifted and the ordinary, the old and the young, the short and the rest) between the beautiful and the plain, an extra dimension to this conflict being added by the fact that Mary-Theresa's looks, slightly lumpy and large-pored, and the ovoid-faced sluggish solemnity of the natural mouth-breather, were perfectly calibrated to set off my mother's hyacinthine looks: her eyelashes were as long and delicate as a young man's; her subtle coloration was thrown into relief by the over-robust blossoming of Mary-Theresa's country complexion; the expressive farouche beauty of her eyes (more than one admirer having blurtingly confessed that until meeting her he hadn't understood the meaning of the term 'lynx-eyed') was only emphasized by the exophthalmic naivety of Mary-Theresa's countenance, which had a look that never failed to be deeply bullyable; added to this was a tension of the type—mysterious and uncategorizable but immediately perceptible, as present and as indecipherable as an argument in a foreign language—that exists between two women who do not 'get on'. This was apparent in the certain *ad hominem* crispness with which my mother gave Mary-Theresa instructions and issued reprimands, as well as Mary-Theresa's demeanour, with just the faintest bat squeak of mimed reluctance as she acted on my mother's ukases, her manner managing to impute an almost limitless degree of wilfulness, irrationality and ignorance of basic principles of domestic science on the part of the spoilt chatelaine of the chaise longue (perhaps I paraphrase slightly). All this was underscored by the contrast with Mary-Theresa's attitude to what my mother would call 'the boys', meaning my father (never boyish, incidentally, not even in the blazered photographs of his youth, which admittedly record a period before most people felt entirely unselfconscious in front of a camera) and me and my brother: Mary-Theresa's manner with us always having a friendly directness that my mother, with finer perceptive instruments than we possessed, I think saw as not being wholly free from all traces of flirtatiousness. (Has any work of art in any medium ever had a better title than *Women Beware Women*?) All this, of course, would be apparent (or not apparent) in dialogues which, if transcribed, would run, in full, as follows:

Mother: Mary-Theresa, would you please change the flower-water.

Mary-Theresa: Yes, Ma'am.

—the live flame of human psychology having flickered away through this exchange like the sparrow flitting through the hall in Bede's history. (I think I have already said that there is an erotics of dislike.) Anyway, notwithstanding that, my mother reacted badly to what happened. It began one sharp morning in April. My mother was at her mirror.

'Darling, have you seen my earrings?'

Remarks of this nature, usually addressed to my father but sometimes absent-mindedly to me or my brother, more, one felt, as local representatives of our gender than as full paternal surrogates, were a routine occurrence. My father was in the small dressing-room next door which opened off their bedroom, engaged in the mysteries of adult male grooming, so much more evolved and sophisticated than the knee-scrubbing, hair-combing and sock-straightening that my brother and I would quotidianly undertake: shaving (with a bowl and jug full of hot water, drawn from the noisy bathroom taps and then thoughtfully carried to his adjoining lair in order to make way for the full drama and complexity of my mother's toilette); eau-de-cologning, tie-tying, hair-patting, cuff-shooting and collar-brushing.

The earrings in question were two single emeralds, each set off by a band of white gold, possessing in my view the unusual quality of being vulgar through understatement; they were the gift of a mysterious figure from my mother's early life, the love-smitten scion of a Midlands industrial family, who (in the version that emerged through veils of 'this weather reminds me of someone I was once very fond of' and 'I always wear them today because it was a special day for someone I'd prefer not to speak about'), had refused to accept the gift back when she attempted to return it, and had subsequently run away to join the Foreign Legion. His relatives only managed to catch him in time because he was struck down in Paris (in the course of what was supposed to be his last meal as a free man) by an infected *moule*. In later life he was knighted for services to industry before dying in a seaplane crash. The gleaming banks of seafood on display at the great Parisian brasseries are like certain politicians in that they manage to be impressive without necessarily inspiring absolute confidence.

'Which earrings?'

'No darling, Maman is busy'—this to me—'the emeralds.'

'Not in the morning!'

'I wasn't going to wear them, darling—I'm looking in the box.'

'Have you tried the box?'

The formulaic, litanic quality of these exchanges perhaps being perceptible in that reply of my father's.

'Of *course* I wouldn't wear them now. I'm not an idiot,' said my mother.

The discovery of the earrings hidden under Mary-Theresa's mattress in the traditional little attic room of the *bonne* was, to my mother especially, a shock. It was the gendarmes who found the cherished jewellery—the gendarmes whom my father had called, reacting to my mother's insistence at least partly in a spirit of exhausted retaliation, a cross between an attempt to show up my mother's as-he-said hysteria and an *après-moi-le-déluge* desire to give up and let the worst happen (the worst being, in his imagination, I don't know quite what; I think he thought either that the earrings would turn up somewhere they had been irrefutably left by my mother—beside the toothpaste, down the side of a chair—or that they would have been stolen by the concierge, an especially sinister Frenchwoman *du troisième age*, evil-looking even by the standards of the type, allegedly a widow though, as my father would say, 'It's very hard to imagine a husband for Mme Dupont, once one accepts that circumstances can be shown to rule out Dr Crippen'). But I think my father had underestimated the French seriousness about property and money. The young gendarme to whom he made the initial report, filling out a form of great complexity, was genuinely and visibly affected by news of the value of the missing item, and turned up at our flat the next day. He first sequestered himself in the drawing-room with my mother, who ordered tea. And then, before beginning his search, he spoke to my brother and me, first together with our mother present and then separately (this arrangement, and my mother's scented departure, smiling and glancing reassuringly and perfect-motherishly backwards, being conveyed between the two of them with an apparently wordless arrangement that in another context would have seemed tanglingly adulterous.) The general overwhelmingness of the occasion was augmented by the feeling that the imputation of theft, once aired, had somehow taken on a life of its own—as if the allegation, when voiced, was, like magnesium, spontaneously combustible when exposed to oxygen. As indeed it turned out to be, though as so often happens with adult dramas that take place in front of children, the first stages were hidden, perceptible only in the form of noises off and in the distortions that affected our day. These began when, after potterings and meanderings around the flat on the part of the gendarme—while we sat in the drawing-room with Mary-Theresa and our mother, my brother as usual daubing away at an indoor easel and I reading, as I peculiarly happen to remember, *Le Petit Prince*—he came back into the room and, avoiding all our gazes, asked my mother if he could speak to her alone for a moment.

Time to draw back the curtains on the creative process. I have been dictating these reflections on winter food on board a ferry during an averagely rough crossing between Portsmouth and St Malo. With the aid of a seductively miniaturized Japanese dictaphone I have been murmuring excoriations of English cooking while sitting in the self-service canteen among microwaved bacon and congealing eggs; I have spoken to myself of our old flat in Bayswater while sitting on the deck and admiring the dowagerly carriage of a passing Panamanian supertanker; I have pushed through the jostling crowd in the video arcade while cudgelling myself to remember whether Mary-Theresa used jam or jelly in her Queen of Puddings, before it struck me (as I tripped over a heedlessly strewn rucksack outside the *bureau de change*) that she had in fact used jam but had insisted on its being sieved—a refinement which, as the reader will not have been slow to notice, I have decided to omit. In all memory there is a degree of fallenness; we are all exiles from our own pasts, just as, on looking up from a book, we discover anew our banishment from the bright worlds of imagination and fantasy.

And now, the prospect of arrival in St Malo is concentrating my mind on the possibility of visiting a restaurant to 'put myself outside' (as my brother used to say) a portion of fish soup. Perhaps, just as every love stands in some relationship to our first love affair—a relation which holds only if one extends the possible nature of the interdependency to include parody, inversion, quotation, pastiche, operatic recasting, as well as slavish and identical reduplication—no restaurant in later life comes entirely unaccompanied by some associations with our first restaurant. And just as one's first love is not automatically or necessarily one's first bed partner, and just as well, one's first restaurant is not or need not be one's literal first restaurant, the place where one ate in public for the first time and paid for the experience (the forgotten motorway service station on a trip north to Auntie's, the first, good-behaviour-rewarding shopping expedition teashop scone), but rather the place where one first encountered the blinding, consoling hugeness of the restaurant *idea*. Stiff, authoritative napery; heavy, gravity-laden crockery; pristine wineglasses, erect and presentable as Guardsmen on parade; a crack regiment of pronged, edged and silent cutlery; the human furniture of the other diners and the uniformed waiters; above all, the awareness that one has finally arrived at a setting designed primarily to minister to one's needs, a bright palace of rendered attention. Hence, perhaps the tug of the mythic which underlies restaurants, which are after all a comparatively recent institution, evolving out of the traveller's inn, via the gradual urbanization of western man, and first appearing in their theatricalized modern lineaments comparatively late, in the last years of the eighteenth century, not long before the Romantic idea of genius. There are certain types of conversation, certain varieties of self-awareness, which take place only in restaurants, particularly those bearing on the psychodynamics of relationships between couples whom (frequent solitary diner-out that I am) I notice often eat out apparently with the specific purpose of monitoring the condition of their affair—as if breaking up, by fixed anthropological principle, could only be done by instalments and in public; as if it were reassuring to witness how many others were also precariously aboard the freighted craft of couplehood; as if all couples were by law compelled to take their place in a tableau of relationship conditions, with every state on display from the initial overextension of eye contact to one of those silences which can only be incubated by at least two decades of attritional intimacy.

I may have been sensitized to all this by my mother. It was with her that I underwent my own restaurant *rite de passage*, and she could be relied upon for very little else as confidently as she could for her sense of occasion. The town, Paris; the restaurant, La Coupole; the cast of characters, my mother and me and our Parisian public and an attendant chorus of bustling, solicitous waiters; the meal, a fish soup followed by the celebrated *curry d'agneau* for her, a simple steak-frites for little me, followed by a lemon tart split between the two of us; my mother's dress, a deliciously expensive black scallop-backed item by a named designer, worn with no jewellery apart from the already mentioned pair of earrings; my own outfit, an entirely adorable little blue sailor suit with white neckings (many were the hot-eyed glances I had no doubt been unheedingly darted—though one was amused to come across, reproduced in a magazine article, a photograph of the original youth who had so affected Thomas Mann, and upon whom he had modelled Aschenbach's *visione amorosa*: the child in question could honestly be described only as a *lump*. Art over life once again.) It may have been in those moments that food crystallized as a lifelong interest for me, through a combination of enjoyment at the spectacle, of the sensations of eating themselves, of the pleasures of demonstrating one's proper public conduct as an ideal son of an ideal mother—the pleasure of appearances raised to the highest possible degree. A commitment to a particular kind of life was decided on for me that evening, as my mother smiled at me across the ruins of the tureened soup and devastated *rouille* and said: 'One day, *chéri*, I am sure you will do great things.'

It will therefore surprise no one to learn that all fish soups and stews have always had an especially high place in my esteem and affections. I have a particularly strong identification with that recipe which fuses the base with the noble, the leftover catch at the bottom of the fisherman's net (the primary source for the fish in

this dish as in most fish stews and soups) with the highest degree
of esculence, delicacy and artistry; that brings together the
unsaleable minnows of the Mediterranean with the fabulous
luxuriousness of saffron (almost as expensive, pound for pound, as
gold, for which it can sometimes seem to be a kind of edible
simile); a dish rooted in the solid traditions of peasant
cookery—perfectly exemplified by the fact that the dish is prepared
in a single pot, the totemic single pot of European and indeed
global peasant cookery, from the subsistence farmer in Connemara
to the muzhik of Omsk—but which also has its noble place in the
ramifying, allusive grammar of French restaurant cooking, the
cuisine which has in its home country reached the greatest degree
of approximation to the full complexity of an articulated language;
in short, I have always been especially keen on bouillabaisse. As
the legendary eater Curnonsky said, 'A great dish is the master
achievement of countless generations.' Bouillabaisse's combination
of luxuriousness and practicality, of romance and realism, is one
that is positable as characteristic of the Marseillaises themselves,
who possess in marked degree that habit of seeming to act up to a
collective stereotype which is often to be found in the inhabitants
of port towns—one thinks of the self-consciously abrasive and
warm-hearted vitality of Naples, the self-consciously waggish
sentimentality of Liverpool, the self-consciously romantic
stevedores of Alexandria or even the self-consciously muscular,
rude and truculent dock-workers of old New York: on this
spectrum the Marseillaises take the place of being self-consciously
romantic about how realistic they are, and just as it can seem as if
the whole of Liverpool is constantly engaged in the description,
celebration and praise of Scouseness, the Marseillaises can appear
to be embarked on a permanent project to enumerate, categorize
and enact their own particular brand of forcefully realistic
méridionalité. Note that even the name of bouillabaisse—from
bouille and *abaisser*, 'boil and reduce'—strikes a note of
swaggering, shrugging, stylized rough practicality, as if to say, it's
a soup—what else are you going to do? It is also present in the
story underlying the myth that bouillabaisse was invented by the
goddess Aphrodite herself, patron saint and founder of that
characterful city; a fiction no doubt superimposed upon the

historical truth that Marseilles was first settled by the Phoenicians, who ,were attracted by its conveniently near-rectangular natural harbour (the city's heart is still the *vieux port*); they brought with them their mythology, their lighthouses and their talent for trading. Aphrodite is alleged to have invented the dish as a way of getting her husband Hephaestus—the crippled smith, patron of craftsmen and cuckolds—to ingest a large quantity of saffron, a then-famous soporific, and to fall asleep, thus permitting the goddess to set off for an assignation with her inamorata Arte (who has always struck me as being, of all the characters in the Greek pantheon, the most unattractively *sweaty*). One point in favour of the Greek myths, as of the Old Testament, is that they do have the virtue of describing the way people actually behave.

My researches have failed to confirm or deny the scientific basis of this folk belief about saffron, which is, by the way, a flower, consisting as it does of the stigmas (the pollen-trapping part) of *Crocus sativus*. It takes more than four thousand of the laboriously (manually) harvested stigmas to provide a single ounce of the spice, the popularity of which is confirmed by the name of the town Saffron Walden, now no doubt a rather dreary market town with the standard appurtenances of lounging skinheads swigging cider on the steps of the graffito-defaced war memorial, and a punitive one-way system. I have never bothered to visit Saffron Walden, notwithstanding the fact that it is not a big detour off the route I usually take from my pied-à-terre in Bayswater to the cottage in Norfolk. This part of England, I often think, must have been at its pleasantest during the period of Roman occupation, when toga'd Romano-Britons could stroll through properly laid-out paved streets past clean buildings to the baths, where they could relax with a leisurely dip, a gossip and perhaps a glass or two of locally grown wine, confident in the knowledge that they were protected from their own countrymen by handsome, polite and heavily armed legionaries. The important thing to remember about saffron from the cook's point of view is that it is enough to use just one or two threads, and more will risk imparting a bitter, unpleasantly 'socky' flavour.

There is considerable debate about whether it is possible to make bouillabaisse away from the Mediterranean and the rocky coves which provide this once-humble dish with its delicious variety of what my father used to refer to as 'little finny blighters'. My own view, which I relate after the consumption of many gloomy alleged bouillabaisses in northern climes, is that the dish does not travel or translate but that, when the basic principles are understood, it can be made to adapt.

Take two pounds of assorted rockfish, ideally bought somewhere on the Mediterranean in a quayside negotiation with a leathery grandfather-and-grandson team who have spent the long day hauling nets aboard in steep, baking coves, their tangible desire for the day's first pastis in no way accelerating the speed or diminishing the complexity of the bargaining process. There must be at least five different kinds of fish including of course the canonical *rascasse*, an astonishingly ugly fish whose appearance always reminds me of our Norwegian cook, Mitthaug. Also necessary are gurnard; monkfish/angler fish/*lotte*/*baudroie* (the same thing, *baudroie* being the fish and *lotte* its tail as used in cooking; and another child-frightener it is too); and a wrasse or two, either the *girelle* or the wonderfully named *vieille coquette*, which I first ate in the company of my mother. Clean the fish and chop the big ones into chunks. Organize two glasses of Provençale olive oil and a tin of tomatoes; alternatively you can peel, seed and chop your own tomatoes. Personally, canned tomatoes seem to me to be one of the few unequivocal benefits of modern life (dentistry, the compact disc). Sweat two cloves of chopped garlic in one glass of the oil, add the tomatoes, add six pints of what in England would be chlorinated former effluent (also known as 'water') and boil furiously. Put in the firmer-textured of the fish and the second glass of oil and boil hard for fifteen minutes. Add the softer-textured fish and cook for five minutes. Serve whole fish and big chunks on large soup-plate-type plates and serve the broth separately with croutons and *rouille*. I can't be bothered to go into details about the *rouille*.

Note that bouillabaisse is one of the only fish dishes to be boiled quickly. This is to compel the emulsification of the oil and water; it is in keeping with the Marseillaise origin of the dish that in it oil is not poured over troubled water but violently forced to amalgamate with it. Notice also that bouillabaisse is a controversial dish, a dish which provokes argument and dissent, canonical and non-canonical versions, focusing on issues such as the aforementioned geographically conditioned possibility of making the dish at all, the desirability or otherwise of adding a glass of white wine to the oil and water liaison, the importance or unthinkability of including in the dish fennel or orange peel or thyme or cuttlefish ink or severed horse's heads. (On which my personal verdicts are respectively 'yes', 'no', 'yes', 'no', 'why not', 'yes if you wish to make the bouillabaisse *noir* of Martigues', and 'only joking'.) Some dishes seem to be charged with a psychic energy, a mana, which makes them attract attention, generate interest, stimulate debate, inspire controversy and debates about authenticity. The same is true of certain artists. I am not thinking of my brother.

The discovery among Mary-Theresa's possessions of my mother's earrings (found hidden under the mattress by the gendarme already mentioned; it was as if Mary-Theresa had been acting out one of the failed impersonations in the legend of the princess and the pea) was a shock, of course, and the scene that ensued was very terrible, not least, one gathered, because of the vehemence and passion with which she categorically asserted her innocence. (But then, innocence is such a *problematic* quality, don't you find?) The news was broken to us children in that way that adult scandals always are—mediated to one's childish self by a sense of things unspoken, by small anomalies in the texture of the everyday, by a feeling of parental distractions and absences, by the knowledge that heated conversations are taking place just out of earshot. So one knew, from the time of one's father's arrival home in the early afternoon—'dropping in on the home front' was what he reported himself as doing—that something was up. At about six o'clock, by which time my brother and I had been alerted by all sorts of major distortions to the daily routine (non-presentation of tea by Mary-Theresa, my mother instead distractedly and unalibiedly constructing sandwiches of, I remember noting, a startlingly irregular thickness of bread; non-presence of Mary-Theresa in her putting-the-boys-down-for-their-afternoon-nap role; non-presence of Mary-Theresa in a supervisory capacity during our afternoon rough-and-tumble; non-praising by Mary-Theresa of whatever my brother had got up to in the afternoon, her hysterical cry of 'look at what Barry's done now' as she held up his latest daubing or smear being welcomely and conspicuously absent; and finally non-preparation of dinner by Mary-Theresa, what seemed like a slight delay in proceedings gradually extending into a bona fide gastric emergency), until my father intervened with his gravely radical tidings.

'Boys, I have some bad news.'

The word 'boys' inevitably prefaced some announcement of more than usual import—'Boys, your mother is staying for a while in a sort of clinic.' In this case:

'Mary-Theresa has been rather naughty, and she has had to leave us.'

'But Papa!'

'Please don't ask any more questions, boys. Your mother is very upset, and it is important that you show you are strong for her.'

Needless to say it did not take too long to piece together the real story, not least because my parents' official declaration of a wall of secrecy had to contend unsuccessfully with my mother's histrionic impulses. She spent the next few days, as she was in certain circumstances prone to do, standing for minutes at a time gazing at the restored earrings in her ears (via a mirror), and was not above muttering, as if to herself, the single word 'Betrayed . . .' Uniquely, that evening, my father cooked, serving a surprisingly competent sorrel omelette that he must have learned somewhere on his travels, much as he had been taught to juggle by a Neapolitan aristocrat while waiting in a queue to clear customs during a government employees' work-to-rule in Port Said.

Luckily that evening was not one of the times I had part-emptied the gas canister.

GRANTA

ANDREW O'HAGAN
HOW IT ENDS

Pensioners dancing on the Garroch Head sludge boat   MURDO MACLEOD

The Clyde used to be one of the noisiest rivers. Thirty or forty years ago you could hear the strike of metal against metal, the riveter's bedlam, down most of the narrow channel from Glasgow, and at several other shipbuilding towns on the estuary. There was a sound of horns on the water, and of engines turning. Chains unfurled and cargoes were lifted; there was chatter on the piers. But it is very quiet now. Seagulls murmur overhead, and nip at the banks. You can hear almost nothing. The water might lap a little, or ripple when pushed by the wind. But mostly it sits still.

This quietness is broken, five days a week, by the passage of the two ships which carry one of the Clyde's last cargoes: human effluent, sewage, sludge.

Glaswegians call these ships the sludge boats. Every morning, they sail west down the river to turn, eventually, south into the estuary's mouth, the Firth, where they will drop their load into the sea. By this stage of the voyage, their elderly passengers may be dancing on the deck, or, if the weather is wet or windy, playing bingo in the lounge. Underneath them, a few thousand tons of human sewage (perhaps some of their own, transported from their homes) will be slopping in the holds.

There was a time when passengers and cargo set sail from the Clyde to New York, Montreal, Buenos Aires, Calcutta and Bombay in liners equipped to carry awkward things like railway locomotives and difficult people like tea planters. And now, almost alone upon the river, this: tons of shit accompanied by an average complement of seventy old-age pensioners enjoying a grand day out, and travelling free.

This morning it was the ladies—and several gentlemen—of the Holy Redeemers Senior Citizens' Club of Clydebank who were taking a trip down the river. I'd watched them ambling on to the boat from the wharf at Shieldhall sewage works, each of them with a plastic bag filled with sandwiches and sweets. Now I could hear the party arranging itself on the deck above me, as I stood down below to watch the sludge being loaded into the ship's eight tanks. It came from the wharf through an enormous red pipe, then into a funnel, and then from the funnel into a hopper, which channelled the sludge evenly through the ship's basement. It took about an hour and thirty minutes to load up. As the ship filled—with wakeful passengers and tired sludge—a little fountain of perfume sprinkled silently over the hopper's top.

We were on board the *Garroch Head*, a handsome ship named after the point near the dumping ground forty miles downstream, and built on the Clyde, as was her sister ship, the *Dalmarnock* (named after a sewage works). The *Garroch Head* can carry three and a half thousand tons of sludge; the *Dalmarnock* three thousand tons. They are not particularly old ships—both were launched in the 1970s—but neither seems likely to survive the century. After 1998, the process of dumping at sea will be outlawed by a directive from the European Union on grounds of ecology and public health. And yet this quiet disposal, this burial of a city's intimate wastes in ninety fathoms halfway between the islands of Bute and Arran, once seemed such a neat and clean solution.

Until the 1890s, Glasgow's untreated sewage went straight into the river's upper reaches, where it bubbled under the surface and crept ashore as black mud. Civic concern arose with the stench; the population was still growing in a city made by the first industrial revolution and popularly described as 'the workshop of the world'. In 1889, the city's engineer, Alexander Frew, read a paper on the sewage question to the Glasgow Philosophical Society, and then addressed increasingly heated questions about what was to be done. He opposed dumping at sea, and suggested instead that the sewage be spread along the banks of the Clyde, where it would come to form fine agricultural land. The city rejected this scheme, though a feeling persisted that something *useful* (and profitable) might be done with Glasgow's swelling effluent; in London at that time, the Native Guano Company of Kingston-upon-Thames appeared to be setting a trend with this sort of thing. Glasgow's own brand, Globe Fertilizer, was popular for a short while. But here, science was ahead of the game—or behind it—with new artificial fertilizers that were more powerful and cheaper than the processed human stuff.

How did other cities arrange their disposal? A delegation went from Glasgow to Paris to find out, and there discovered a great tunnel on either side of the river Seine. Sewage poured out of pipes into these tunnels, which then poured into the Seine some miles from the city. The Seine, however, was clean when compared with the Clyde, because (as the delegation noted) the current carried the effluent away from the city to less fortunate towns further downstream, and then to the sea. The Clyde, on the other hand, was tidal; sewage went with the ebb and came back up with the flood—a mess that, like an unwanted stray dog, could not be shooed away. There was also another reason for the Seine's relative purity, which perversely had to do with Glasgow's greater progress in sanitation. Paris had six hundred thousand closets, or lavatories, but only a third of them were waterclosets; the rest were dry, their waste carried away by night-soil carts to fields and dumps. Glasgow, thanks to its climate and municipal reservoirs and pipes, had most of its lavatories flushed by water. It had wet sewage rather than dry, and much more of it to get rid of.

In 1898, nine years after the Paris trip, another delegation travelled south, this time to London, where they were shown the system of sewers, sewage works and, lastly, sewage ships which carried the capital's waste to its destination far out in the Thames estuary. They were impressed, and by 1910 Glasgow had a similar system in place—the second-largest (after London) in the world, with three great sewage works sending their produce down the Clyde in ships.

The passengers came later, just after the First World War, when a benevolent but cost-conscious Glasgow city council (then called the Glasgow Corporation) decided that convalescing servicemen would benefit from a day out on the Clyde. Cruising on pleasure steamers up and down the estuary and across to its islands was then Glasgow's great summer pastime; the sludge boats offered the city council the prospect of killing two birds with one stone. Their voyages were already paid for out of the rates. The servicemen could travel free. It was seen as an expression of socialist goodwill—allied with the enlightened Victorian municipalism that had given Glasgow its lavish water supply and so many public parks. The vessels were rebuilt to carry passengers, fitted out with more lifeboats and saloons, equipped with deck quoits. By and by, their traffic in convalescing servicemen died away, to be replaced, thanks to the charitable offices of Glasgow Corporation, by old people who couldn't afford cruises on the regular steamships, but who may have been encouraged by the doctor to take the air.

And so it was, in the summer of 1995, that I came to be travelling with the Clydebank Holy Redeemers on top of three and a half thousand tons of sludge.

Everything—or everything visible to the passenger—on the *Garroch Head* was scrupulously clean. The wooden table and chairs in the lounge shone with polish; the urinals gleamed; the deck was as free of dirt as any deck could be. The haphazard filth and toxic stews of Glasgow were kept well out of sight. There was a sense among the crew that it was this opposition of cleanliness to filth that carried them and their ship forward on each voyage.

We sailed past the grass and rubble where the shipyards used to be—Connells and Blythswood to starboard, Simons and Lobnitz to port—and I talked to a woman who was leaning on the ship's rail and enjoying the breeze. She was called Mary Kay McRory, she was eighty, and she had a big green cardigan pulled across her chest. Her eyes ran, but she laughed a lot as she spoke. She said the first time she had sailed on the Clyde was in 1921, when she had travelled as a six-year-old with her family on the steamer that took cattle and people from Derry in Ireland to Glasgow, and very seldom took the same ones back again. Mary Kay's father was escaping some bother in Donegal; he heard of work in Glasgow, came over and was employed right away as a lamplighter. Then he summoned his wife and the six children. 'We came away from Donegal with biscuits,' Mary Kay said. 'Everybody would throw biscuits over the wall to you. They were good biscuits. The food over there was good.'

She had worked as a waitress, when the city was still full of tearooms, and then on the Glasgow trams for twenty-five years. I asked her if Glasgow had changed much, and she got me by the arm. 'Ye can say what ye like,' she said, 'but there's no poverty now, none.' She talked a lot about sanitation, about toilets and baths, in the way many old Glaswegians do. Those who remember lavatories shared with neighbours and trips to the public bathhouse tend to talk more about these matters than people like me who grew up thinking it was nothing special to have porcelain bits at the top of the stairs stamped ARMITAGE SHANKS.

Plastic bags were being rustled in the lounge. Out of them came the day's supplies: sandwiches of white bread cut into quarters and filled variously with slates of corned beef, chicken breast, shiny squares of gammon, salmon paste and cheese spreads. And then the treats to follow: Paris buns, Blue Riband biscuits, Tunnock's Teacakes, Bourbon creams. Some of the women dropped sweeteners into their tea and stirred melodically for a long time after. Others placed ginger snaps at the edge of their saucers, or unwrapped tight wads of shortbread, ready for distribution. Neat stacks of white bread and sweet acres of treats stretched on the table, in front of every passenger. All the mouths were going—shredding meat and sloshing tea—like washing machines on a full load.

This was not lunch for the Holy Redeemers; merely elevenses.

Sludge, in the particular sense of our sludge boat's cargo, comes about like this. The sewage pumped into Glasgow's three sewage works is twice screened. The first screening takes out large objects—lumps of wood, rags, metal—that somehow find their way into the sewers. The second screening extracts smaller, abrasive materials such as glass and sand. Then comes the first separation process, designed to make the organic component of the sewage sink to the bottom of the tank (just as sediment will settle in a bottle of wine). They call this the stage of primary settlement. The heavy stuff at the bottom is called raw sludge; the clearer liquid above is settled sewage.

The raw sludge is not ready to dispose of; it needs further modification and is subject to biochemical breakdown. Some of it goes through a process called digestion. Bacteria are allowed into the holding chambers, where they feed energetically on the proteins and carbohydrates, diminishing the organic matter until the sludge is fit to be spread on farmland or made ready for dumping at sea. Then, at the works near the wharf at Shieldhall, the sludge is 'settled' one last time, to increase the content of sinkable solids in the watery mix. The stuff in the hold has passed through many systems—biological and mechanical—and it will have no final rest from the biological, even at the bottom of the sea. It degrades there to feed marine life (the fishing near the dumping ground is said to be fairly good) and continue its journey through the ecosystem.

There has, however, been an awful lot of it dumped, and all in the same place. In the first year of the sludge boats, 213,867 tons were carried down the Clyde. In 1995, the figure was 1.8 million tons. The total for this century is 82.6 million tons. The seabed at the dump's centre is said to be damaged, its organisms contaminated. The EU has delivered its verdict. Glasgow needs a new venue for the sludge, and old ideas are being re-examined. Fertilizer, for example. Sludge is rich in nitrates (four per cent), phosphate (three per cent) and potassium (one per cent), and full of nutrients—it could do a good job on the land, and farmers seem willing to try it for free. It is also well suited to grass-growing and is already being spread on derelict industrial sites to prepare them for reclamation. A new product range—sludge cakes, sludge pellets—will be tried on the waste ground that was once the Ravenscraig steelworks, the largest and last of Scotland's steel plants, where the soil has been poisoned by decades of metal wastes. Sludge used there could make a meadow grow.

We passed Greenock, which used to make ships and sugar, and then veered left into the Firth proper. The *Garroch Head* was going at a fair pelt now, and most of the passengers had their eyes down, playing a restive round or two of bingo. Some were nibbling still at the corners of buns and sandwiches. From the saloon porthole the water looked silver, as if some giant shoal of mackerel swam just beneath the surface. The islands of Great and Little Cumbrae stood out, like two large boulders only recently dropped into the sea.

We passed them. Up on the bridge, they were slowing the vessel down, ready to discharge their load. We had reached the dumping ground, and as soon as the position was right a crewman on the bridge flicked a switch, and I heard a little rumble. The valves were opening. I thought I could feel the cargo starting to be pulled by gravity from its tanks.

I went down from the bridge to the deck nearest the water, and saw the first of the billowing columns. Fierce puffs, great Turner clouds of wayward brown matter, rose up and spread in an instant over the surface. The waters of the Firth were all at once rusty and thick, and the boat was an island in a sea of sludge. This was all in the first few minutes.

We moved off, leaning to port, aiming to complete a full circle as the sludge descended. A group of pensioners stood in a row looking out, covering their mouths and noses with white hankies. All the worst odour of a modern city, until now stored and battened down, was released in this time-stopping, comical stench. I looked up at the coast and wondered for a second where it had all begun, because this was an ending, and the sense of an ending was as palpable and strong as the brew in the sea before us.

The ship turned about and headed home. Its emptying had taken ten minutes. Back in the saloon, the pensioners were dancing to a song called 'Campbeltown Loch, I Wish Ye Were Whisky'. My tea sat just where I'd left it, and I was happy to notice it was still quite warm.

NOTES ON CONTRIBUTORS

CHITRITA BANERJI is the author of *Life and Food in Bengal*.

GEOFFREY BEATTIE's book *On the Ropes—Boxing as a Way of Life* will be published next year.

J. M. COETZEE's novels include *Waiting for the Barbarians, Life and Times of Michael K*, winner of the 1983 Booker Prize, and *The Master of Petersburg*, winner of the 1995 *Irish Times* International Fiction Prize.

GILES FODEN is deputy literary editor of the *Guardian*. 'Idi's Banquet' is his first published fiction.

SEAN FRENCH's latest novel is *The Dreamer of Dreams*, published by Granta Books.

ROMESH GUNESEKERA's novel, *Reef*, was shortlisted for the 1994 Booker Prize and is published by Granta Books.

JOHN LANCHESTER is deputy editor of the *London Review of Books*. 'The Gourmet' is taken from his novel, *The Debt to Pleasure*, which will be published by Picador in the UK and Henry Holt in the United States.

WILLIAM LEITH is film critic for the *Mail on Sunday*.

NORMAN LEWIS is the author of thirteen novels and nine works of non-fiction. He is currently working on a further volume of autobiography.

ANDREW O'HAGAN is the author of *The Missing*.

AGNES OWENS's collection of short stories *People Like That* will be published by Bloomsbury next year.

JANE ROGERS is the author of five novels, including *Mr Wroe's Virgins* and *Promised Lands*.

AMARTYA SEN is a professor of economics and philosophy at Harvard. His books include *Poverty and Famines* and *Hunger and Public Action*.

LAURA SHAPIRO is a senior writer at *Newsweek* and the author of *Perfection Salad: Women and Cooking at the Turn of the Century*.

JOAN SMITH is the editor of *Hungry For You: An Unconventional Anthology of Food*, which will be published by Chatto & Windus.

JOHN STURROCK has chosen and translated a collection of shorter pieces by Georges Perec, to be published by Penguin.

GRAHAM SWIFT's novels include *Waterland* and *Ever After*. 'The Butcher of Bermondsey' is taken from his latest novel, *Last Orders*, which will be published next year by Picador in the UK and Knopf in the United States.

MARGARET VISSER is the author of *Much Depends on Dinner, The Rituals of Dinner* and *The Way We Are*.